Greetings from Javier Jaén Studio
Counter-Print Books

FIRST IMPRESSIONS COUNT
FIRST IMPRESSIONS COUNT
FIRST IMPRESSIONS COUNT
FIRST IMPRESSIONS COUNT
FIRST IMPRESSIONS COUNT
FIRST IMPRESSIONS COUNT
FIRST IMPRESSIONS COUNT
FIRST IMPRESSIONS COUNT
FIRST IMPRESSIONS COUNT
FIRST IMPRESSIONS COUNT
FIRST IMPRESSIONS COUNT
FIRST IMPRESSIONS COUNT
FIRST IMPRESSIONS COUNT
FIRST IMPRESSIONS COUNT
FIRST IMPRESSIONS COUNT

I was born the same year that Joan Miró died, *TIME* magazine chose the computer as the machine of the year and *The A-Team* was shown for the first time. That same year, Pope John Paul II withdrew the Catholic Church's condemnation of the astronomer Galileo Galilei, I just read it on *Wikipedia*. I share birthdays with Bruce Springsteen, Ray Charles, Julio Iglesias and the Roman Emperor Caesar Augustus. I grew up, as much as I could, in one of the many social housing areas in the suburbs of Barcelona. In the 1970s they welcomed emigrants who changed rural environments for prosperous industrial estates. This was also the case for my family. My father fixed cars, while my mother raised two children. I am the little brother of a musician with a degree in telecommunications. We lived on the eleventh floor of a grey building. Two floors below lived my aunt and my cousins, we were somewhat of a large family. They were all born before me. Family anecdotes that end with a "you were not born yet" are still remembered. For one reason or another, I've always been surrounded by people older than me. I spent hours and hours distracted in my room, well-channeled boredom can be very stimulating and productive. Perhaps the excess of stimuli today is one of our great ills. Although I put on many variety

Nací el mismo año en el que murió Joan Miró, la revista *TIME* eligió al ordenador como máquina del año y se emitió por primera vez el *Equipo A*. Ese mismo año el papa Juan Pablo II retiró la condena de la Iglesia católica contra el astrónomo Galileo Galilei, lo acabo de leer en *Wikipedia*. Comparto cumpleaños con Bruce Springsteen, Ray Charles, Julio Iglesias y el emperador romano César Augusto. Crecí todo lo que pude en una de las muchas ciudades de viviendas sociales del extrarradio de Barcelona. En los años setenta acogieron a los emigrantes que cambiaron entornos rurales por prósperos polígonos industriales. También fue el caso de mi familia. Mi padre arreglaba coches mientras mi madre ponía en marcha a dos hijos. Soy el hermano pequeño de un músico licenciado en telecomunicaciones. Vivíamos en la undécima planta de un bloque de pisos de color gris. Dos plantas más abajo vivían mi tía y mis primas, éramos algo así como una familia numerosa. Todos nacieron antes que yo. Se siguen recordando las anécdotas familiares que acaban con un "tú aún no habías nacido". Por una u otra razón, siempre me he visto rodeado de personas mayores que yo. Pasaba horas y horas distraído en mi habitación, el aburrimiento bien canalizado puede ser muy estimulante y productivo. Quizá el exceso de estímulos es hoy uno de

shows at home, what I really wanted was to be a pastry chef. I never had the profile of a child artist, I did not show particular ability for drawing or writing and I only learned to play *Happy Birthday* with one finger on the piano. I do not remember with nostalgia the moment in which my colleagues chose the members of their teams for sports competitions. They say out there that all your life you are who you were in the schoolyard. Cue the violins. For survival, I had to find my way not to be invisible. We want to be loved, to be accepted by the tribe, and sometimes we do really weird things to get it.

The day the first computer came into the house, my downstairs neighbour jumped out of the window. For both of us it was a decisive event in our lives. I am convinced that they are not connected facts, but they happened in the same instant. Although I wanted a video game console, my parents bet on a *PC*. An apparently small decision like that, meant that instead of growing up with *Super Mario*, my time was spent with archaic drawing and music programs. I did not identify them as real interests until years later. You don't have to be in a hurry for the seeds to bear fruit, or even expect them to always do so. At school, I spent more time on the front page of my

nuestros grandes males. Aunque hacía muchos espectáculos de variedades domésticos, realmente yo quería ser pastelero. Nunca tuve el perfil de niño artista, no demostré particular habilidad por el dibujo o la escritura y solo aprendí a tocar *Cumpleaños feliz* con un dedo al piano. No recuerdo con nostalgia el momento en el que mis compañeros elegían los integrantes de sus equipos para competiciones deportivas. Dicen por ahí que toda tu vida eres quien fuiste en el patio del colegio. Dentro violines. Por supervivencia tuve que encontrar mi manera de no ser invisible. Queremos que nos quieran, que la tribu nos acepte, y a veces hacemos cosas realmente extrañas para conseguirlo.

El día que entró el primer ordenador en casa, saltó por la ventana mi vecino de abajo. Para ambos fue un evento decisivo en nuestras vidas. Estoy convencido de que no son hechos conectados, pero pasaron en el mismo instante. Aunque yo quería una videoconsola, mis padres apostaron por un *PC*. Una decisión aparentemente pequeña como esa, hizo que en vez de crecer junto a *Super Mario*, lo hiciera con arcaicos programas de dibujo y música. No los identifiqué como intereses reales hasta años más tarde. No hay que tener prisa para que las semillas den frutos, ni siquiera esperar que siempre lo hagan. En la escuela dedicaba

work than on the inside. Soon I started to "design" for my classmates with the help of my computer, markers, scissors and my cousins' printer. When asked about my first design assignment, I never know what to answer. I see it as absurd as asking a comedian what his first joke was. Every child expresses himself in some graphic form, some adults stop doing it.

As usually happens in life, things did not always go as expected: I did not become a pastry chef. To be honest, I have never had a plan, everything has been a fabulous coincidence. Often the so-called good luck is actually created by oneself and we are ourselves responsible for creating scenarios in our life where things are prone to happen. It looks oddly like those *YouTube* chain reaction videos. *Rube Golberg machines* where a ping-pong ball throws a salt shaker, which makes a toothbrush jump through the air, throws domino pieces, activates a fan, moves a paper cup, that blows a trumpet, that feeds the parakeet. Sometimes the longest road is also the most fun.

From the day I was born until today I have dedicated myself to various things. I have been a student, a shelf-stacker in a supermarket, a dresser of hotel events rooms, a video store clerk, a factory assembly line

más tiempo a la portada de los trabajos que a su interior. Pronto empecé a "diseñar" para mis compañeros con ordenador, rotuladores, tijeras y la impresora de mis primas. Cuando me preguntan por mi primer encargo de diseño, nunca sé qué contestar. Lo veo tan absurdo como preguntarle a un cómico cuál fue su primer chiste. Todo niño se expresa en alguna forma gráfica, algunos adultos dejan de hacerlo.

Como suele ocurrir en la vida, las cosas no salieron como esperaba: no me convertí en pastelero. Para ser sincero, nunca he tenido un plan, todo ha sido una fabulosa casualidad. A menudo la mal llamada buena suerte es en realidad creada por uno mismo, dibujando escenarios propensos a que sucedan los actos que se desean. Se parece extrañamente a esos videos de *YouTube* de reacciones en cadena. *Máquinas de Rube Golberg* donde una pelota de ping-pong tira un salero, que hace que salte por los aires un cepillo de dientes, que tira unas piezas de dominó, que activan un ventilador, que mueve un vaso de papel que hace sonar una trompeta que da de comer al periquito. A veces el camino más largo es también el más divertido.

Desde el día que nací hasta hoy me he dedicado a varias cosas. He sido estudiante, reponedor en un supermercado, montador de

worker, a secretary at a language academy, a group leader for exchange students in England, an excursion guide for the elderly, radio host, wedding DJ, graphic designer, illustrator and teacher. I have changed my address thirteen times, I have studied in nine educational centres and I have one hundred and sixty-four countries to visit if we count the Vatican City. If not, only one hundred and sixty-three.

I like to be open to what the Germans call *zeitgeist* and I don't mind accepting that my opinions can be changing and polyhedral. As I understand it, even from a cellular perspective, I am not the same as I was ten years ago. *Amazon's* algorithm is very confused with this, and results in it suggesting accessories for the car I don't drive or buying a garden irrigation system for the garden that I don't have.

Music was always important in my house. I am not exaggerating when I say that in each room there was a small sound system. There was even a mirror ball in my brother's room. The exquisite soundtrack ranged from huge hits from *Dire Straits* to the popular *Megamix* records of the 1980s. Perhaps this was my first contact with the concept of *collage*, where the whole is more than the sum of its parts. The first

salones en un hotel, dependiente de videoclub, trabajador en la cadena de montaje de una fábrica, secretario en una academia de idiomas, monitor de adolescentes en Inglaterra, guía de excursiones para la tercera edad, locutor de radio, DJ en bodas, diseñador gráfico, ilustrador y profesor. He cambiado de domicilio trece veces, he estudiado en nueve centros educativos y me faltan ciento sesenta y cuatro países por visitar si contamos la Ciudad del Vaticano. Si no, solo ciento sesenta y tres.

Me gusta ser permeable a lo que los alemanes llaman *zeitgeist* y no me importa aceptar que mis opiniones puedan ser cambiantes y poliédricas. Según tengo entendido, incluso desde una perspectiva celular, no soy el mismo que hace diez años. El algoritmo de *Amazon* está muy confundido con eso, y lo mismo me sugiere sutilmente accesorios para el coche que no conduzco, como que compre un sistema de riego para el jardín que no tengo.

La música siempre fue importante en mi casa. No exagero cuando digo que en cada habitación había un pequeño sistema de sonido. En la habitación de mi hermano incluso había una bola de espejos. La exquisita banda sonora iba desde grandes éxitos de *Dire Straits* a los populares discos *Megamix* de los años 80. Quizá éste fue mi primer contacto con el concepto

graphic design memory I have is the cover of *Pink Floyd's Wish You Were Here* album. The design was done by Storm Thorgerson but at the time I didn't know that. Nor did I know that such a profession existed. I only knew that this image terrified me and at the same time, I couldn't stop looking at it. It was an image so different from all the others, so iconic, so brave, that he didn't even need to put the group's name on the cover. It had a great impact on me and became my strange gateway to surrealism, where elements are extracted from their usual context, located in dream spaces or where reality is deformed through symbolic visual montages. Surrealists also extended the principle of collage to the assembly of incongruous found objects. His influence on my work still lingers.

At the age of 12 we moved to the next city. A couple of streets away from home were the facilities of a small local radio station. I signed up for one of their broadcasting courses. The teacher reluctantly accepted me. It was not a children's course and the next youngest student was twice my age. I liked it so much that I spent more than 10 years collaborating with the station. Once again surrounded by people much older than me and believing I have a lot to prove. I did everything: music shows, interviews, impersonations,

de *collage*, donde el todo es más que la suma de sus partes. El primer recuerdo memorable de diseño gráfico que tengo es la portada del disco *Wish You Were Here* de *Pink Floyd*. El diseñador fue Storm Thorgerson pero en ese momento yo no lo sabía. Tampoco sabía que existía tal profesión. Solo sabía que esa imagen me daba terror y a la vez, no podía parar de mirarla. Era una imagen tan diferente a todas las demás, tan icónica, tan valiente, que ni siquiera necesitaba poner el nombre del grupo en la cubierta. Tuvo en mí un gran impacto y se convirtió en mi extraña puerta de entrada al surrealismo, donde se extraen elementos de su contexto habitual, se ubican en espacios oníricos o se deforma la realidad a través de simbólicos montajes visuales. Los surrealistas también extendieron el principio del collage al ensamblaje de objetos encontrados. Su influencia en mi trabajo todavía perdura.

Con 12 años nos mudamos a la ciudad de al lado. A un par de calles de casa estaban las instalaciones de una pequeña emisora de radio local. Me apunté a uno de sus cursos de radiodifusión. La profesora aceptó a regañadientes. No era un curso para niños y el siguiente alumno más joven me doblaba la edad. Me gustó tanto que pasé más de 10 años colaborando con la emisora, una vez más rodeado de gente mucho mayor que yo y creyendo

and even a humour show with friends. Fortunately, there was hardly any internet, and the only record that remains of all that is some cassette tapes hidden in a shoe box. I spent adolescence convinced that I wanted to be a journalist. I combined two great passions, the radio and editing the high school magazine, which added to the stupidity of the age, led me to a resounding school failure, having to repeat courses twice. At the age of 20, I combined high school with theatre classes and precarious jobs. I think I had my first existential crisis. I lost interest in the radio while a new chain of coincidences led me to sign up to study graphic design, without having any idea what it was about. I loved it. At that time I understood that what I had was a serious motivation problem and I needed to overcome it. Although I am now embarrassed to look at them, I left a piece of myself in each of the student assignments. Design saved my life.

As I began my working life with my new identity as a designer, the adult world gave me some vertigo and I escaped to northern Greece, where I was a *Unesco* volunteer for about a year. I learned English and the basic steps of *sirtaki*. When I returned, I wanted to continue training and study the different disciplines of audiovisual language and decided on what my partner at

tener mucho por demostrar. Hice de todo: programas musicales, entrevistas, imitaciones, e incluso un magazine de humor con amigos. Afortunadamente, apenas existía internet, y el único registro que queda de todo eso son algunas cintas de cassette escondidas en una caja de zapatos. Pasé la adolescencia convencido de que quería ser periodista. Compaginaba dos grandes pasiones, la radio y editar la revista del instituto, cosa que sumada a la estupidez propia de la edad, me llevaron a un estrepitoso fracaso escolar, teniendo que repetir dos veces de curso. Con 20 años combinaba el bachillerato con clases de teatro y trabajos precarios. Creo que tuve mi primera crisis existencial. La radio y yo dejamos de interesarnos mientras una nueva cadena de casualidades me llevó a apuntarme a estudiar diseño gráfico sin tener absoluta idea de qué se trataba. Me encantó. En ese momento entendí que lo que yo tenía era un grave problema de motivación y lo estaba superando. Aunque ahora me avergüenzo al mirarlos, me dejé la piel en cada uno de los trabajos de estudiante. El diseño me salvó la vida.

Al empezar la vida laboral con mi nueva identidad como diseñador, el mundo de los adultos me dio cierto vértigo y me escapé al norte de Grecia, donde estuve como voluntario de *Unesco* durante cerca de un año. Aprendí inglés

the time, Fine Arts at the *University of Barcelona*, was studying. That same summer I started attending a multitude of courses, workshops, talks and congresses, which I consider as important to my training as the faculty. I met some of my heroes and I could see how sometimes, when you touch a star, you get the glitter on your fingers. I greatly admire talent, but I am no longer a mythomaniac. Those same years I met others who were as hungry for information as I was and who would become good friends and professional colleagues. The first personal illustration projects and the possibility of starting work for newspapers and magazines also emerged at that time. For years I combined university with working in various design studios part-time. I started applying for scholarships to study abroad with the absolute conviction that they would not give me any. They gave me two for the same year. 2010 was a rare and exciting year, I spent six months at *The Cooper Union* in New York and another six months at *Moholy-Nagy University* in Budapest. It was a very important turning point, for what I learned and for what I experienced. The first assignments as a freelancer began to arrive. Once again without a plan, I quit my job and settled on my own in a shared flat. There I started working for international media from a laptop. Soon after, the first offers for conferences and teaching came.

y los pasos básicos del *sirtaki*. Al volver, quise seguir formándome y profundizar en las distintas disciplinas del lenguaje audiovisual y me decidí por lo que estudiaba mi pareja de la época, Bellas Artes en la *Universidad de Barcelona*. Ese mismo verano empecé a asistir a multitud de cursos, talleres, charlas y congresos, que considero tan importantes para mi formación como la facultad. Conocí a algunos de mis héroes y pude comprobar como algunas veces, cuando tocas una estrella, se te queda la purpurina en los dedos. Admiro muchísimo el talento, pero ya no soy mitómano. Esos mismos años conocí a otros que estaban tan hambrientos de información como yo y se convertirían en buenos amigos y colegas de profesión en un futuro. También surgieron en ese momento los primeros proyectos personales de ilustración y la posibilidad de comenzar a trabajar en periódicos y revistas. Durante años compaginé la universidad con el trabajo en varios estudios de diseño a tiempo parcial. Comencé a solicitar becas para estudiar en el extranjero con el absoluto convencimiento de que no me darían ninguna. Me otorgaron dos para el mismo año. 2010 fue un año tan raro como estimulante, pasé seis meses en *The Cooper Union* de Nueva York y otros seis en la *Moholy-Nagy University* de Budapest. Fue un punto muy importante de inflexión, por lo aprendido y por lo vivido. Empezaron a llegar los primeros encargos como *freelance*.

For better or worse, I have never been a conformist (*I can't get no satisfaction*) and at times I have become too obsessed with work (*Harder, Better, Faster, Stronger*). I try to do things the best I know how. Although it often has a high personal cost, I think it makes up for it. Working so many hours at home was not helping me. I am not an organised person and I work compulsively. For my mental health, it was urgent to find timetables and spaces where I could socialise and learn from others. In 2012 I started my first studio. It was a tiny office shared with one of my best friends, lots of useless objects, and a legion of roaches. It always works to romanticise how dramatic your beginnings were, but there were really too many roaches. It only took us four years to move to the place where we work today, also a shared space. I had always understood my work as that of the one-man orchestra, but in 2015 I applied that African proverb that says that if you want to go fast, you must walk alone, but if you want to go far, better do it accompanied. I have no idea where I want to go, but I am convinced that a shared life is better, richer, more fun, and I decided to add "Studio" to my professional name. It was a way to open the door to collaborate with other people, inside and outside of the physical structure. I have the feeling that even as a society, one of the most significant

Una vez más sin un plan, dejé mi trabajo y me establecí por mi cuenta en un piso compartido. Allí empecé a trabajar para medios internacionales desde un ordenador portátil. Poco después llegaron las primeras ofertas para conferencias y docencia.

Por suerte o por desgracia nunca he sido conformista (*I can't get no satisfaction*) y en algunos momentos me he obsesionado demasiado con el trabajo (*Harder, Better, Faster, Stronger*). Intento hacer las cosas lo mejor que sé. Aunque a menudo tiene un coste personal elevado, creo que me compensa. Trabajar tantas horas en casa no me estaba ayudando. No soy una persona ordenada y trabajo compulsivamente. Para mi salud mental era urgente encontrar horarios y espacios donde poder socializar y aprender de otros. En 2012 llegó mi primer estudio. Era una minúscula oficina compartida con uno de mis mejores amigos, montones de objetos inútiles y una legión de cucarachas. Siempre funciona romantizar cuán dramáticos eran tus inicios, pero realmente había demasiadas cucarachas. Solo tardamos cuatro años en mudarnos al lugar donde hoy trabajamos, también un espacio compartido. Siempre había entendido mi trabajo como el del hombre orquesta, pero en 2015 apliqué aquel proverbio africano que dice que si quieres ir rápido, debes caminar solo, pero si quieres ir lejos, mejor

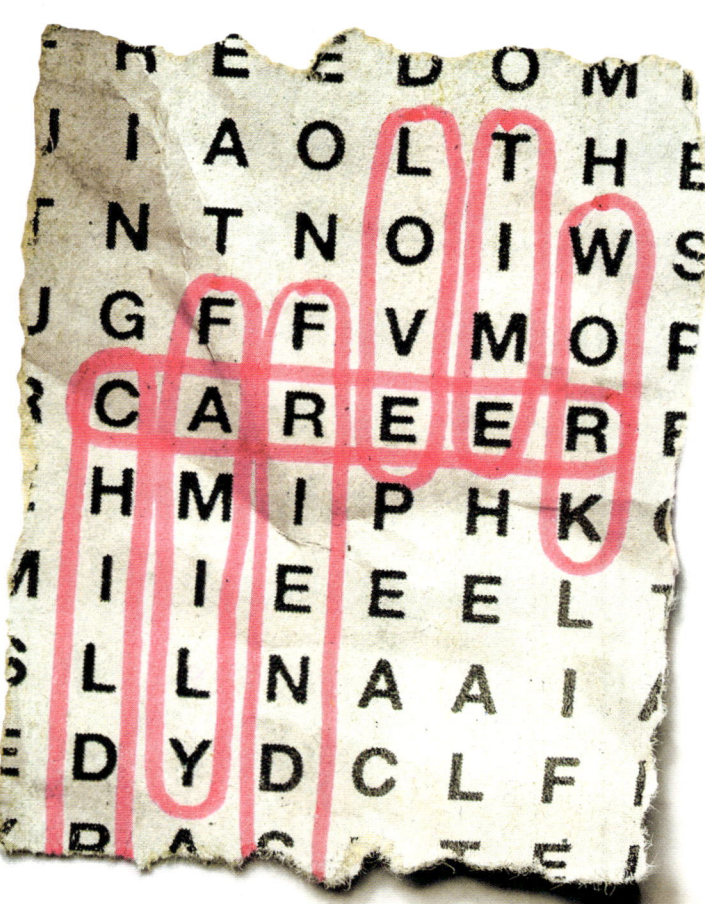

changes in recent years is the discovery of "the others". I want to think that we are learning to listen. Outside discourses and sensitivities make us uncomfortable and at the same time make us grow.

For years I lived with a bittersweet imbalance between my professional and personal life. I was absolutely passionate about what I did, but I was all too aware that work is not everything. However, I didn't have a plan to fix that, but again, a fabulous coincidence occurred. Teaching, I met the one who would be my travelling companion and her wonderful two-year-old girl and we formed a *collage* family. Design saved my life for a second time.

I do not know the paths that have led you, dear reader, to buy this book, but I want to give you my heartfelt thanks. Close to seven billion people have not, it's a downright embarrassing number from a business perspective. It was also by chance that one day I met some English publishers who were kind enough to publish this little time capsule. I have the feeling of being at the end of a vital and professional chapter (and the beginning of the next). Shortly before the age of forty I take the first pause to look back, take a breath and continue walking. As I was told, there is a certain pattern to the vital

hacerlo acompañado. Yo no tengo ni idea de dónde quiero ir, pero estoy convencido de que la vida compartida es mejor, más rica, más divertida, y decidí añadir "Estudio" a mi nombre profesional. Era una manera de abrir la puerta a colaborar con otras personas, dentro y fuera de la estructura física. Tengo la sensación de que incluso como sociedad, uno de los cambios más significativos en los últimos años es el descubrimiento de "los otros". Quiero pensar que estamos aprendiendo a escuchar. Los discursos y sensibilidades no hegemónicas nos incomodan y nos hacen crecer.

Durante años viví con un agridulce desequilibrio entre mi vida profesional y personal. Sentía absoluta pasión por lo que hacía, pero era demasiado consciente de que el trabajo no lo es todo. Tampoco tenía un plan para solucionar eso, y de nuevo, la fabulosa casualidad. Dando clases conocí a la que sería mi compañera de viaje y a su maravillosa niña de dos años y formamos una familia *collage*. El diseño me salvó la vida por segunda vez.

Desconozco los caminos que te han llevado, querido lector, a comprar este libro, pero quiero darte mi más sentido agradecimiento. Cerca de siete mil millones de personas no lo han hecho, es un número francamente vergonzoso desde una perspectiva de negocio. Fueron también las casualidades

moment for a monograph. Although we are scared to recognise it, we always repeat some pattern, we are not as special as we think. *Spotify* knows this and has just recommended me to listen to *El Cantante* by *Héctor Lavoe*. I keep looking for exciting ways to explain stories, my own or others, and for new languages that are as stimulating for me as for everyone else. I make John Baldessari's mantra *"I will not make any more boring art, I will not make any more boring art, I will not make any more boring art"* my own. Every day I doubt more. I think certainties lead nowhere. Or maybe they do. I have no idea.

las que llevaron a que un día conociese a unos editores ingleses que tuvieron a bien publicar esta pequeña cápsula del tiempo. Tengo la sensación de estar al final de un capítulo vital y profesional (y al principio del siguiente). Poco antes de los cuarenta años hago la primera pausa para mirar atrás, tomar aliento y seguir caminando. Según me contaron, existe un cierto patrón en el momento vital para la primera monografía. Aunque nos asuste reconocerlo, siempre repetimos algún patrón, no somos tan especiales como creemos. *Spotify* lo sabe y me acaba de recomendar escuchar *El Cantante* de *Héctor Lavoe*. Sigo buscando maneras excitantes de explicar historias, propias o ajenas y lenguajes que sean tan estimulantes para mí como para los otros. Hago mío el mantra de John Baldessari *"I will not make any more boring art, I will not make any more boring art, I will not make any more boring art"*. Cada día dudo más. Creo que las certezas no llevan a ningún lugar. O quizá sí. No tengo ni idea.

(p.2) CDN, 2019. *(p.3)* Cafuertera I, 2009. *(p.4)* New York Times Magazine, 2016. *(p.5)* Cafuertera II, 2009. *(p.6)* CDN, 2017. *(p.7)* Cafuertera III, 2009. *(p.10)* First Impressions Count, 2013. *(p.13)* New York Times Magazine, 2017. *(p.14)* Afinar, 2009. *(p.17)* New York Times Magazine, 2019. *(p.18)* CDN, 2018. *(p.21)* CDN, 2018. *(p.22)* The Time is now, 2014. *(p.25)* How to Untie a Tie, 2013. *(p.26)* New York Times Magazine, 2015. *(p.29)* I'm Feeling Lucky, 2012.

Where do we come from?

Google Search   I'm Feeling Lucky

What are we?

Google Search   I'm Feeling Lucky

Where are we going?

Google Search   I'm Feeling Lucky

Goya, 2023.

According to *Google*, there is a "Javier Jaén" who is dedicated to sports marketing, another works at the Red Cross, another is a personal trainer, another a cardiologist and another claims to be a top model. I mainly dedicate myself to translation. I translate concepts and stories into images. For my work I use the main resources of graphic design, illustration or photography as my key ingredients, although I don't feel like a graphic designer, illustrator or photographer. I try to see them as disciplines that help me dress up ideas. Before I was worried about being accepted into a single professional family, today it frees me a lot not to be. I am interested in the concept of communication that uses any possible language.

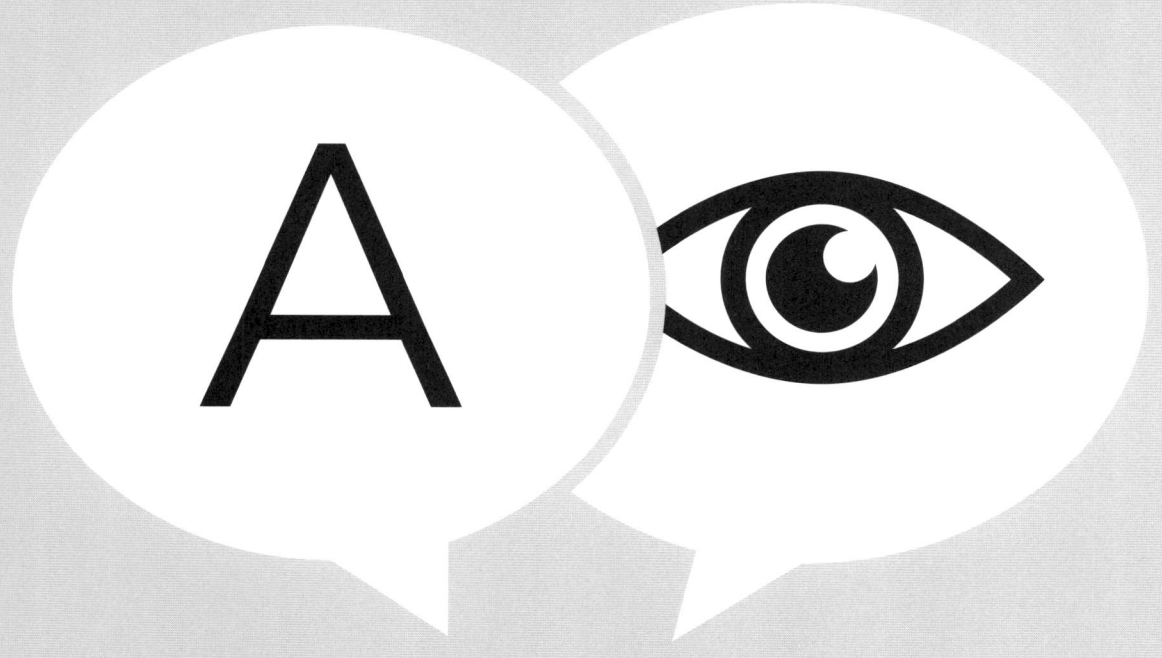

Según *Google*, hay un "Javier Jaén" que se dedica al marketing deportivo, otro trabaja en la Cruz Roja, otro es entrenador personal, otro cardiólogo y otro dice ser top model. Yo me dedico principalmente a la traducción. Traduzco conceptos e historias en imágenes. Para mi trabajo utilizo como ingredientes principales los recursos propios del diseño gráfico, la ilustración o la fotografía, aunque no me siento diseñador gráfico, ilustrador o fotógrafo. Intento verlas como disciplinas que me ayudan a vestir ideas. Antes me preocupaba ser aceptado en una sola familia profesional, hoy me libera mucho no estarlo. Estoy interesado en el concepto de comunicación que utiliza cualquier lenguaje posible.

I usually work from a premise **(A)**. It can be an article for an editorial illustration, a text for a book cover or the taste of a tomato sauce to design a label. It is relatively easy to find images associated with ideas. **(B)** A ladder to talk about improvement, a light bulb to talk about creativity or a puzzle piece to talk about almost anything. Although they are very effective solutions, they are usually in the territory of the obvious and cliché and end up being imprecise or unexciting. I try to flee from the representation of the human figure, I am interested in making the images as universal as possible. I don't think my job is to win an originality contest using all the fireworks available to me, but I do try to make it genuine and honest. It's not worth cheating or taking shortcuts, at least not all the time. Paul Rand said that you don't have to try to be original, just try to be good. I try to make a small jump **(C)** translating the premise into an image that is understandable, and in some way stimulating, either graphically or conceptually. **(D)** Very often we tend to lean towards graphic representations that are too far from their meaning, making it difficult for the viewer/reader/consumer/user to decipher the image.

Habitualmente trabajo a partir de una premisa **(A)**. Puede ser un artículo para una ilustración editorial, un texto para la portada de un libro o el sabor de una salsa de tomate para diseñar su etiqueta. Es relativamente sencillo encontrar imágenes asociadas a ideas. **(B)** Una escalera para hablar de superación, una bombilla para hablar de creatividad o una pieza de puzzle para hablar de casi cualquier cosa. Aunque son soluciones muy efectivas, suelen estar en el territorio de lo obvio y el cliché y acaban siendo poco precisas o excitantes. Intento huir de las representaciones de figura humana, me interesa que las imágenes sean lo más plurales y universales posibles. No creo que mi trabajo sea ganar un concurso de originalidad utilizando todos los fuegos artificiales a mi alcance, pero sí que intento que sea genuino y honesto. No vale hacer trampas ni tomar atajos, al menos no todo el tiempo. Decía Paul Rand que no hay que intentar ser original, hay que procurar hacerlo bien. Trato de hacer un pequeño salto **(C)** traduciendo la premisa en una imagen que sea comprensible, y de alguna manera estimulante, ya sea gráfica o conceptualmente. **(D)** Muy habitualmente tendemos a representaciones gráficas que están demasiado alejadas de su significado, dificultando que el espectador/lector/consumidor/usuario pueda descifrar la imagen.

Love

A **B**

Let's see it with an example. If I have to represent a concept as beautiful and complex as love **(A)**, a correct and valid solution could be to use a heart **(B)**. In a hypothetical search for originality we could change its habitual type of representation, turning it into a square heart, or make it out of stars. However, you can't make a silk purse out of a sow's ear. I try to approach the projects by asking the reader to decipher a small puzzle **(C)** making the image their's forever. If we go one step further **(D)** and instead of butterflies in the stomach, we use two ants kissing, we are using insects as in the previous case, but making it very difficult to understand. Only who knows the code will be able to reveal the message. Although it is a somewhat dangerous strategy, well used it can generate a lot of complicity.

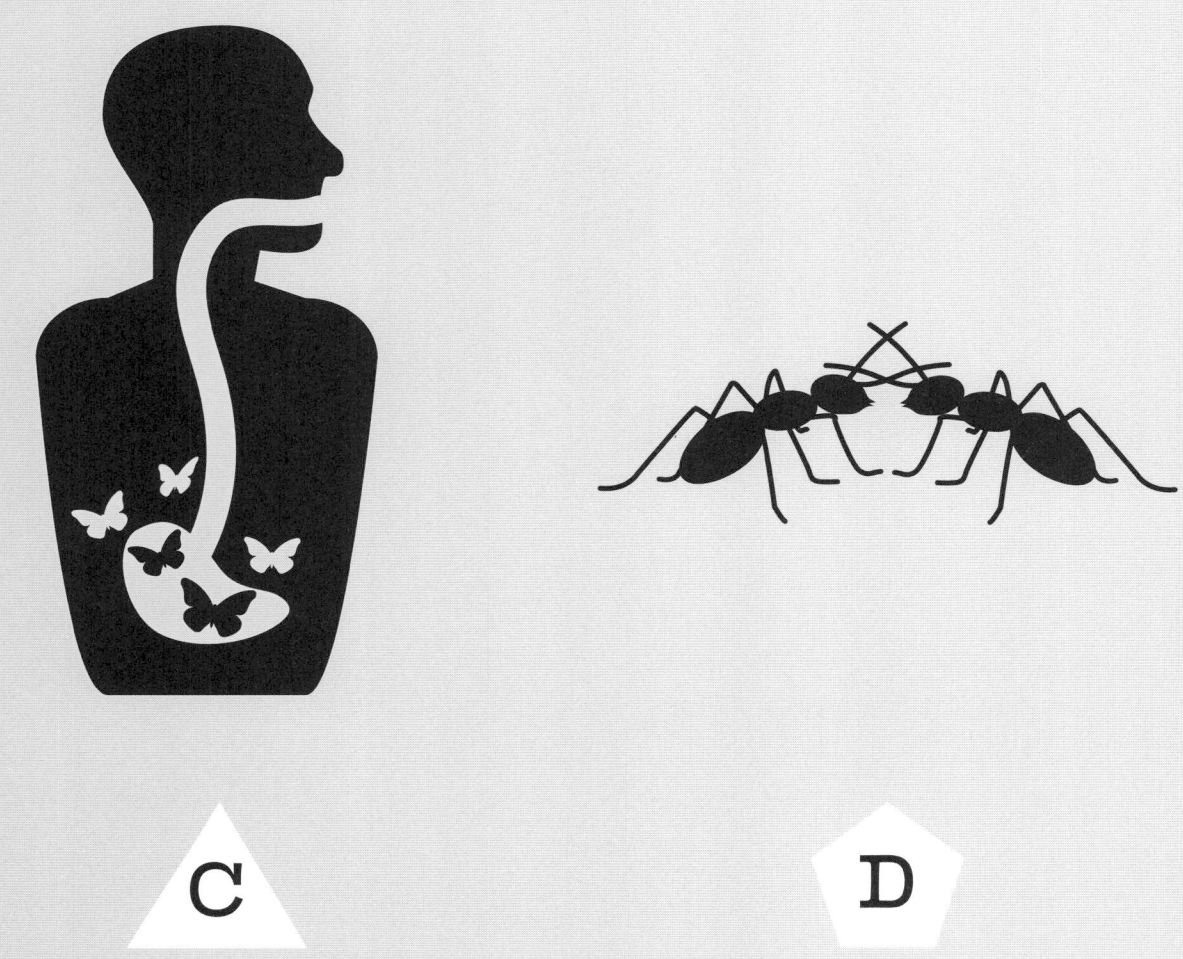

Veámoslo con un ejemplo. Si tengo que representar un concepto tan bonito y complejo como el amor (A), una solución correcta y válida podría ser utilizar un corazón (B). En una pretendida búsqueda de la originalidad podríamos cambiar su forma habitual de representación, convirtiéndolo en un corazón cuadrado, o hecho con estrellas. Aunque la mona se vista de seda, mona se queda. Intento abordar los proyectos haciendo descifrar al lector un pequeño enigma (C) haciendo suyas las imágenes para siempre. Si vamos un paso más allá (D) y en lugar de mariposas en el estómago, utilizamos dos hormigas besándose, estamos utilizando insectos como en el caso anterior, pero dificultando mucho su comprensión. Solo aquél que conozca el código podrá desvelar el mensaje. Aunque es una estrategia algo peligrosa, bien utilizada puede generar mucha complicidad.

Hat, 2020.

Barcelona Creative Commons Film Festival

In 2010 I received one of my first commissions to design a poster. I was happy, bears like honey, cats like balls of wool, and designers like making posters.

It was a new film festival. They did not select their films by style, genre or subject, but because they were licensed under *Creative Commons*. These licenses offer the author of a work a simple way to grant the public permission to share, use or reinterpret the work. I knew next to nothing about that field. One of the things that interests me most about this profession is the possibility of permanently diving into unknown waters. The challenge here was how to translate the concept of the festival into an image. If it were horror movies, a knife and a lot of blood would have done the job. For a comedy festival, bright colours and dancing letters could help, at least in an unsophisticated first attempt. But how do you graphically represent legal licenses? The image speaks of cinema shared and understood in a different way, but — now that no one is listening to us — it is the kind of poster that works for 80% of film festivals. I think that although it works graphically, it is excessively generic and not very specific. My job should be like that of a tailor making a custom suit for each project.

En 2010 recibí uno de mis primeros encargos para diseñar un cartel. Estaba feliz, a los osos les gusta la miel, a los gatos los ovillos de lana, y a los diseñadores hacer carteles.

Era un nuevo festival de cine. No seleccionaba sus películas por estilo, género o temática, sino por estar licenciadas en *Creative Commons*. Estas licencias ofrecen al autor de una obra una manera simple de otorgar permiso al público para compartir, usar o reinterpretar su trabajo. Yo no sabía casi nada de ese campo. Una de las cosas que más me interesa de esta profesión es la posibilidad de bucear permanentemente en aguas desconocidas. El reto aquí era cómo traducir el concepto del festival en una imagen. Si fuese de cine terror, un cuchillo y mucha sangre hubiesen hecho el trabajo. Para un festival de comedia, colores brillantes y letras que bailan podrían ayudar, al menos en un primer estadio poco sofisticado. Pero, ¿cómo representar licencias legales gráficamente? La imagen habla del cine compartido y entendido de otra manera, pero —ahora que no nos oye nadie— es un cartel que sirve para el 80% de festivales de cine. Creo que aunque gráficamente funciona, es excesivamente genérico y poco específico. Mi trabajo debería ser como el de un sastre que hace un traje a medida para cada proyecto.

BccN

1a Mostra Cinema Creative Commons
Barcelona 14 i 15 de maig 2010

The festival was a success, and although nobody expected it, the project ended up lasting more than ten years. To date, it has been my longest relationship. In 2011, I made the poster while studying in Budapest. The image was based on one of the phrases that was used to explain the concept behind these type of "copy me, remix me" licenses, brought to its ultimate conclusion. In 2012, *BccN* was held at the Museum of Contemporary Art in Barcelona. The image of that year represented a pair of padlocks turned into glasses with which to see a world free of restrictive licenses. Since we had the real object, we asked the museum to display it during the festival and surprisingly they accepted. Another strange door opened for me, this time in a museum. In 2013, the *leitmotif* was the power of collaboration in projects. However, I was not being too consistent with the theme. I was alone in the studio hooking plastic eyes onto a piece of paper, photographing it and doing the graphic design of the poster. So since 2014, I have a rule for this project to collaborate with someone in the production of the festival image. That same year I collaborated with a television production company and a bodypainting artist who painted the hands of the festival team, forming a big collaborative vision.

El festival fue un éxito, y aunque nadie lo esperaba, el proyecto acabó durando más de diez años. Hasta la fecha, ha sido mi relación sentimental más larga. En 2011, hice el cartel mientras estudiaba en Budapest. La imagen se basó en una de las frases que se utilizaba para explicar el concepto detrás de ese tipo de licencias "copy me, remix me" llevado a las últimas consecuencias. En 2012, *BccN* pasó a realizarse en el Museo de Arte Contemporáneo de Barcelona. La imagen de ese año representaba un par de candados convertidos en gafas con las que ver un mundo libre de licencias restrictivas. Como teníamos el objeto real, pedimos al museo exponerlo durante la celebración del festival y sorprendentemente aceptaron. Otra extraña puerta de entrada, esta vez en un museo. En 2013, el *leitmotiv* era la fuerza de la suma en proyectos colaborativos. No estaba siendo demasiado coherente en el proceso. Estaba yo solo en el estudio enganchando ojos de plástico en un papel, fotografiándolo y haciendo el diseño gráfico del cartel. Así que desde 2014 me marqué como norma para este proyecto colaborar con alguien en la producción de la imagen del festival. Ese mismo año colaboré con una productora de televisión y una artista de *bodypainting* que pintó las manos del equipo del festival formando una gran mirada plural, y ahora sí, colaborativa.

(1) BccN, 2011. +Adèle De Keyzer. (2) BccN, 2012. (3) BccN, 2013. (4) BccN, 2014. +Several Studio.

In 2015, the focus of interest of the festival was opened beyond the movies and began to talk about open source projects. We imagined an open eye as a strand of DNA. As all the previous posters had been based on real objects, I spoke with a sculptor, who in turn put me in contact with someone who made a primitive 3D print. It was a slow, complicated and expensive process, with results far from those desired. The image is so retouched that someone asked me why we hadn't done it digitally. He was absolutely right. Sometimes you win, sometimes you learn. I do not believe in romanticising the process if it is not at the service of the result. In 2016, the theme revolved around public domain projects. After repeating the same assignment for several years there is a part of the brain that begins to dry up, I'm not sure which hemisphere it is hiding in. I was having one of those creative crises when I was invited to give a lecture in Zurich. Walking and thinking about how to solve the poster, I ended up by chance at the *Cabaret Voltaire*, which was celebrating its centenary. The image of a performance by Hugo Ball made me imagine how his costume would look from an elevated point of view, and it ended up being the trigger for the image of the festival. Six *Ken* dolls in wooden hats did the rest of the work.

En 2015, el foco de interés del festival se abría más allá de las películas y se empezaba a hablar de proyectos de código abierto. Imaginamos un ojo abierto como una cadena de ADN. Como todos los carteles anteriores se habían basado en objetos reales, hablé con un escultor, que a su vez me puso en contacto con alguien que hacía una primitiva impresión 3D. Fue un proceso lento, complicado y caro, con resultados muy lejos de los deseados. La imagen está tan retocada que alguien me preguntó por qué no la habíamos hecho digitalmente. Tenía toda la razón. A veces se gana, a veces se aprende. No creo que en la romantización del proceso si no está al servicio del resultado. En 2016 el eje temático giraba en torno a los proyectos de dominio público. Tras repetir el mismo encargo durante varios años hay una parte del cerebro que empieza a secarse, no estoy seguro de en qué hemisferio se esconde. Estaba pasando una de esas crisis creativas cuando me invitaron a dar una conferencia en Zúrich. Paseando y pensando en cómo solucionar el cartel, acabé por casualidad en el *Cabaret Voltaire*, que celebraba su centenario. La imagen de una actuación de Hugo Ball me hizo imaginar cómo se vería su traje desde un punto de vista cenital, y acabó siendo el desencadenante de la imagen del festival. Seis muñecos *Ken* con sombreros de madera hicieron el resto del trabajo.

(1) BccN, 2015. +Frank Viloria, Martí Baltà. (2) BccN, 2016. (3) BccN, 2017. +Lucas Doerre. (4) BccN, 2018. +Playful, Simón Sepúlveda.

In 2017, we thought about what was the particularity that differentiated this film festival from all the others, the fact of sharing as an affective act. We understood that perhaps sharing is one of the purest forms of love. That year I worked with a German 3D artist who ended up becoming one of the studio's regular collaborators, although we have never met in person.

In 2018, a good part of the festival's programme had a political angle and we worked with the idea of free culture as an act of protest. The work was done in collaboration with an Argentine studio. For the last edition of the festival, in 2019, we collaborated with another 3D modeler from Barcelona. Thinking that energy can neither be created nor destroyed; rather, it can only be transformed, we realised that perhaps something similar happens with cinema and culture. It touches you, moves you and transforms you forever.

En 2017, pensamos en cuál era la particularidad que diferenciaba este festival de cine respecto a todos los otros, el hecho de compartir como acto afectivo. Entendimos que quizá compartir es una de las formas más puras de amor. Ese año trabajé con un artista 3D alemán que acabó convirtiéndose en uno de los colaboradores habituales del estudio, aunque nunca nos hemos visto en persona.

En 2018, buena parte de la programación del festival tenía ángulo político y trabajamos con la idea de cultura libre como acto de protesta. El trabajo se hizo en colaboración con un estudio argentino. Para la última edición del festival, en 2019, colaboramos con otro modelador 3D de Barcelona. Pensando en que la energía ni se crea ni se destruye, si no que se transforma, nos dimos cuenta de que quizá pasa algo similar con el cine y la cultura. Te tocan, te mueven y te transforman para siempre.

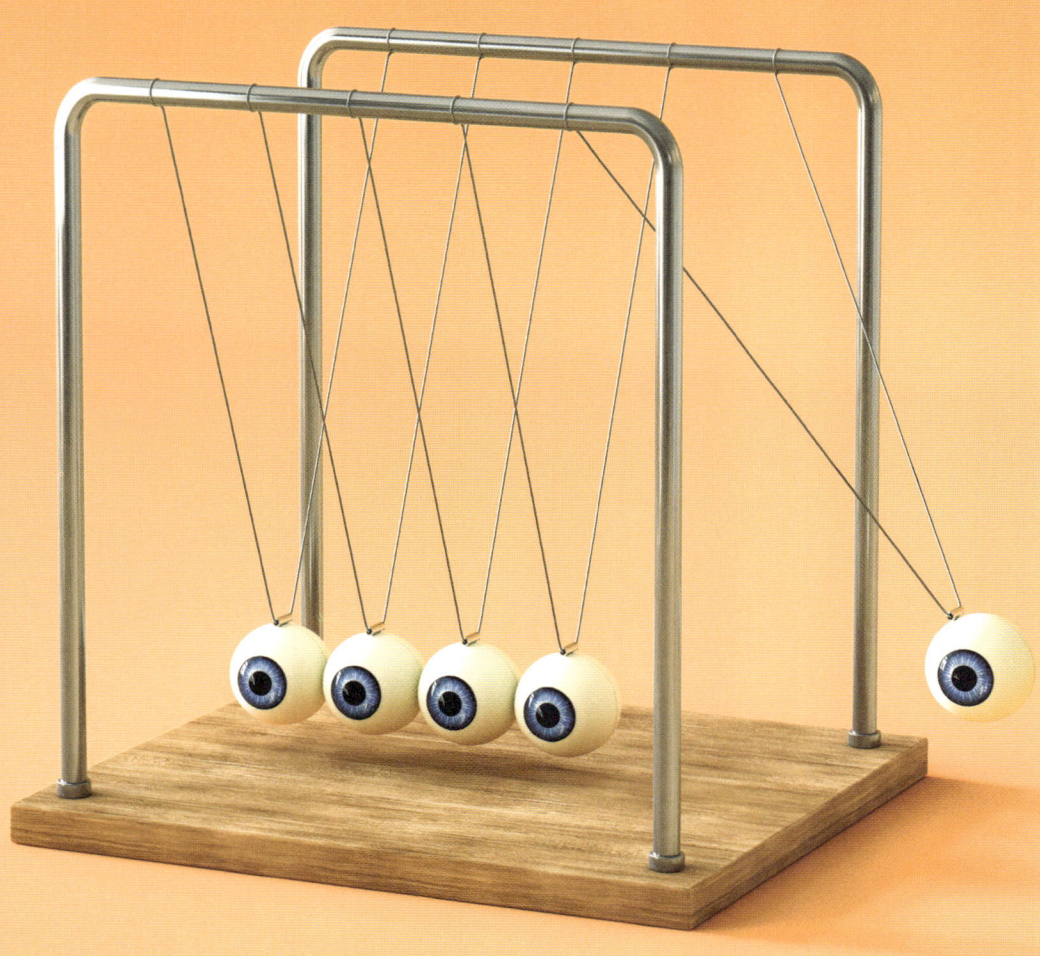

BccN

Barcelona
Creative Commons
Film Festival
25—29 Juny 2019

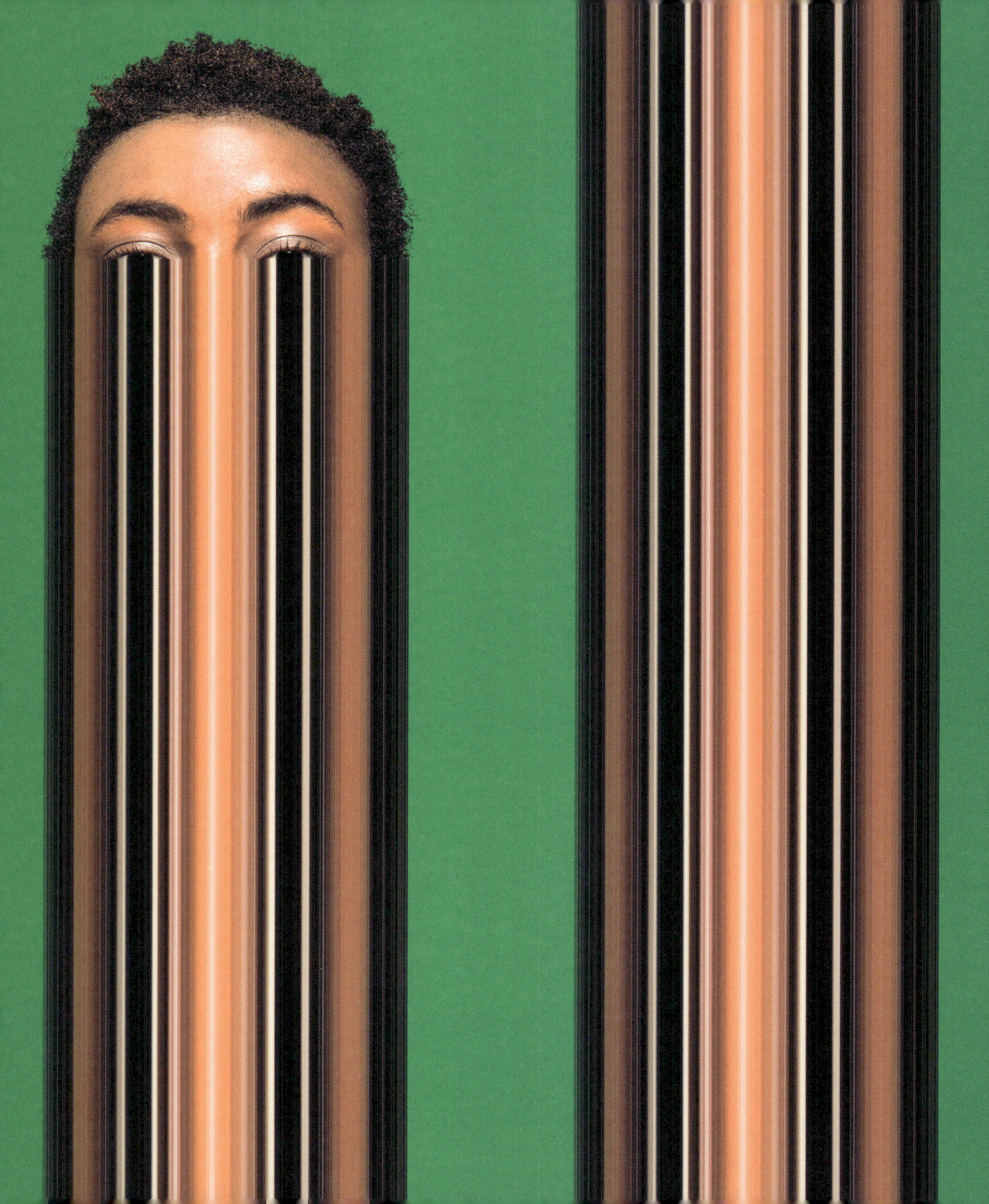

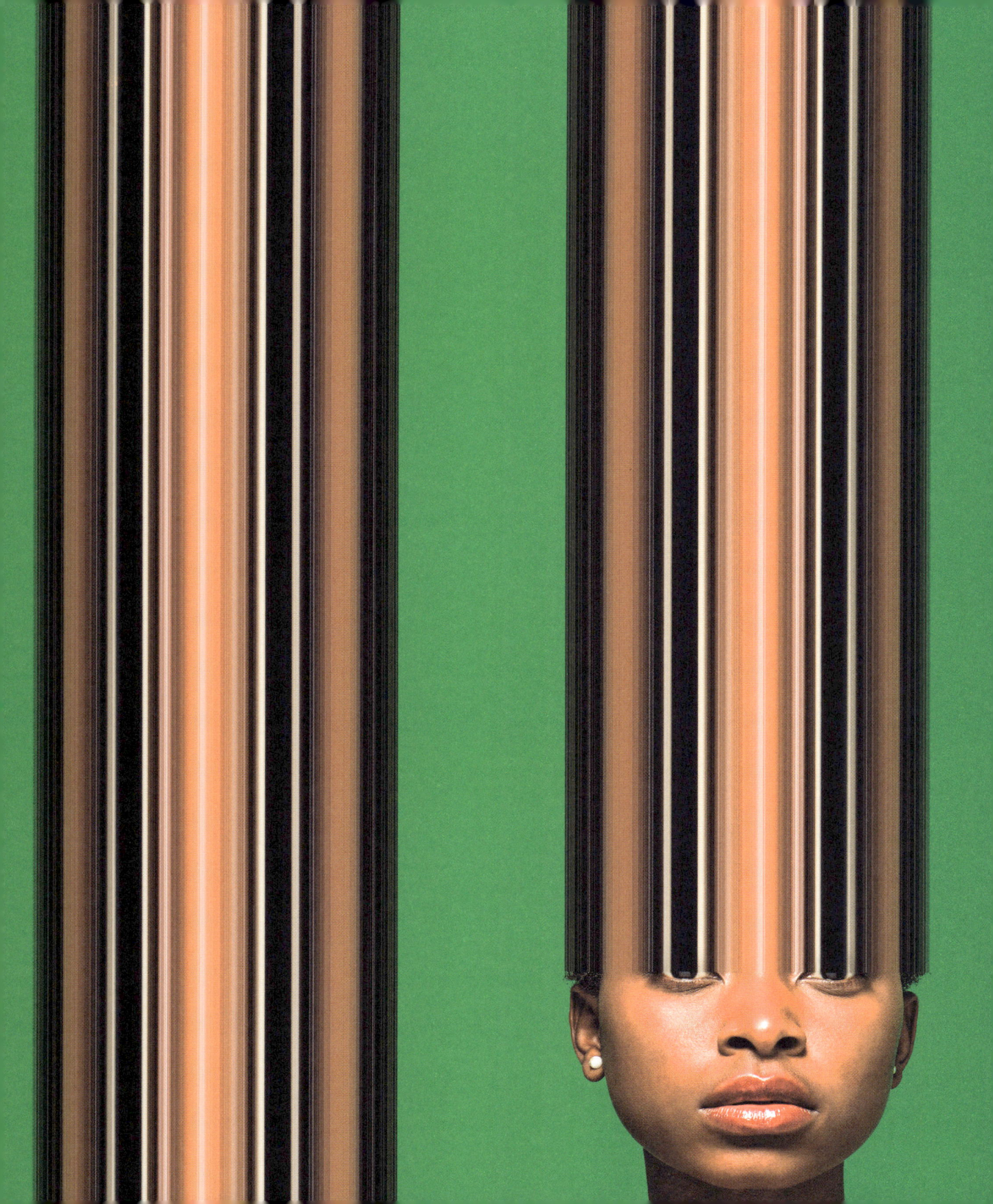

The New York Times Magazine, 2023. Inside the 'Blood Sport' of Oscars Campaigns. War rooms. Oppo dumps. Eight-figure budgets. How the quest for awards-season glory got so cutthroat. Text Irina Aleksander. AD Claudia Rubín.

*International
Women's Film Festival
of Barcelona, 2013.*

(Previous spread) The New York Times, 2022. How Horror Stories Help Us Cope With Real Life. Scary movies, books and podcasts can help people think through how they would respond to threats and prepare them for worst-case scenarios. Text Melinda Wenner Moyer. AD Sarah Williamson.
(This spread) Twin Peaks, 20th Anniversary, 2012. **(1)** Log Lady T-Shirt. **(2)** Poster.

Centro Dramático Nacional

In the 2017–2020 seasons, we worked on the identity, communication and signage of the *National Dramatic Centre of Spain*. The *CDN* is a centre of production and public theatre creation. It is based in two theatres in Madrid.

I have always been interested in the strange relationship between reality and fiction. Theatre is an extension of life beyond what we call reality. To tell the truth, the actors lie. They change their identity with clothes, wigs and makeup. They recite words that someone wrote on paper. They move through cardboard sets illuminated by an electric sun. If you kill on stage, you don't really kill; if you kiss on stage, you don't really kiss, but whatever happens on stage is always looking for true emotions.

We proposed that the *CDN* communication convey that same paradox, a place where you can travel back in time, give life to inanimate objects, resuscitate, fly or sing of sadness.

En las temporadas 2017–2020, trabajamos en la identidad, comunicación y cartelería del *Centro Dramático Nacional de España*. El *CDN* es un centro de producción y creación teatral pública. Tiene su sede en dos teatros de Madrid.

Siempre me han interesado las extrañas relaciones entre realidad y ficción. El teatro es una extensión de la vida más allá de lo que llamamos realidad. Para contar la verdad, los actores mienten. Cambian su identidad con ropas, pelucas y maquillajes. Hacen suyas palabras que alguien escribió en un papel. Se mueven por decorados de cartón iluminados por un sol eléctrico. Si se mata en un escenario, no se mata de verdad; si se besa en un escenario, no se besa de verdad, pero cuanto sucede en él busca siempre emociones verdaderas.

Propusimos que la comunicación del *CDN* trabajase con esa misma paradoja, un lugar en el que se puede viajar en el tiempo, dar vida a objetos inanimados, resucitar, volar o cantar de tristeza.

The season launch was preceded by an action on the streets of Madrid. Posters were placed announcing the mysterious disappearance of a fish. Seeing him, passers-by were asked to question it and they created a surprise, a smile, a doubt. They stopped, they looked around, and if they called the indicated phone number, after a long applause, a voice indicated to them that, at that very moment, a new season of theatre had begun with them as protagonists.

That same lost fish ended up in a spot to announce the programme of the season. It also became an icon of Madrid and an *Instagram* star by turning the theatre's own facade into a giant fish tank.

El lanzamiento de temporada vino precedido por una intervención en las calles de Madrid. Se colocaron carteles anunciando la misteriosa desaparición de un pez. Al verlo, a los transeúntes se les planteaba una pregunta, una sorpresa, una sonrisa, una duda. Se detenían, miraban a su alrededor, y si llamaban al teléfono indicado, tras un largo aplauso, una locución les indicaba que, en ese mismo instante, una nueva temporada de teatro había comenzado con ellos como protagonistas.

Ese mismo pez perdido acabó en un spot para anunciar la programación de la temporada. También se convirtió en un icono de Madrid y en una estrella de *Instagram* al convertir la fachada del teatro en una pecera gigante.

(Next spread) A Nanouk Films + Javier Jaén Studio Production, 2017. CD Javier Jaén. Filmmakers Salvador Sunyer, Josep Prat. Executive Prod Salvador Sunyer. Prod Dir Sandra Olalde. Head of Prod Lucia Andrés. Prod Assistant Greta Diaz. Dir of Photography Pau Muñoz. AD Núria Guàrdia. Art Assistant Roger Guàrdia. Technical and Material Support Carlos Muñoz. Gaffer Pau Ramirez. Colourist Lluís Velamazán. Creative Support Álvaro Carmona. Assistant Dir Alex Macías. Music The Fucked Up Beat. Script Marta Lallana. Sound Design Miquel Mestres. Sound Mix Angel Sound. Still Photo Marta Lallana. Post-prod Josep Prat. Prod Estudio Javier Jaén Ester Ferruz.

PERDIDO

PERDIDO EN ESTA ZONA. POR FAVOR ROGAMOS PONERSE EN CONTACTO INMEDIATAMENTE SI DISPONEN DE CUALQUIER TIPO DE INFORMACIÓN.

911 547 450 | 911 547 450 | 911 547 450 | 911 547 450 | 911 547 450 | 911 547 450

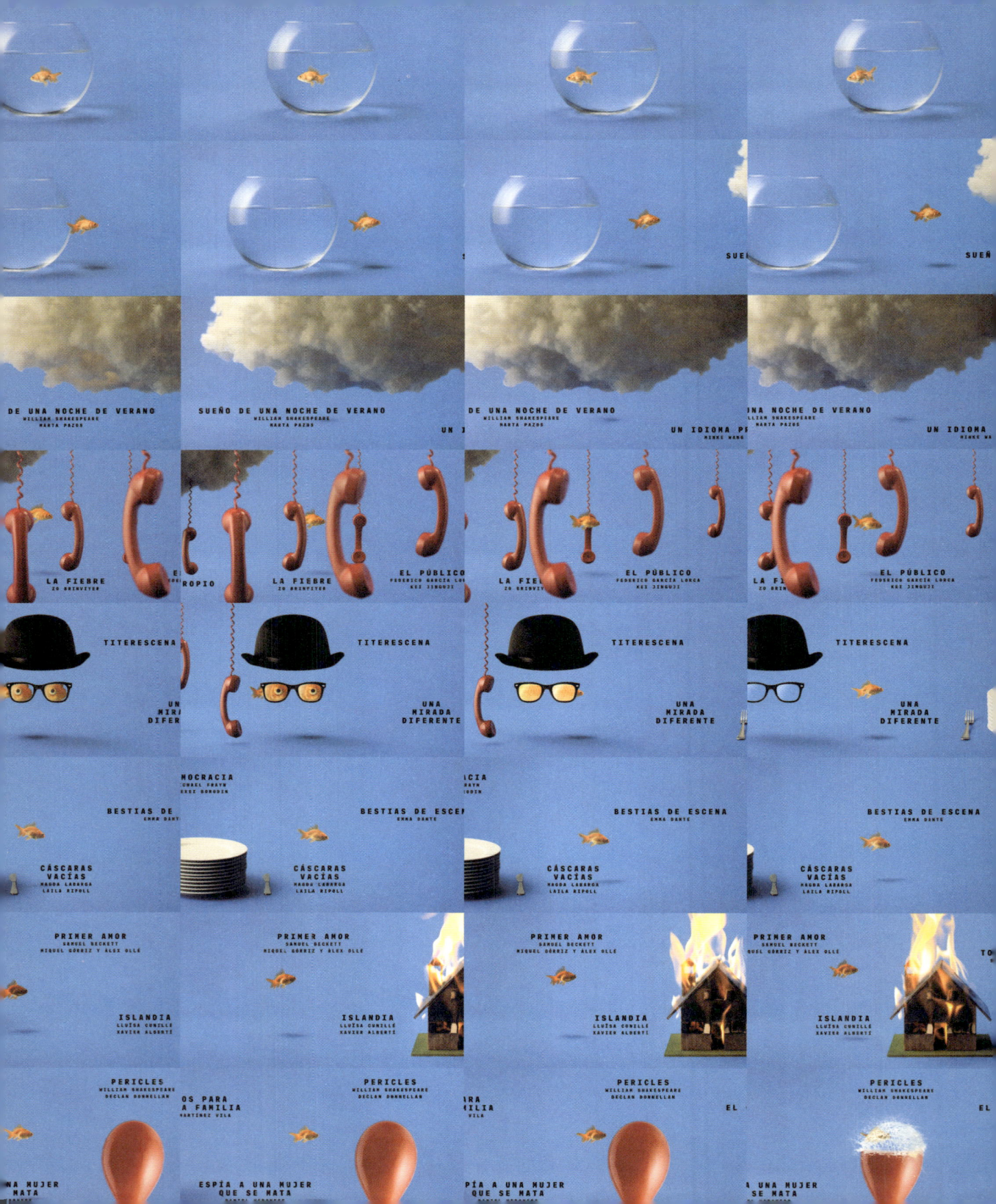

During three seasons we have designed more than 100 theatre posters. They have been developed with a language that allows adaptation as many times as necessary and that still continues to be attractive and recognisable. One of the challenges of this project was to create a system where each work could have its own graphic identity and, at the same time, coexist coherently with the rest of the centre's productions.

We work with ingredients flexible enough to fit works of all kinds, from drama to comedy to children's shows or conferences.

Limitations can help us a lot in a job. I always work with conditions; deadlines, budget, format, and of course the subject. I find it difficult to work with absolute freedom. We need limits to try to transgress them. I find it very stimulating to turn the constraints around and use them as a challenge, so I set myself some basic rules:

- Use a single font.
- Flexibility in composition.
- Colour as an expressive element.
- The object as a symbolic element.

Durante tres temporadas hemos diseñado más de 100 carteles de teatro. Se ha trabajado con un lenguaje que permitiese declinarse tantas veces como fuese necesario y que, aún así, continuase siendo atractivo y reconocible. Uno de los retos de este proyecto era crear un sistema donde cada obra pudiese tener una identidad gráfica propia y a la vez, convivir coherentemente con el resto de producciones del centro.

Trabajamos con ingredientes suficientemente flexibles para encajar obras de todo tipo, desde el drama a la comedia pasando por espectáculos infantiles o congresos.

Las limitaciones pueden ayudarnos mucho en un trabajo. Siempre trabajo con condiciones; plazos de entrega, presupuesto, formato, y por supuesto el tema. Me cuesta trabajar con absoluta libertad. Necesitamos límites para intentar transgredirlos. Encuentro muy estimulante dar la vuelta a las constricciones y utilizarlas como reto, así que me autoimpuse algunas normas básicas:

- Utilizar una sola tipografía.
- Flexibilidad en la composición.
- El color como elemento expresivo.
- El objeto como elemento simbólico.

Posters, 2017–2020.

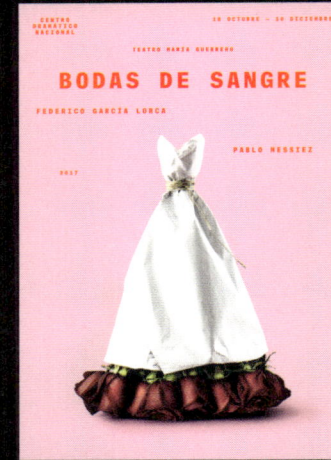
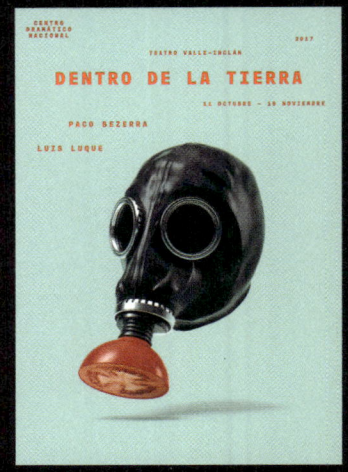
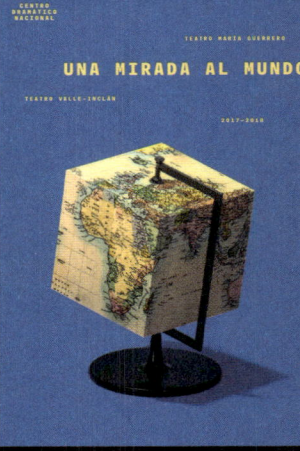
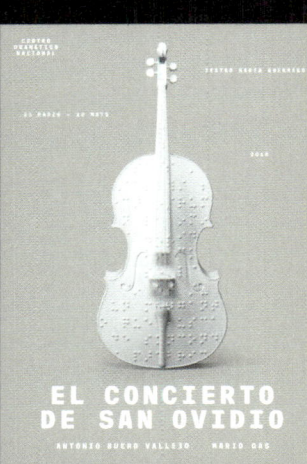
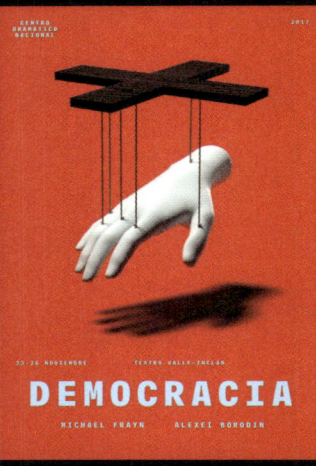
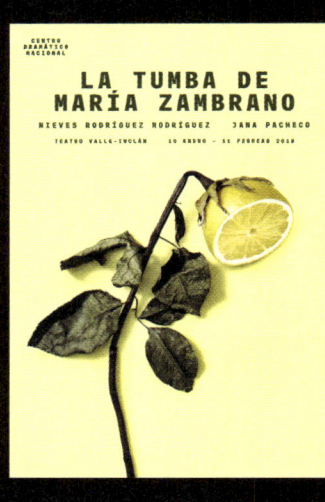

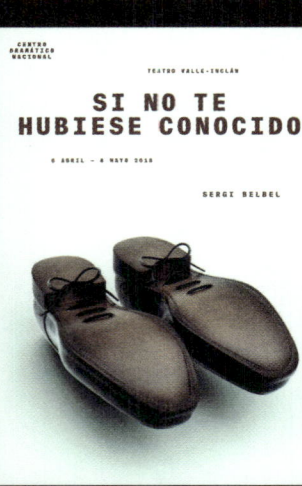

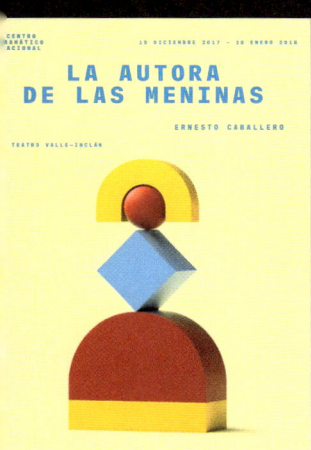

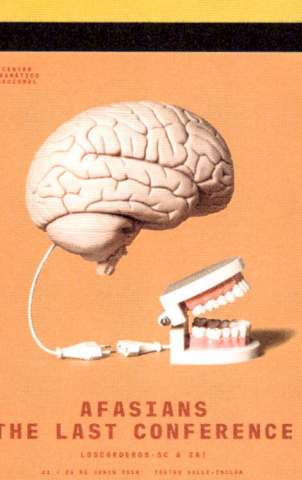
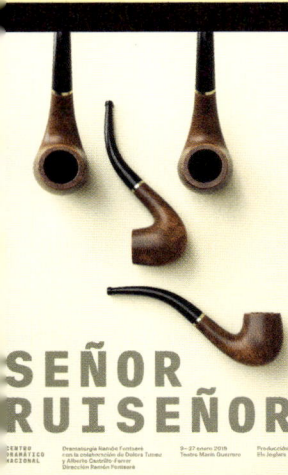
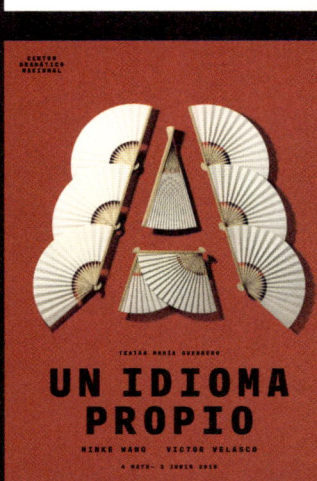

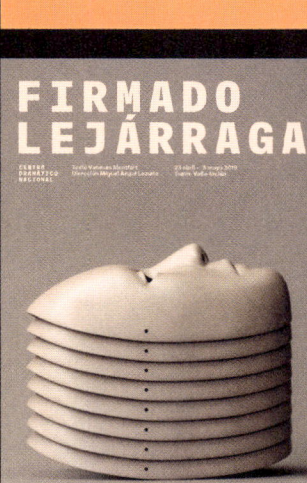

Posters, 2017–2020.

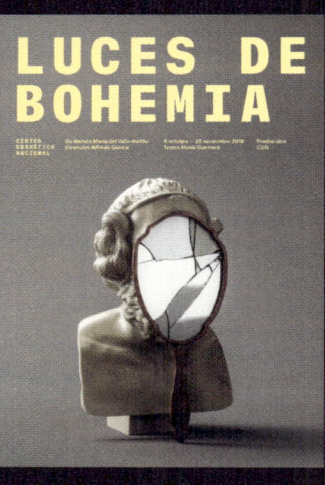

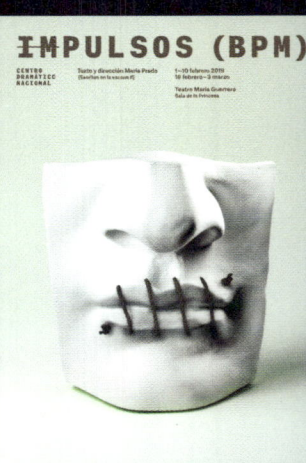

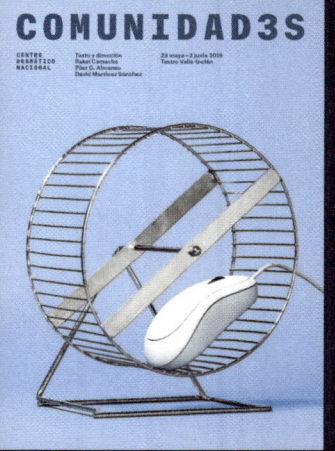

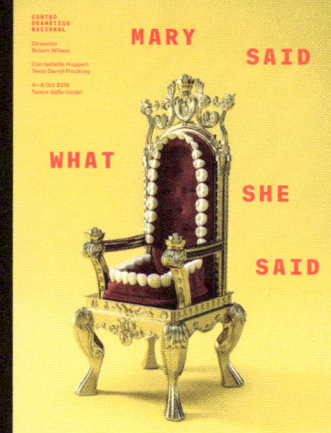
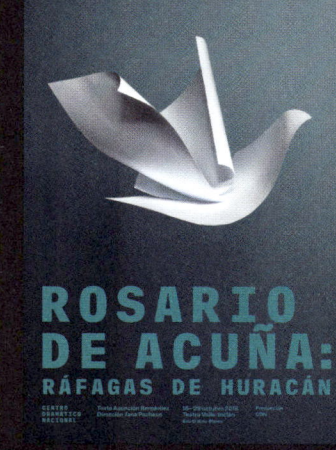

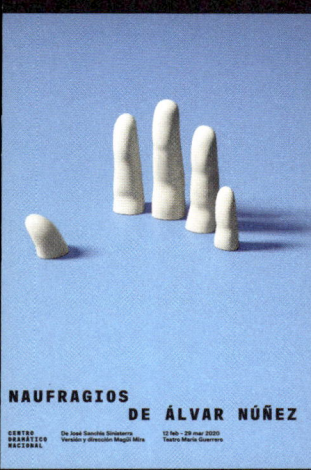

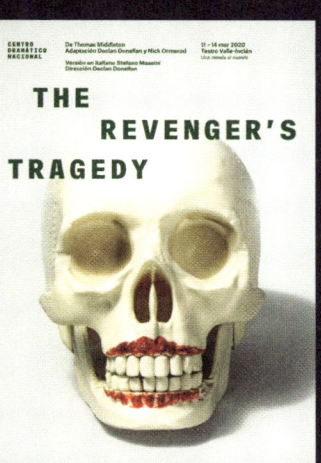

(1) *DDB Worldwide*, 2021. Unexpected Works. AD Fabien Donnay and Maximilien Guibert.
(2) *All Those Food Market*, 2022. Festival of artisans and gastronomic entrepreneurs in Barcelona.
(Next spread) **(1)** *Arts, Emotions and Creativity. International Meeting*. Centro Botín Santander,
(2) *Ajuntament de Barcelona*, 2021. Campaign for City and Science Biennial.

CCCB

The Center for Contemporary Culture of Barcelona (*CCCB*) enccurages interdisciplinary dialogue and critical reflection on the social, political and cultural issues of cur time.
I have had the opportunity to work on the communication of their exhibitions. Beyond the poster, we think about how the graphics will live on social networks, postcards, canvases, buses, bags, notebooks, press announcements, audiovisuals or a fridge magnet.
I try to distill the information to be conveyed until I come up with an image that is both precise, recognisable and versatile.

For the exhibition *"Quantum"* we use a *matryoshka* in the communication. Quantum physics can be understood as a Russian doll, where each layer represents a level of observation of the subatomic world.

"Mars, The Red Mirror" offered a broad vision of the planet Mars, covering topics such as future colonisation plans or its impact on literature and cinema. The exhibition poster hides the promise of a fascinating journey. In the image, you can see the reflection of the planet on the helmet of an astronaut, creating an optical illusion that appears to be a smile.

The exhibition *"Science Friction. Living Among Companion Species"* revolved around the symbiotic and interdependent relationships of all organisms on Earth, and the collaborations, exchanges, and mutations that result from them. For the communication, we envisioned a new species that challenged the fuzzy boundaries in biological classification.

El Centre de Cultura Contemporània de Barcelona (*CCCB*) fomenta el diálogo interdisciplinario y la reflexión crítica sobre las cuestiones sociales, políticas y culturales de nuestro tiempo. He tenido la oportunidad de trabajar en la comunicación de sus exposiciones. Más allá del cartel, pensamos en cómo vivirá la gráfica en redes sociales, postales, lonas, autobuses, bolsas, libretas, anuncios de prensa, audiovisuales o un imán de nevera. Intento destilar la información a transmitir hasta dar con una imagen que sea a la vez precisa, reconocible y versátil.

Para la exposición *"Cuántica"* utilizamos una *matrioshka* en la comunicación. La física cuántica puede entenderse como una muñeca rusa, donde cada capa representa un nivel de observación del mundo subatómico.

"Marte, el espejo rojo" ofrecía una amplia visión del planeta, abarcando temas como los planes futuros de colonización o su impacto en la literatura y el cine. El cartel de la exposición esconde la promesa de un viaje fascinante. En la imagen, se puede apreciar el reflejo del planeta sobre el casco de un astronauta, creando una ilusión óptica en la que parece verse una sonrisa.

La exposición *"Ciencia f(r)icción. Vida entre especies compañeras"* giraba en torno a las relaciones simbióticas e interdependientes de todos los organismos de la Tierra, y de las colaboraciones, intercambios y mutaciones que se derivan de ellas. Para la comunicación, imaginamos una nueva especie que desafiaba los difusos límites en la clasificación biológica.

Quàntica
Exposició al CCCB
10 abril—24 setembre 2019

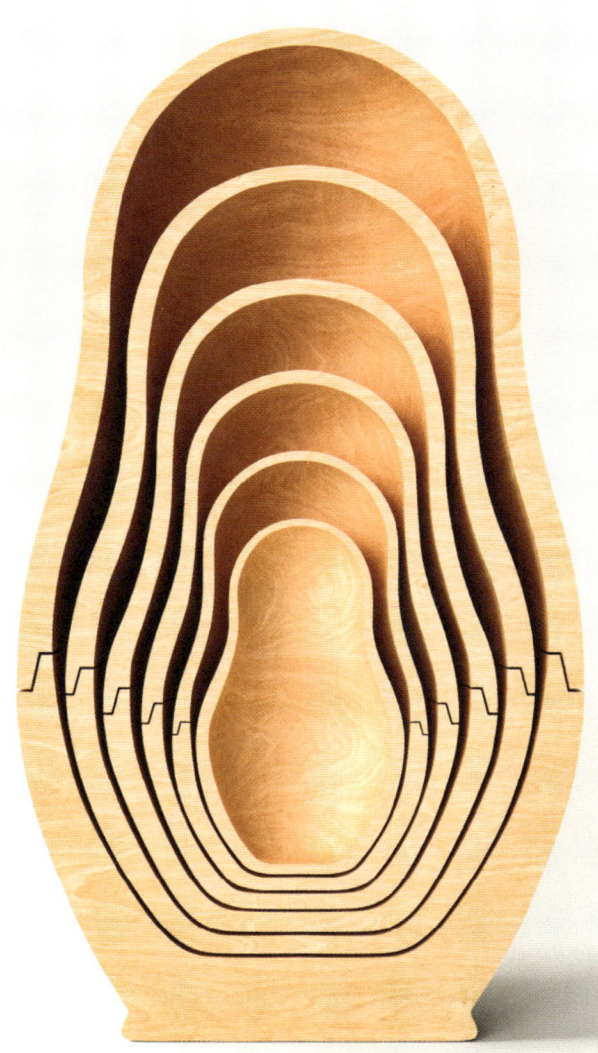

"Brains" presented the human brain as the most complex and enigmatic object known and the challenges of its study. Creativity arises when neural connections are activated in new and surprising ways. Similarly, fireworks are created through the activation of chemical compounds that release energy and create an explosion of light and colour.

For the graphics of the exhibition "AI: Artificial Intelligence" we based the identity on the infinite monkey theorem, where it is stated that an ape typing randomly on a typewriter for an unlimited time would eventually produce a masterpiece. This can be seen as an analogy for how AI today generates content by combining automatically learned and processed language patterns. As of the publication date of this book, we are not able to predict its impact at a social, cultural or economic level. In a personal capacity, the robot monkey is a kind of self-portrait. For the creation of the images, I used AI tools for the first time. Under my instructions they have generated endless and dazzling possibilities, but they have left me with the strange feeling of becoming the primate who ends up getting it right without really knowing what he is doing.

"Cerebro(s)" presentaba el cerebro humano como el objeto más complejo y enigmático conocido y los desafíos de su estudio. La creatividad surge cuando las conexiones neuronales se activan de nuevas y sorprendentes maneras. De forma similar, los fuegos artificiales se crean a través de la activación de compuestos químicos que liberan energía y generan una explosión de luz y color.

Para la gráfica de la exposición "IA: Inteligencia Artificial" nos basamos en el teorema del mono infinito, donde se plantea que un simio tecleando al azar en una máquina de escribir durante un tiempo ilimitado eventualmente produciría una obra maestra. Esto puede ser visto como una analogía de cómo hoy la IA genera contenido mediante la combinación de patrones de lenguaje aprendidos y procesados de manera automática. A fecha de la publicación de este libro no somos capaces de predecir su impacto a nivel social, cultural o económico. A título personal, el mono robot es una suerte de autorretrato. Para la creación de las imágenes, empleé por primera vez herramientas IA. Bajo mis instrucciones han generado infinitas y deslumbrantes posibilidades, pero me han dejado la extraña sensación de convertirme en el primate que acierta sin saber demasiado bien qué está haciendo.

(p.77) Quantum. CCCB, 2019. *(p.79)* Mars, The Red Mirror. CCCB, 2021. *(p.80-81)* Science Friction. Living Among Companion Species. CCCB, 2021. *(p.82-83)* Brains. CCCB, 2022. *(p.84-85)* AI: Artificial Intelligence. CCCB, 2023.

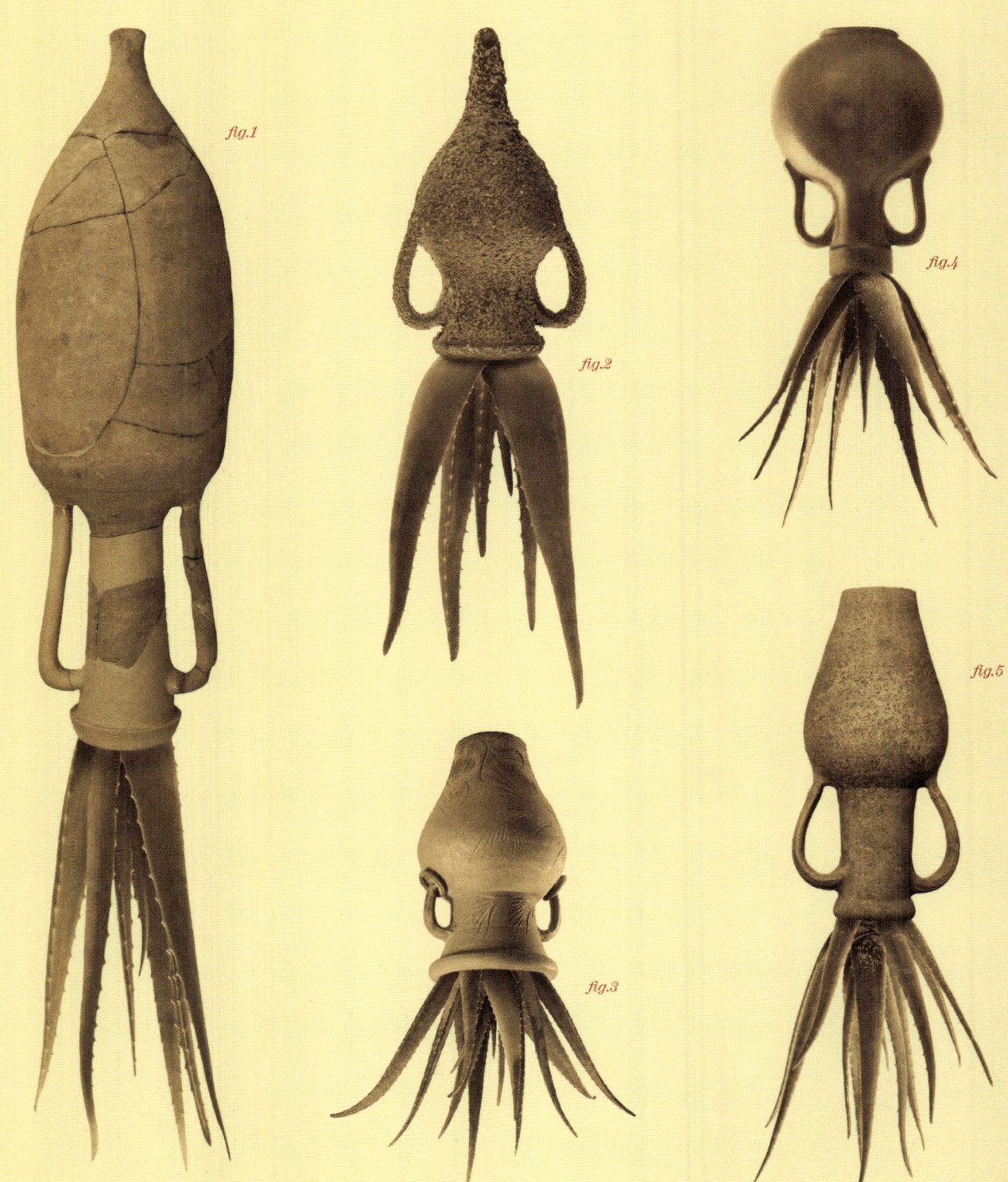

Der vermessene Mensch

During the German colonial era in South West Africa, present-day Namibia, imperial troops committed the first genocide of the 20th century against the Herero, Nama and Ovambanderu peoples. The Germans murdered tens of thousands of people and took their remains in the name of science, guided by racial principles. The skulls and skeletons were used in anthropological studies with which it was intended to prove white supremacy. They were also used to justify colonisation and domination of subject peoples.

Designing the poster for the film "Measures of Men" (*StudioCanal*, 2023) by Lars Kraume was a challenging, emotionally intense and incredibly rewarding process. The objective was to create a poster that represented the theme of the film in a powerful but respectful way, avoiding explicit and sinister images.

I started the process by researching photographs of human zoos, exhibits of African people that took place in Europe between the 17th and 20th centuries, and I ended up focusing on a close-up of the protagonist, dressed in her colourful, traditional costume and looking straight at the camera. Above it, an oversized German Gothic typeface. Deliberately disconnected from the image as a sign of oppression, aggressiveness and invasion of physical and personal territory.

Durante la época colonial alemana en África Sudoccidental, actual Namibia, las tropas imperiales cometieron el primer genocidio del siglo XX contra los pueblos Herero, Nama y Ovambanderu. Los alemanes asesinaron a decenas de miles de personas y tomaron sus restos en nombre de la ciencia, guiados por principios raciales. Los cráneos y esqueletos fueron utilizados en estudios antropológicos con los que se pretendía acreditar la supremacía blanca. También se utilizaron para justificar la colonización y el dominio de los pueblos sometidos.

Diseñar el cartel de la película *"Der vermessene Mensch"* (*StudioCanal*, 2023) de Lars Kraume fue un proceso desafiante, emocionalmente intenso e increíblemente enriquecedor. El objetivo era crear un cartel que representara el tema de la película de manera impactante pero respetuosa, huyendo de imágenes explícitas y siniestras.

Inicié el proceso investigando fotografías de zoos humanos, exhibiciones de personas africanas que tuvieron lugar en Europa entre los siglos XVII y XX, y terminé centrándome en un primer plano de la protagonista, vestida con sus coloridos trajes tradicionales y mirando directamente a cámara. Sobre ella, una sobredimensionada tipografía gótica alemana. Deliberadamente inconexa con la imagen en señal de opresión, agresividad y de invasión del territorio físico y personal.

Madres Paralelas

Pedro Almodóvar revolutionised Spanish culture, opening new avenues in the representation of social issues and sexual identity with a fresh, free narrative and with a unique aesthetic universe. His movie posters are a relevant part of his artistic legacy. Not only as an advertising tool, but also as an artistic expression that has turned them into huge cultural icons. I recognise these posters and their creators as an important influence in my training as a designer.

The *Parallel Mothers* (*El Deseo*, 2021) project was very exciting from the beginning. The film talks about motherhood, mourning and memory. Among the proposals presented were hugs, tears and different representations of pain and sorority. For the campaign, two posters were chosen. One introduced the film to the media and the public, and the other presented it in movie theaters and on social platforms.

Instagram censored the first for showing an eye-shaped lactating nipple crying milk, considering it erotic or pornographic content. This decision caused a great uproar in the media and networks, generating public debates about the sexualisation of the female body, censorship, freedom of expression or the moral decisions made by algorithms. The controversy went viral internationally, turning the image into a symbol beyond the film. Such was the media and social pressure that *Instagram* was forced to publicly apologise and allow its publication.

Pedro Almodóvar revolucionó la cultura española abriendo nuevas vías en la representación de temas sociales y de identidad sexual con una narrativa fresca, libre y con un singular universo estético. Los carteles de sus películas son parte relevante de su legado artístico. No solo como herramienta publicitaria, sino también como una expresión artística que los ha convertido en enormes iconos culturales. Reconozco estos carteles y a sus autores como influencia importante en mi formación como diseñador.

El proyecto de *Madres Paralelas* (*El Deseo*, 2021) fue muy emocionante desde el primer momento. El film habla sobre la maternidad, el duelo y la memoria. Entre las propuestas presentadas había abrazos, lágrimas y diferentes representaciones de dolor y sororidad. Para la comunicación se escogieron dos carteles. Uno daba a conocer la película a los medios y al público y el otro la presentaba en salas de cine y plataformas.

Instagram censuró el primero por mostrar un pezón lactante en forma de ojo que llora leche, considerándolo contenido erótico o pornográfico. Esta decisión provocó gran revuelo en medios y redes, generando debates públicos sobre la sexualización del cuerpo femenino, la censura, la libertad de expresión o las decisiones morales tomadas por algoritmos. La controversia se viralizó internacionalmente, convirtiendo la imagen en un símbolo más allá de la película. Tal fue la presión mediática y social que *Instagram* se vio obligado a disculparse públicamente y permitir su publicación.

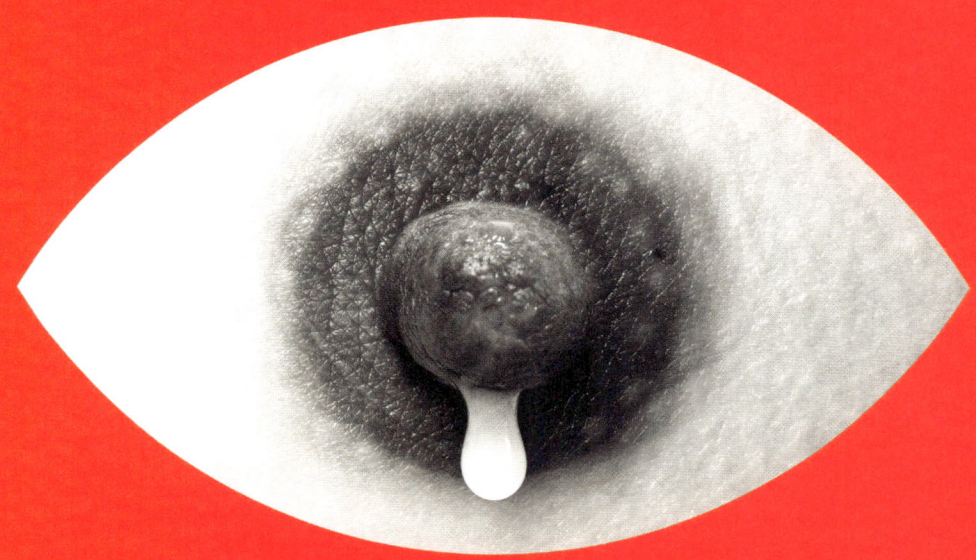

LA VANGUARDIA
Un pezón goteando leche, el gráfico e icónico cartel de Almodóvar para 'Madres paralelas'

Diario16
Instagram muestra su lado más mojigato y retira el cartel de la última película de Almodóvar

npr
Instagram Apologizes After Removing A Movie Poster Because It Shows A Nipple

OPOVO
Instagram tira do ar cartaz do novo filme de Pedro Almodóvar

Variety
Instagram Apologizes to Pedro Almodóvar for Poster Censorship, Filmmaker Responds

ABC
Almodóvar gana la partida: Instagram recula y permite la publicación del cartel de 'Madres paralelas'

el Periódico
Almodóvar publica amb polèmica el cartell de 'Madres paralelas', la seva nova pel·lícula

FRANCE 24
Instagram 'sorry' after pulling poster for new Almocovar film

Libération
Le téton de l'affiche du prochain Almodóvar n'échappe pas à la censure d'Instagram

ara
Polèmica amb el cartell de 'Madres paralelas', el nou film de Pedro Almodóvar

Le Parisien
Pour un téton, Instagram supprime l'affiche du nouveaufilm de Pedro Almodóvar puis s'excuse

GLAMOUR
Penélope Cruz comparte el póster de 'Madres Paralelas' y su 'realismo' lo hace viral

The New York Times
Almodóvar has conquered the algorithm

EL MUNDO
Instagram censura el cartel de Madres Paralelas

TIMES MALTA
Instagram 'sorry' after pulling poster for new Almodovar film

EXCELSIOR
Instagram se disculpa con Almodóvar por censurar póster de 'Madres Paralelas'

Público
El pezón del cartel de la última película de Almodóvar es ya un icono del año

MARCA
El cartel de 'Madres Paralelas', película de Pedro Almodóvar, reta a la censura con un pezón goteando leche

EL UNIVERSAL
Instagram retira cartel de cinta de Almodóvar: un pezón derramando una gota de leche

Pravda
Instagram sa ospravedlnil Almodóvarovi za cenzúru plagátu k jeho filmu

EL PAÍS
Almodóvar libera el pezón

BAZAAR
El pezón del cartel de 'Madres paralelas' de Almodóvar gana la batalla de la censura en Instagram

NATIONAL COALITION AGAINST CENSORSHIP
INSTAGRAM CENSORS, THEN UNCENSORS, ALMODÓVAR MOVIE POSTER

Bloomberg
Instagram Apologizes for Almodóvar Film's Poster Censorship

Esquire
El pezón de Almodóvar: el director vence a Instagram ante la censura del póster de 'Madres paralelas'

Fotogramas
ALMODÓVAR AGRADECE EL APOYO TRAS LA POLÉMICA POR EL CARTEL DE 'MADRES PARALELAS'

La Voz de Galicia
Polémica por la censura del cartel de la nueva película de Almodóvar

HUFFPOST
Almodóvar: "Hay que estar alerta antes de que las máquinas decidan qué podemos hacer"

NEWS.am
Instagram-ը հետաձգել է Պեդրո Ալմոդովարի «Զուգահեռ մայրեր» ֆիլմի պաստառը, այն համարել են հանդուգն

The Guardian
Instagram apologises after Almodóvar poster censorship row

Daily Mail
Poster for Penelope Cruz movie Parallel Mothers showing a lactating nipple is censored by Instagram

COSMOPOLITAN
La censura sui capezzoli colpisce pure Pedro Almodóvar, e lui si schiera con #freethenipple

The Washington Post
Pedro Almodóvar warns against algorithms in Instagram row

USA TODAY
Pedro Almodóvar declares 'victory' after Instagram reinstates film poster featuring nipple

豆瓣
海报中的哺乳期乳头遭到审查，Instagram向导演阿莫多瓦致歉

The Jakarta Post
Instagram removes poster for new Almodovar film

NACIONAL
Poster novog filma Pedra Almodovara nevjerojatno je uzbudljiv

Le Point
L'affiche d'un film d'Almodóvar retirée d'Instagram à cause d'un téton

Cuba
Instagram se disculpa por quitar póster de la película de Pedro Almodóvar "Madres paralelas"

DEADLINE
Instagram Backtracks After Taking Down Poster For Pedro Almodovar's Venice Opener 'Parallel Mothers'

CNN Prima NEWS
Instagram smazal režisérů Almodóvarovi plakát k filmu. Byla na něm bradavka

INDEPENDENT
Parallel Mothers: Instagram apologises after taking down lactating nipple poster

NEW YORK POST
New Penelope Cruz film poster showing leaking nipple censored online

Clarín
Pedro Almodóvar desafía la censura de Instagram con el afiche de su nueva película

N1
Poster novog filma Pedra Almodovara izazvao polemike na društvenim mrežama

Rolling Stone
Instagram Apologizes After Banning Pedro Almodóvar Movie Poster Over Nipple Artwork

IndieWire
Instagram Apologizes for Banning Almodóvar's 'Parallel Mothers' Poster, Featuring Lactating Nipple

BBC
Instagram says sorry for removing Pedro Almodovar film poster

DR
Stjerneinstruktør fik fjernet billede af mælkedryppende bryst på Instagram: Nu får han en undskyldning

LOS ANDES
Pedro Almodóvar: el cineasta que esta semana le ganó a Instagram

VULTURE
Instagram Is 'Really Sorry' for Putting the Madres Paralelas Poster in Horny Jail

Newsweek
Penélope Cruz Movie Poster Featuring Lactating Nipple Censored on Instagram

sky news
Instagram apologises for removing Penelope Cruz film poster showing lactating nipple

W
Instagram Apologizes For Censoring Pedro Almodóvar's Nipple Film Poster

Courrier international
Le téton de la discorde. L'affiche du nouveau film d'Almodóvar censurée par Instagram

CINEMANÍA
"Un algoritmo nunca tendrá corazón": Pedro Almodóvar agradece el apoyo al póster de 'Madres paralelas'

Las manos de los maestros.
J.M. Coetzee, 2016.
AD Nora Grosse.
Penguin Random House.

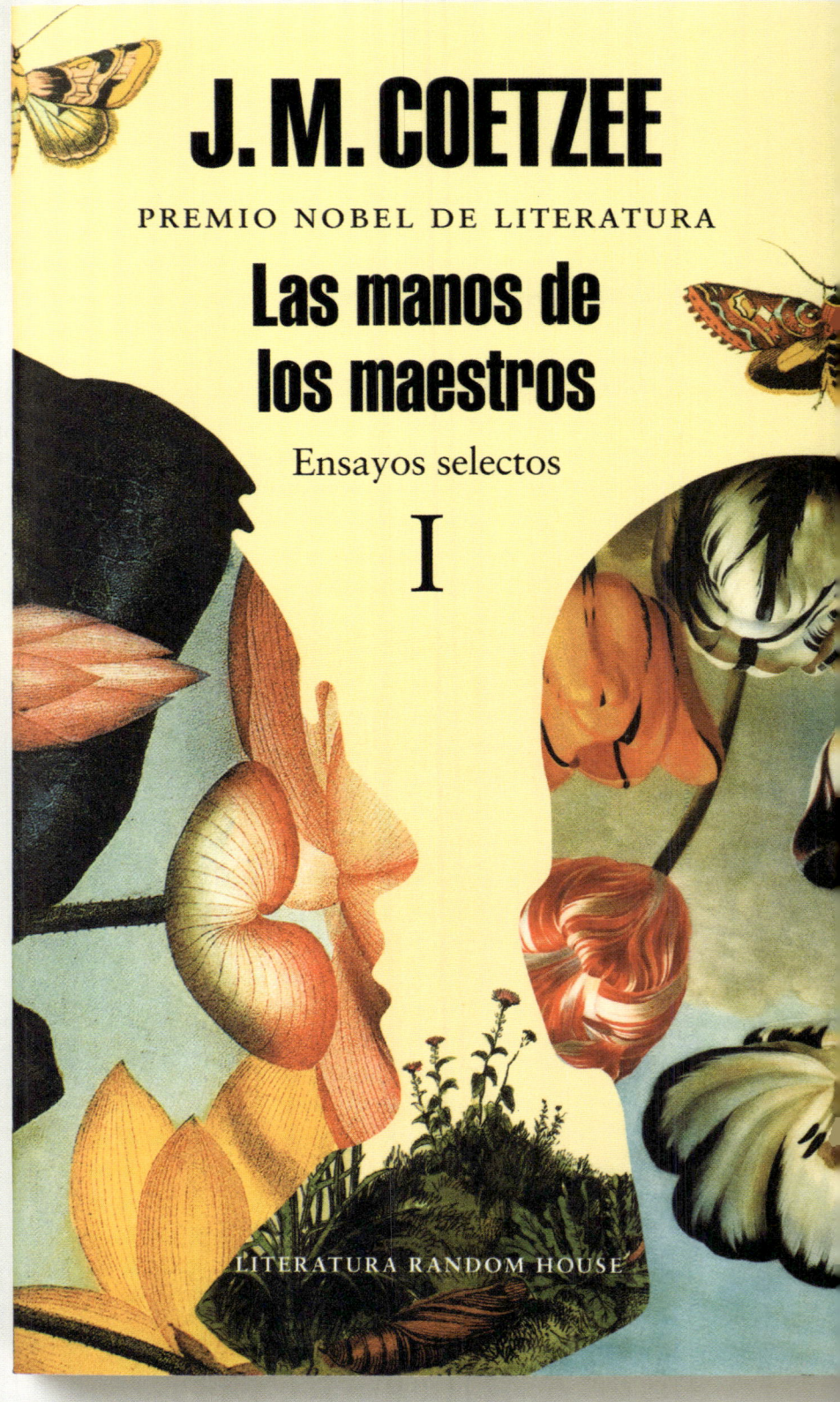

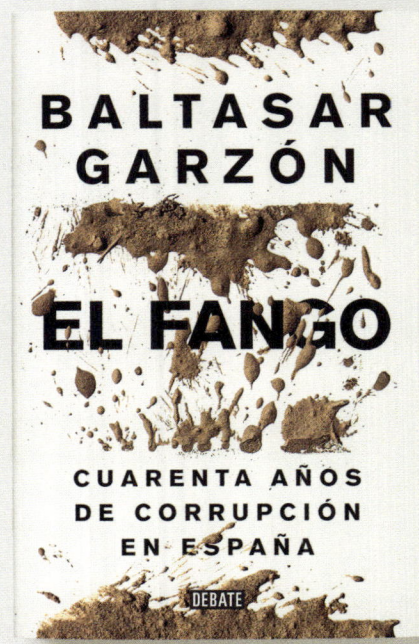
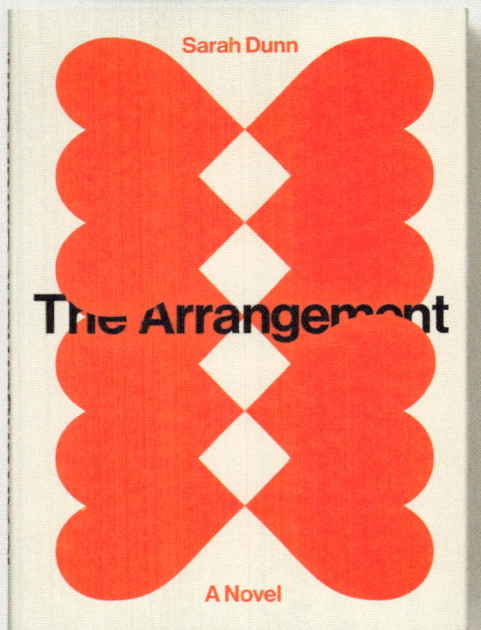
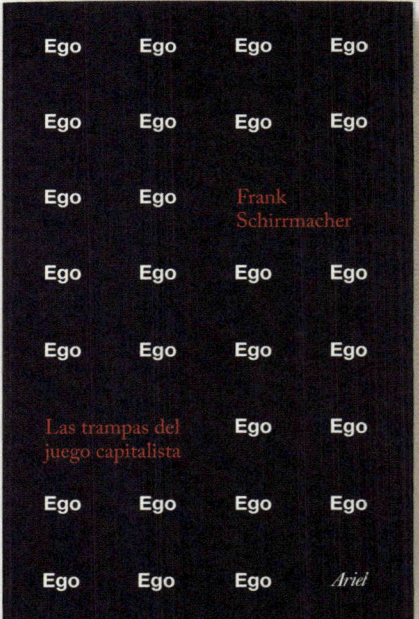

(1) *Nemesis*, Misha Glenny, 2015 (Not published). **(2)** *El Fango*, Baltasar Garzón, 2015. Penguin Random House. AD Nora Grosse. **(3)** *The Arrangement*, Sarah Dunn, 2016 (Not published). **(4)** *Ego, Las trampas del juego capitalista*, Frank Schirrmacher, 2014. Ariel. AD Mauricio Restrepo.

(1) *Autobiografía de un Cobarde*, Alfredo Gómez Cerdá, 2015. **(2)** *La Gran Búsqueda*, Sylvia Nasar, 2012. Debate. Random House Mondadori. AD Ferran López (Not published). **(3)** *És l'hora dels adéus?*, Xavier Sala i Martín, 2014. Penguin Random House. **(4)** *La Guillotina*, Simone Van Der Vlugt, 2017. Ediciones SM. AD Lara Peces.

A.M. Cassandre,
Mª Ángeles Domínguez, 2010.
Gràffica. AD Victor Palau.

Saul Bass, Ainhoa Fernández
y Mª Ángeles Domínguez, 2011.
Gràffica. AD Victor Palau.

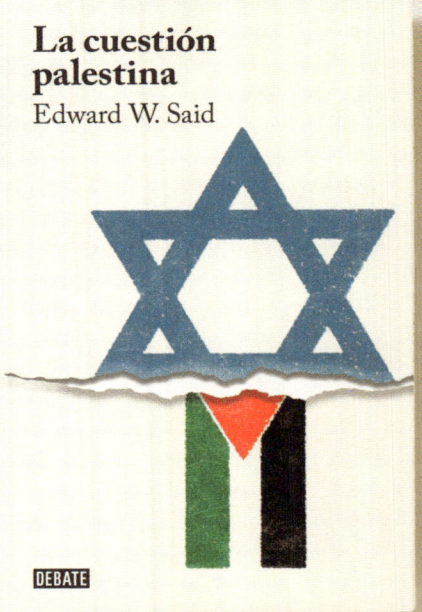

(1) *The Hell of Good Intentions: America's Foreign Policy Elite and the Decline of U.S. Primacy*, Stephen M. Walt, 2018. Farrar, Straus and Giroux. **(2)** *Ashenden o El agente secreto*, W. Somerset Maugham, 2010. Random House Mondadori. **(3)** *Al filo de la navaja*, W. Somerset Maugham, 2010. Random House Mondadori. **(4)** *La cuestión palestina*, Edward W. Said, 2011 (Not published).

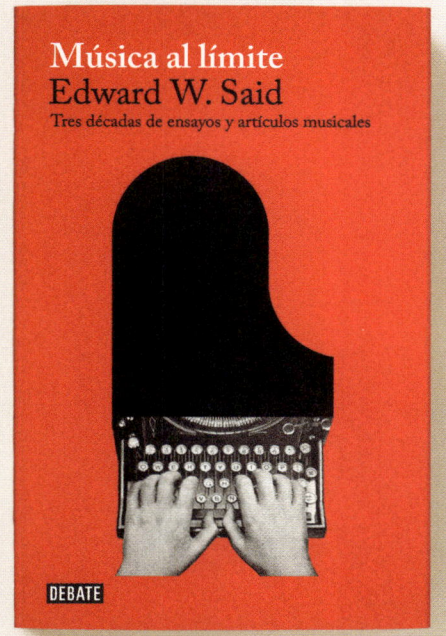
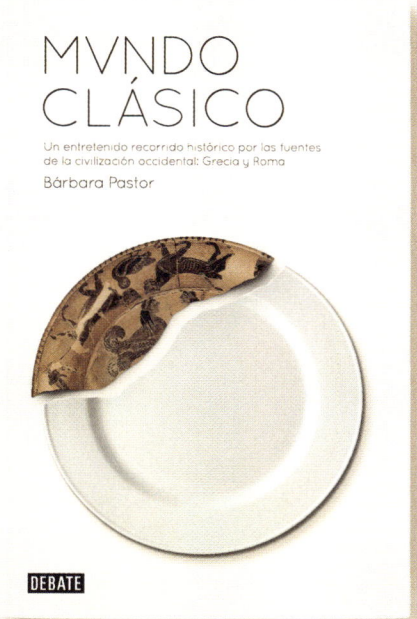

(1) *Antología poética*, Mario Benedetti, 2019. Penguin Random House. **(2)** *Piratas de lo público*, Antón Losada, 2013. Editorial Planeta. **(3)** *Música al límite, Tres décadas de ensayos y artículos musicales*, Edward W. Said, 2010. Debate. Random House Mondadori. **(4)** *Mundo Clásico*, Bárbara Pastor, 2010. Debate. Random House Mondadori (Not published).

Humor, Terry Eagleton, 2021. Taurus.

El último sueño, Pedro Almodóvar, 2023. Reservoir Books.

Adiós a las armas, Una crónica del final de ETA, Antoni Batista, 2011. Debate. Random House Mondadori.

Barcelona Poesia 2019

This is one of those dream assignments, so much that it almost killed me. Fortunately, I was already bald at 20. At some point during every project I still have anxiety and stomach pain (also doing this book). My grandfather used to say he slept with one eye open, some nights it happens to me too. I think everyone will realise that I am a fraud and a security guard will accompany me to the exit door. It is the well-typified impostor syndrome. Apparently it severely whips sectors similar to mine. Fighting these villains and translating them into positive energy is one of the most important daily tasks.

In 2019, the Barcelona City Council commissioned me to design communications for the Poetry Festival and I wanted to do it well. It was difficult for me to run away from the cliché images; the feather, the cloud, the dried flowers, the clock, the chess pieces… The list of toxic metaphors is long, I recommend using them only in an emergency. I was looking for poetry somewhere unexpected, I even proposed using Leo Messi in the poster. Poetry does not have to be synonymous with idealised beauty. In the same way that we don't only paint flower meadows and blue skies, we can enjoy non-harmonic sounds, bitter flavours or the blackest darkness in controlled doses. I wanted to represent poetry as a synonym for emotion, whatever the emotion is. Many times, working from contrast works for me. To talk about something gigantic I use an ant, for something quick, a turtle. In this case, we represent emotion with a cold interpretation of the bristling epidermis.

Este es uno de esos encargos soñados. Tanto, que casi acaba conmigo. Afortunadamente ya me había quedado calvo a los 20. En algún momento de los proyectos sigo teniendo ansiedad y dolor de estómago (también haciendo este libro). Mi abuelo decía dormir con un ojo abierto, algunas noches a mí también me pasa. Pienso que todos se darán cuenta de que soy un farsante y un agente de seguridad me acompañará a la puerta de salida. Es el bien tipificado síndrome del impostor, aparentemente azota con severidad a sectores similares al mío. Luchar contra estos villanos y traducirlos en motores positivos es una de las tareas diarias más importantes.

En 2019, el Ayuntamiento de Barcelona me encargó la comunicación del Festival de Poesía y yo quería hacerlo bien. Me resultaba muy difícil huir de las imágenes cliché; la pluma, la nube, las flores secas, el reloj, las piezas de ajedrez… La lista de metáforas tóxicas es larga, recomiendo utilizarlas solo en caso de emergencia. Buscaba poesía a algún lugar que no le fuese propio, incluso planteé utilizar a Leo Messi en el cartel. La poesía no tiene por qué ser sinónimo de una belleza idealizada. De la misma manera que no sólo pintamos prados con flores y cielos azules, podemos disfrutar de sonidos no armónicos, de sabores amargos o de la más negra oscuridad en dosis controladas. Quería representar la poesía como sinónimo de emoción, sea cual sea. Muchas veces, me funciona trabajar desde el contraste. Para hablar de algo gigantesco utilizo una hormiga, para algo rápido, una tortuga. En este caso, representamos emoción con una fría interpretación de la epidermis erizada.

BARCELONA POESIA
8 — 16 MAIG 2019

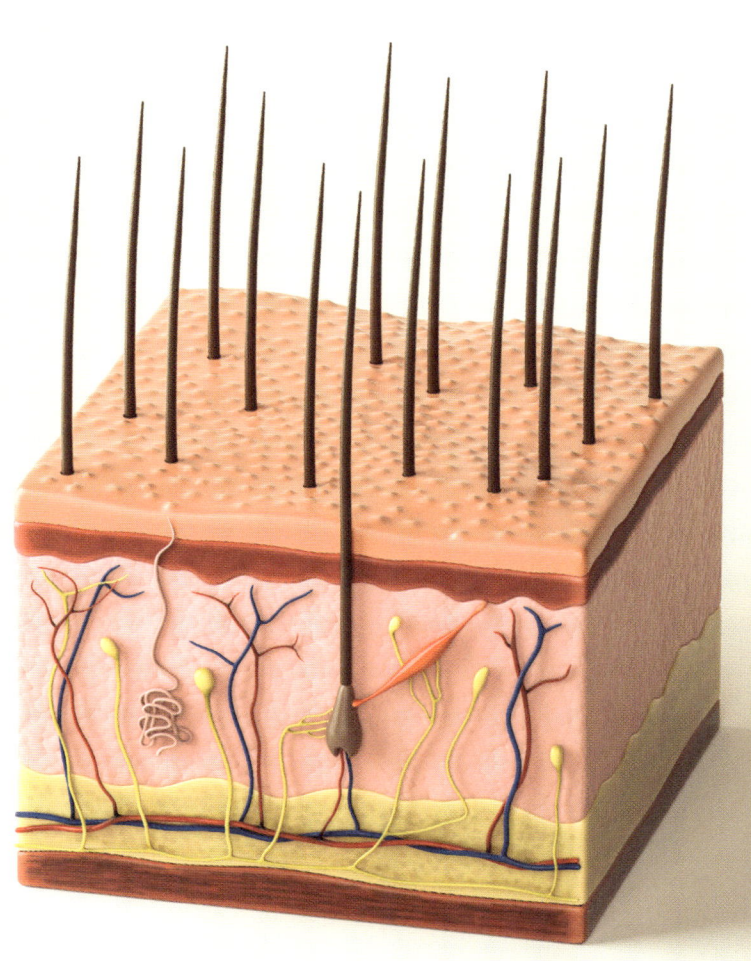

Love of Lesbian

Warner Music commissioned me at the end of 2019 to design the new *Love of Lesbian* album. The work explores the theme of suicide and invites us to reflect on the meaning of life, an *epic journey towards nothingness*. They asked me for a forceful and clean cover that would question the viewer. They talked about a clear design, without artifice and the symbolic power of the memorable covers of *Hipgnosis*.

The project was developed in 2020 during the *COVID-19* pandemic and lockdown, so the production of the image could not be a real photograph. This huge limitation helped to explore new expressive possibilities and new work tools.

It finally went on sale in 2021, in a post-lockdown society experiencing a complex and challenging transition to the "new normal". Many of us feel anxious and worried about the future as we adjust to new forms of work, education, and socialisation.

The cover image, recontextualised in time, acquired new readings that made it uncomfortably contemporary.

Warner Music me encargó a finales de 2019 el diseño del nuevo disco de *Love of Lesbian*. La obra explora el tema del suicidio e invita a un momento reflexivo sobre el sentido de la vida, un *Viaje épico hacia la nada*. Me pedían una portada contundente y limpia que interpelara al espectador. Se habló de un diseño diáfano, sin artificios y del poder simbólico de las memorables portadas de *Hipgnosis*.

El proyecto se desarrolló en 2020 durante la pandemia de *COVID-19* y el confinamiento, así que la producción de la imagen no podía ser una fotografía real. Esa gran limitación ayudó a explorar nuevas posibilidades expresivas y nuevas herramientas de trabajo.

Salió finalmente a la venta en 2021, en una sociedad post-confinamiento que experimentaba una transición compleja y desafiante a la "nueva normalidad". Muchos nos sentimos ansiosos y preocupados por el futuro, mientras nos adaptábamos a nuevas formas de trabajo, educación y socialización.

La imagen de portada, recontextualizada en el tiempo, adquiriría nuevas lecturas que la hacían incómodamente contemporánea.

V.E.H.N.

LOVE *of* LESBIAN

Musika Música

In 2019 I was in charge of the communication of a great classical music festival in Bilbao. The theme of this edition was the cultural and musical contribution of London and New York. In many cases, I approach the work from a reinterpretation of the sum of concepts. In this case, trying to match so many elements resulted in a *Dr. Frankenstein* creation. What do all the elements of the sum have in common? Music, travel and an urban history.

The first of the proposals we worked with was a treble clef metro map. I showed it to the client and they didn't like it at all. That was great, it helped me keep looking for the right tone and image. You have to learn not to fall in love too much with the first ideas, they usually evolve into new and better solutions.

In a second proposal, we focused on what differentiates the three cities. We thought of a series of clocks in which the hands were replaced by a conductor who, waving his arms, indicated the different hours of London, New York and Bilbao. It didn't work either, perfect.

We continued working with the idea of a journey. How does music travel? I have a childhood memory of accompanying my brother to the music school and seeing with some fascination the shapes of the empty instrument boxes stacked at the entrance. He was trying to guess which instrument they housed. Looking at the suitcases I saw that some stringed instruments were anthropomorphic in shape and seemed to want to tell

En 2019 me encargaban la comunicación de un gran festival de música clásica en Bilbao. Esa edición tenía como eje temático la contribución cultural y musical de Londres y Nueva York. En muchos casos, abordo el trabajo desde una reinterpretación de la suma de conceptos. En este caso, intentar unir tantos elementos daba como resultado una creación del *Dr. Frankenstein*. ¿Qué tienen en común todos los elementos de la suma? La música, el viaje y una historia urbana.

La primera de las propuestas con la que trabajamos era un mapa de metro en forma de clave de sol. Lo enseñé al cliente y no le gustó en absoluto. Eso fue buenísimo, me ayudó a seguir buscando el tono y la imagen adecuada. Hay que aprender a no enamorarse demasiado de las primeras ideas, por lo general evolucionan en nuevas y mejores soluciones.

En una segunda propuesta, trabajamos poniendo el foco en qué diferencia a las tres ciudades. Pensamos en una serie de relojes en los que se sustituían las agujas por un director de orquesta que moviendo sus brazos, indicaba el diferente horario de Londres, Nueva York y Bilbao. Tampoco funcionó, perfecto.

Seguimos trabajando con la idea de viaje ¿Cómo viaja la música? Tengo el recuerdo de infancia de acompañar a mi hermano al conservatorio y ver con cierta fascinación las formas de las cajas vacías de los instrumentos apiladas en la entrada. Intentaba adivinar qué instrumento albergaban. Mirando las maletas vi que algunos instrumentos de cuerda tenían forma

me something. Finally we had it. An urban story, two cello suitcases meet in the same destination. We do not need to represent the place where the festival happens explicitly in the image. The Eiffel Tower does not appear in all the posters for events that happen in Paris. In this case, forcing the presence of NY and London did not help the poster either and it was information that would already appear in the text. What does not add, often subtracts.

For the construction of the image, I first thought about buying several cello suitcases and photographing still lifes where they would create a dialogue. Seeing their price I changed my mind and we did everything digitally. I liked causing a little short circuit in the process, to talk about classical music, we would use the latest technology.

antropomórfica y parecían querer contarme algo. Ya lo teníamos. Una historia urbana, dos maletas de violonchelo se encuentran en un mismo destino. No necesitamos representar el lugar donde sucede el festival explícitamente en la imagen. No en todos los carteles de eventos que suceden en París aparece la Torre Eiffel. En este caso, forzar la presencia de NY y Londres tampoco ayudaba al cartel y era una información que ya aparecería en el texto. Lo que no suma, a menudo resta.

Para la construcción de la imagen, primero pensé en comprar varias maletas de violonchelo y fotografiar bodegones donde dialogaran. Al ver su precio cambié de idea y lo hicimos todo digitalmente. Me gustaba provocar un pequeño cortocircuito en el proceso, para hablar de música clásica, utilizaríamos lo último en tecnología.

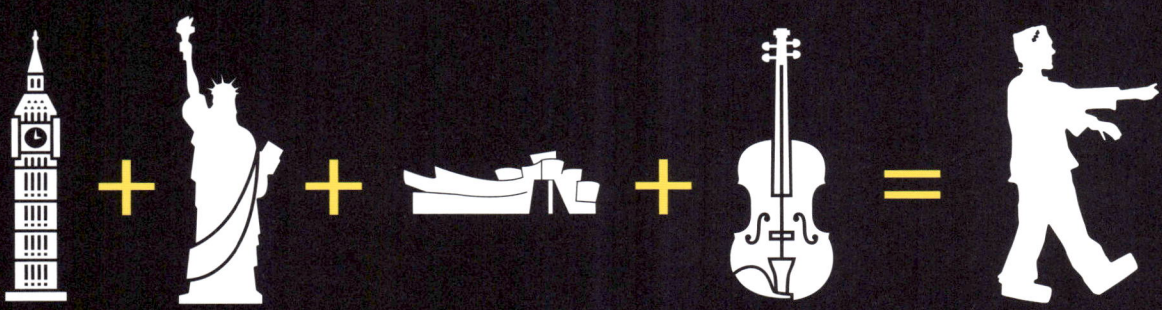

Center for Urban Pedagogy.
Annual Benefit, 2013.
AD Sam Holler.

Titerescena.
CDN, 2019.

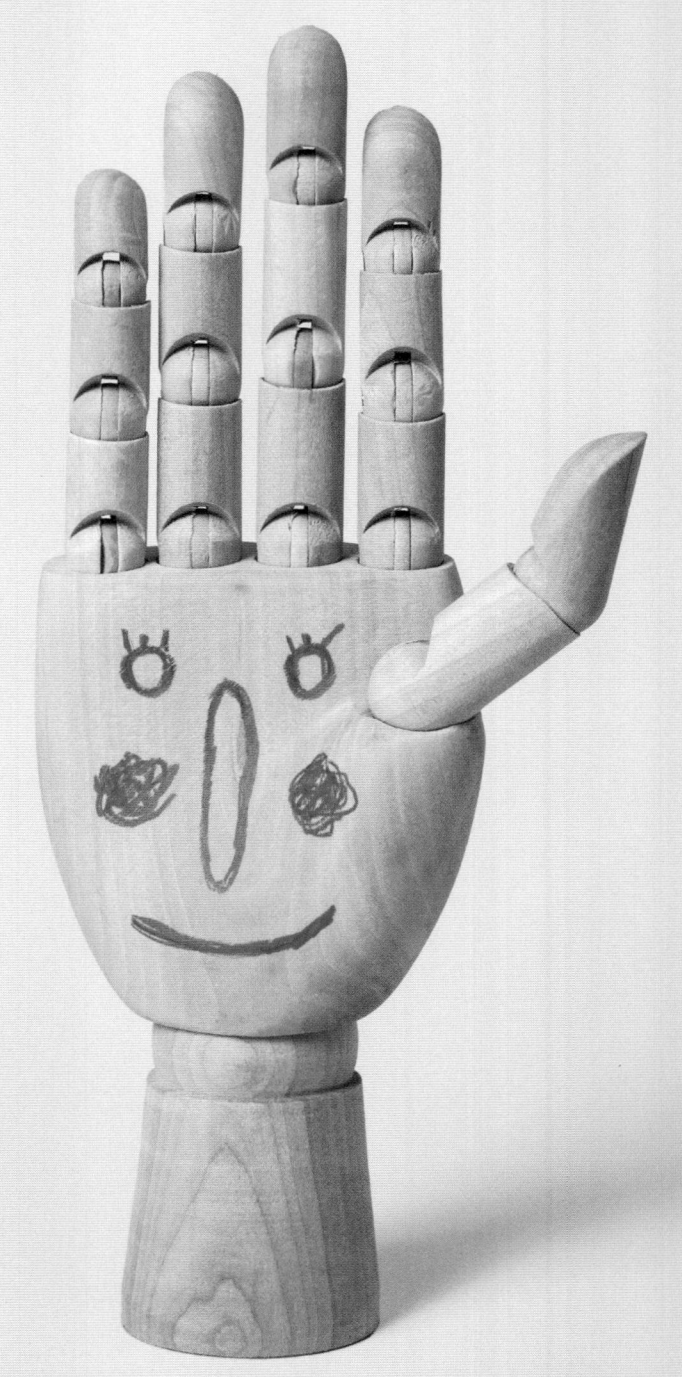

Singlot Comedy Festival,
2015. El Terrat.

Legaris Wine,
Time without clocks,
2020. + Rosàs.

Solvia

In 2016 I was working on an advertising agency's campaign for a bank's real estate agency. They used this house *(a)* in their communication, and although it worked very well, the idea was to reinterpret it in such a way that it was a very versatile element and had a more adult look. It was necessary to generate a system that could function as a language for countless static and moving applications. Our proposal was *(b)* to keep the essentials while respecting the graphic legacy of the brand. Coco Chanel used to say that before leaving the house, you should look at yourself in the mirror and take off an accessory, we were a little rougher and we ended up removing the walls and doors as well.

En 2016 estuve trabajando en la campaña de una agencia de publicidad para la inmobiliaria de un banco. Utilizaban esta casa *(a)* en su comunicación, y aunque funcionaba muy bien, la idea era reinterpretarla de forma que fuese un elemento muy versátil y que tuviese un aspecto más adulto. Había que generar un sistema que pudiese funcionar como lenguaje para infinidad de aplicaciones estáticas y en movimiento. Nuestra propuesta fue *(b)* quedarnos con lo esencial respetando el legado gráfico de la marca. Decía Coco Chanel que antes de salir de casa, deberías mirarte al espejo y quitarte un accesorio, nosotros fuimos algo más toscos y acabamos quitando las paredes y las puertas también.

(Next spread) TV Spots. *Solvia Real State*, 2016. **(1)** *Tetris*. **(2)** *Shapes*. **(3)** *Polaroid*. Agency S,C,P,F, Graphic Prod Estudio Javier Jaén. CD Toni Segarra, Paco Badia. AD Albert Morera, Laura Soler. CW Dalmau Oliveras. Account Mgmt Helena Grau, Carla Gorin, Marta García. Prod Susanna Bergés. Dir MANSON. Spot Prod CANADA. Prod Luna Esquerdo. **(4)** *Piano*. Agency S,C,P,F. Graphic Prod Estudio Javier Jaén. CD Toni Segarra, Paco Badia. AD Albert Morera, Laura Soler. Account Mgmt Helena Grau, Carla Gorin, Marta García. Prod Susanna Bergés. Dir Albert Sala. Prod Andreu Vidal (Malditos) & Luis Delgado (The Mushroom Company). Prod Blanca Ballesté. Prod Mgmt Nacho Piñar. AD Julieta Lasarte. Jose Tirado. DOP Marc Miró.

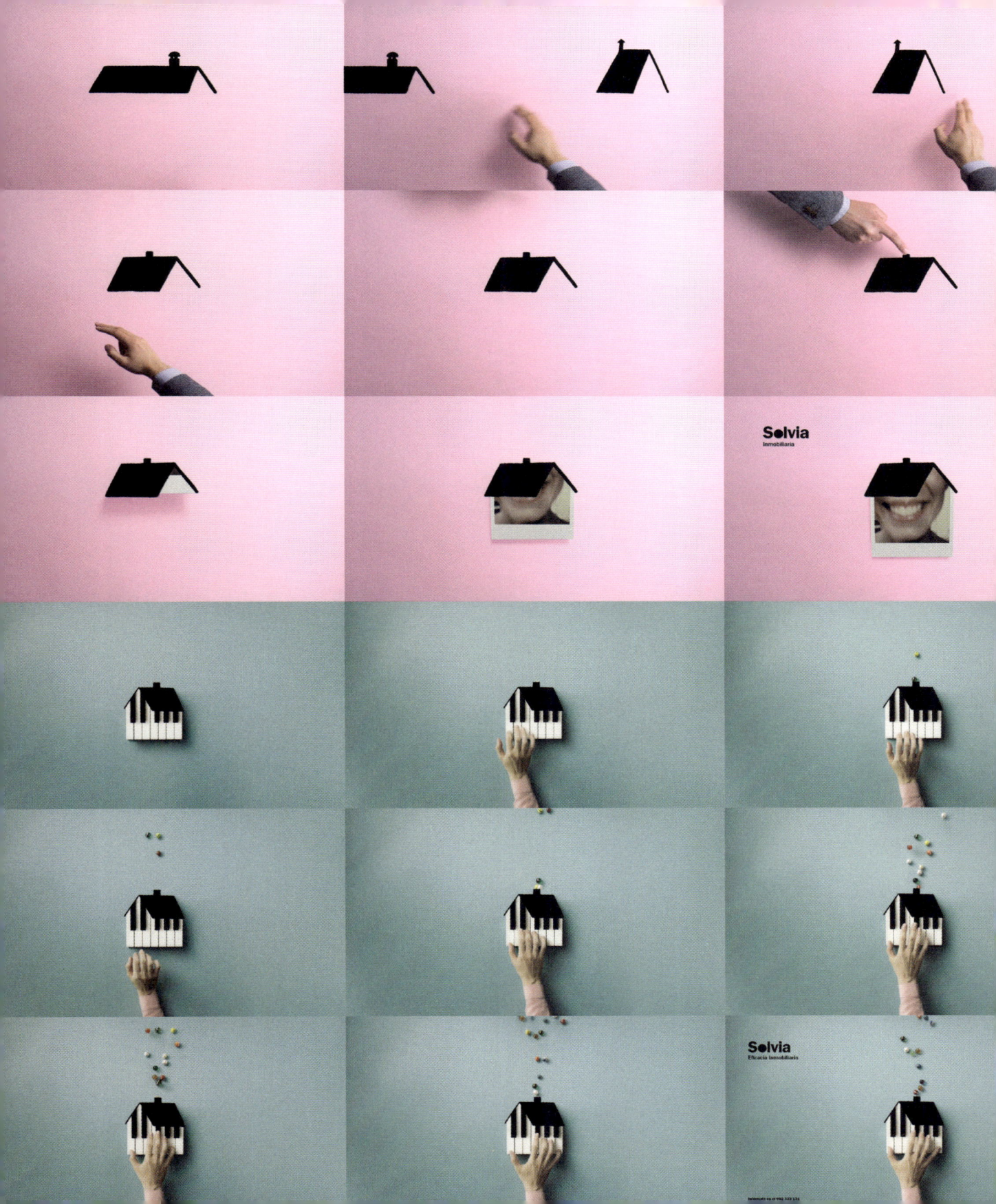

Louis Vuitton, 2017. TV Spot. MY LV World Tour Campaign. ACNE.

Camper

I'm interested in honest advertising, which shows the best side of the product, of course, but without too many tricks. These are not shoes to fly or to flirt with. *These boots are made for walking, and that's just what they'll do*. The simple act of moving generates an interesting trail. Duchamp masterfully portrayed this in his *Nude Descending a Staircase*. The campaign of 2017–2019 "simply" portrays the product from all angles, in still life, inspired by kinetic art.

Me interesa la publicidad honesta, que enseñe la mejor cara del producto, por supuesto, pero sin demasiados trucos. Estos no son zapatos para volar o para ligar más. *These boots are made for walking, and that's just what they'll do*. El simple hecho de movernos genera un rastro interesante. Duchamp lo retrató magistralmente en su *Desnudo bajando una escalera*. Las campañas de 2017–2019 "simplemente" retratan el producto desde todos sus ángulos en bodegones inspirados por el arte cinético.

CAMPER

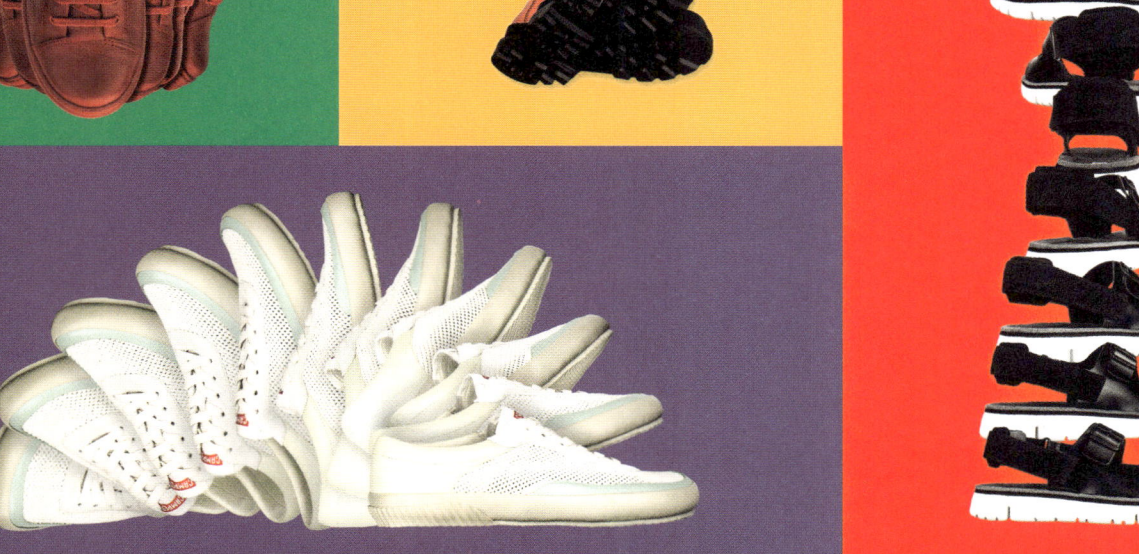

Kill the Bear.
Palm Angels,
2018–2020.

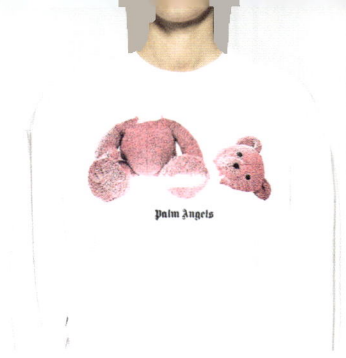
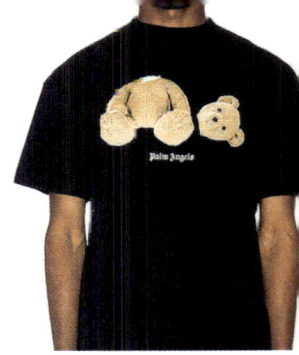

Extra! Extra!

My work has always been linked in one way or another to the events of our time. I have found a refuge for my graphic comments in newspapers and magazines.

If it is scary to face a blank page, imagine a whole newspaper. Every morning they look like that. Before night falls, however, its pages are full of texts, photographs, infographics, illustrations and advertising that in many cases pays for all of the above. A small miracle that happens every 24 hours.

We need journalism to combat darkness, order chaos, rank the drama, encourage critical thinking and do it with the utmost objectivity, intelligence, beauty and independence possible. (I know, I know…) The media is so important that too many times it has been used for dubious purposes, manipulating information, perpetrating stereotypes, or responding to corporate interests. As we know, thanks to photojournalist Peter Parker, great power carries great responsibility.

I have been fortunate to find media, publishers and art directors with whom I have always been able to work freely, but with rigour and a high level of demand. I find it a luxury and a precious challenge to have a small space from which to contribute to public debate and the cultural climate.

Mi trabajo ha estado siempre vinculado de una manera u otra a la actualidad. He encontrado un refugio para mis comentarios gráficos en periódicos y revistas.

Si da miedo enfrentarse a una página en blanco, imagínate un diario entero. Cada mañana tienen ese aspecto. Antes de que caiga la noche, sus páginas están llenas de textos, fotografías, infografías, ilustraciones y de publicidad que en muchos casos paga todas las anteriores. Un pequeño milagro que sucede cada 24 horas.

Necesitamos al periodismo para combatir la oscuridad, ordenar el caos, jerarquizar el drama, incentivar el pensamiento crítico y hacerlo con la máxima objetividad, inteligencia, belleza e independencia posible. (Ya, ya sé…) Los medios de comunicación son tan importantes que demasiadas veces se han utilizado con dudosos fines, manipulando información, perpetrando estereotipos, o respondiendo a intereses corporativos. Según sabemos gracias al fotoperiodista Peter Parker, un gran poder conlleva una gran responsabilidad.

He tenido la suerte de encontrar medios, editores y directores de arte con los que he podido trabajar siempre con total libertad, pero con rigor y alto nivel de exigencia. Me parece un lujo y un precioso reto disponer de un pequeño espacio desde donde contribuir al debate público y al clima cultural.

An editorial illustration commission usually begins with an email. In my case, face-to-face meetings are less common. When that mail arrives, there is always a little flip to the heart. Usually you did not expect it, it can arrive at any time of the day or night, while you were working on another project or while you were up a coconut tree. Furthermore, this commission is usually urgent, very urgent. Learning to discern between the urgent and the important is another of my pending subjects. If all goes well, that first email includes the necessary information to start working. In an ideal world, it should include the text to be illustrated, the technical aspects, size, colour, budget and delivery dates.

The first step is to learn to read the text in detail, looking for the particularity that crystallises the essence of the article. Reading comprehension is crucial for an editorial illustrator. Some people find it helpful to sketch or summarise articles until they are distilled within a couple of sentences. It is the moment to learn more about the subject, it can be reading other articles, looking for related images or watching documentaries. Now it's time to think about how to translate all that content into an image that is worthy of the famous 1000 words. It is logically one of the most complex parts of the process, and you have to find ways to grease the machinery. Sometimes it is with a coffee, other times it is with a walk, but usually it ends up just sitting and working until you have it. Monsters only exist in your head. Editorial illustration projects usually have delivery times ranging from hours to approximately three days, so you can not take too long on that walk.

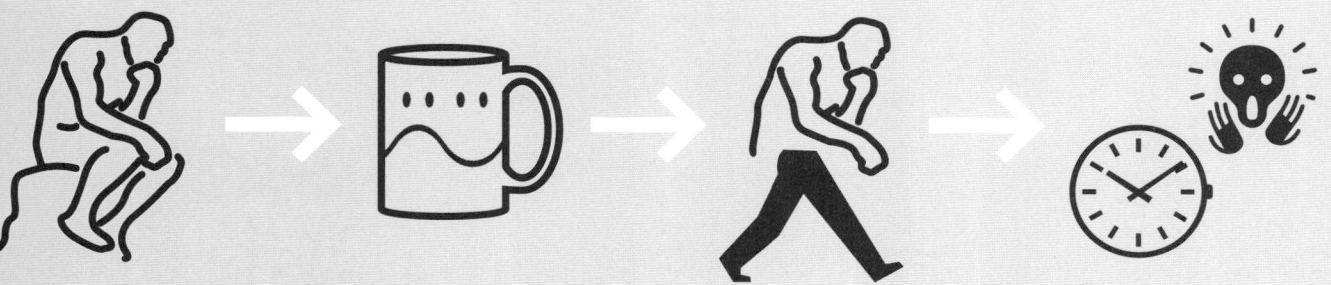

Un encargo de ilustración editorial suele empezar con un e-mail. En mi caso, cada vez son menos comunes las reuniones cara a cara. Cuando llega ese correo, siempre hay un pequeño vuelco al corazón. Por lo general no te lo esperabas, puede llegar en cualquier momento del día o de la noche, mientras trabajas en otro proyecto o mientras estás subido a un cocotero. Además, ese encargo es habitualmente urgente, muy urgente. Aprender a discernir entre lo urgente y lo importante es otra de mis asignaturas pendientes. Si todo va bien, ese primer mail incluye la información necesaria para empezar a trabajar. En un mundo ideal, debería incluir el texto a ilustrar, los aspectos técnicos, tamaño, color, presupuesto y fechas de entrega.

El primer paso es aprender a leer el texto detalladamente, buscando la particularidad que cristaliza la tesis del artículo. Trabajar la comprensión lectora es crucial para un ilustrador editorial. A algunas personas les funciona hacer esquemas o resúmenes de los artículos hasta dejarlos en un par de frases. Es el momento de informarse más del tema, puede ser leyendo otros artículos, buscando imágenes relacionadas o viendo documentales. Ahora toca pensar cómo traducir todo ese contenido en una imagen que valga las famosas 1000 palabras. Es lógicamente una de las partes más complejas del proceso, y hay que buscar formas de engrasar la maquinaria. A veces es con un café, otras veces es con un paseo, pero habitualmente acaba bastando con sentarse y trabajar hasta que lo tienes. Los monstruos solo existen en tu cabeza. Los proyectos de ilustración editorial suelen tener unos plazos de entrega que van desde las horas a los tres días aproximadamente, así que uno no se puede demorar demasiado en ese paseo.

In a first phase, I usually send one to four sketches. They choose the one they like the most, which by the way, does not usually coincide with the one I would have chosen. It is important to present only the ideas with which one is comfortable. It is not necessary to send 30 mediocre ideas, the aim is quality. Sometimes I send ideas that I know will not be chosen, but that help me open new dialogues for future projects. The client only knows what you already did, but not what you want to do. Now it's time to produce the final image. In my case, sometimes this part turns into a fantastic search of shops of all kinds. It is not always a romantic process, I also work with digital tools, image banks or joining forces with collaborators. I try to use any material and technique that is at the service of the concept and the form. That part can sometimes be lengthened more than desired and it is then time to accelerate in order to be able to deliver without too much panic. If you do not deliver on time, not only have you not given a solution, you have also generated a problem in an immense chain of professionals. It is a good shortcut to get blacklisted. A newspaper or magazine is always the result of a collective work. It is important to maintain a positive attitude and be open to suggestions, try to be a person with whom it is easy and pleasant to collaborate. If the final delivery has gone well and there are no last-minute changes, the magic moment comes when you see the work published. The first time I was published in *The New York Times* I had to run outside to celebrate. I have not done it again, but it was an incredible feeling. To finish, we only have to exchange our ideas for chickens, apples or whatever the agreed payment system is.

This would be the anatomy of a single commission, but in a real week several projects overlap in different stages of the process and everything looks dangerously like the number of spinning plates in the circus. The juggler runs from plate to plate making them turn, hoping that none falls. I have not yet succeeded, but I have heard that it is important to learn to be organised.

En una primera fase, suelo enviar de uno a cuatro esbozos. Escogen el que más le gusta, que por cierto, no suele coincidir con el que yo habría elegido. Es importante presentar solo las ideas con las que uno se siente cómodo. No es necesario enviar 30 ideas mediocres, prima la puntería. Algunas veces envío ideas que sé que no serán escogidas, pero que me ayudan a abrir nuevos diálogos para futuros proyectos. Solo conocen lo que ya hiciste, pero no lo que quieres hacer. Ahora toca producir la imagen final. En mi caso, a veces esta parte se convierte en un fantástico juego de pistas por comercios de todo tipo. No siempre es un proceso romántico, también trabajo con herramientas digitales, bancos de imágenes o sumando fuerzas con colaboradores. Intento utilizar cualquier material y técnica que esté al servicio del concepto y la forma. Esa parte a veces se puede alargar más de lo deseado y llega el momento de acelerar para poder entregar sin demasiados sobresaltos. Si no llegas a tiempo, no solo no has dado una solución, además has generado un problema en una inmensa cadena de profesionales. Es un buen atajo para entrar en la lista negra. Un periódico o revista es siempre el resultado de un trabajo colectivo. Es importante mantener una actitud positiva y abierta a sugerencias, tratar de ser una persona con la que sea fácil y agradable colaborar. Si la entrega final ha ido bien y no hay cambios de última hora llega el momento mágico de ver el trabajo publicado. La primera vez que publiqué en *The New York Times* tuve que salir a la calle a correr para celebrarlo. No lo he vuelto a hacer, pero fue una sensación increíble. Solo nos queda cambiar nuestras ideas por gallinas, manzanas o por cualquiera que sea el sistema de pago acordado.

Esta sería la anatomía de un solo encargo, pero en una semana real se superponen varios proyectos en diferentes estadios del proceso y todo se parece peligrosamente al número de los platos giratorios en el circo. El malabarista va corriendo de plato en plato haciéndolos girar esperando que no caiga ninguno. Todavía no lo he conseguido, pero he oído que es importante aprender a organizarse.

In case you haven't read today's news, let me summarise:
En el caso de que no hayas leído las noticias de hoy, permíteme un resumen:

The New York Times Magazine, 2014. Are We Missing the Big Picture on Climate Change? Stories about smaller environmental problems can distract us from the slow-motion calamity that will eventually threaten every living being. Text Rebecca Solnit. AD Frank Augugliaro.

The New York Times Magazine, 2014. Is the 'Anthropocene' Epoch a Condemnation of Human Interference or a Call for More? When some climate scientists began saying we'd entered a new epoch, they meant to draw attention to human effects on climate. Text Wesley Yang. AD Frank Augugliaro.

9/15 ottobre 2020 | n. 1379 · anno 27 | internazionale.it | 4,00 €

Ogni settimana il meglio dei giornali di tutto il mondo

Arundhati Roy
La ferocia dell'India

Scienza
Quando la lingua inciampa

Stati Uniti
Il presidente è malato e il paese non sta meglio

Internazionale

Dove va a finire la nostra plastica

I rifiuti plastici che arrivano da tutto il mondo sono un incubo per l'Africa. Ma le multinazionali occidentali sostengono che non tocca a loro smaltirli

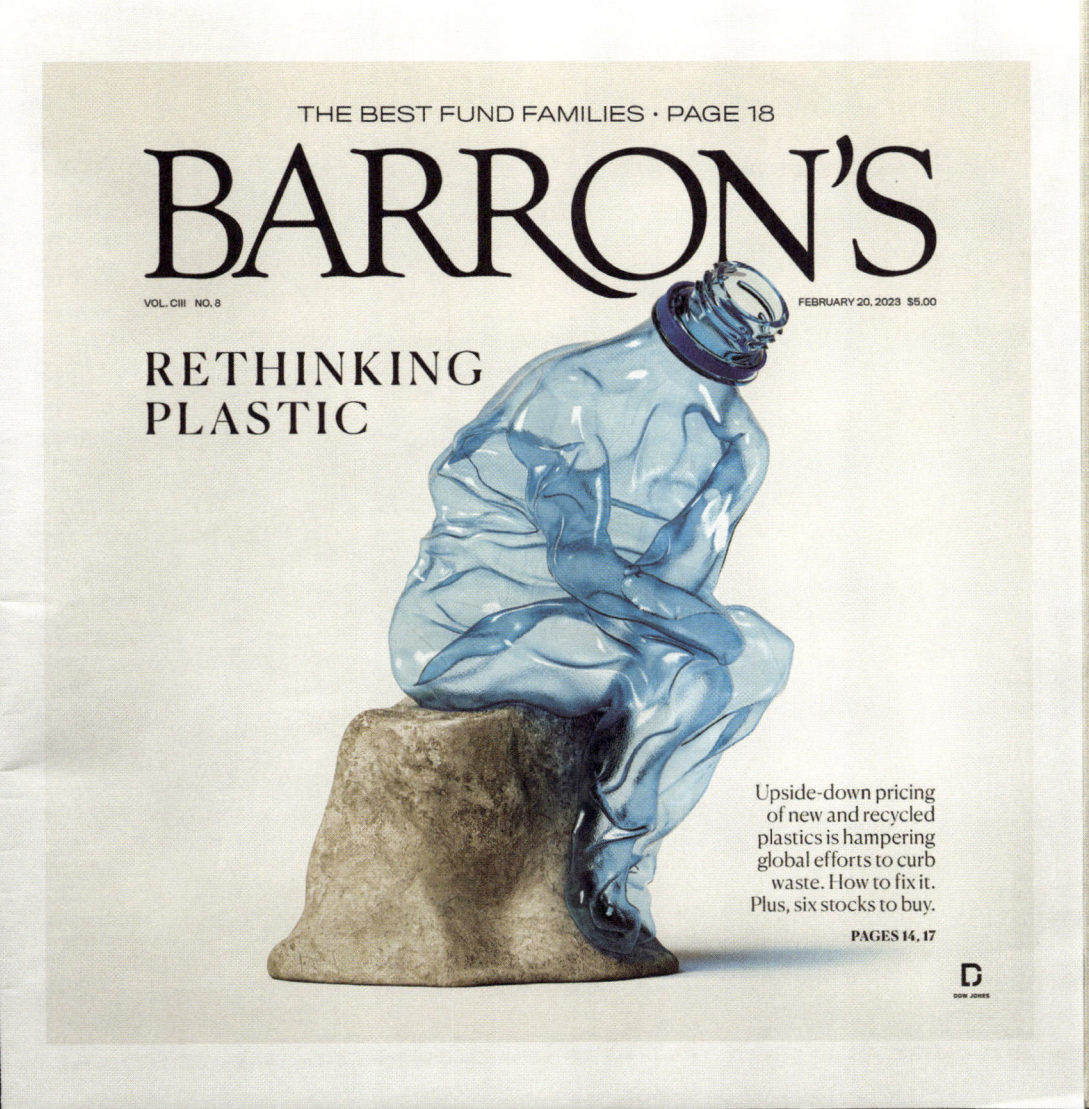

(1) *Internazionale*, 2020. Where does our plastic end up. Plastic waste coming from around the world is a nightmare for Africa. But Western multinationals claim that it's not for them to dispose of them. AD Maysa Moroni. **(2)** *Barron's*, 2023. Rethinking Plastic. AD Lynne Carty.

(1) *The New York Times Magazine*, 2014. The Dark Side of Zootopia. Modern zookeeping's longstanding trend toward cage-free, 3-D dioramas is influencing the way we shape natural habitats too. Text Charles Siebert. AD Jason Sfetko. **(2)** *Touch Wood*, 2019. **(Next spread)** *Greenpeace Magazin*. **(1)** Globalization, 2019. **(2)** I Eat Flowers, 2018. AD Kerstin Leesch, Cale Garrido.

greenpeace magazin.

2.18 März – April
konstruktiv.kritisch.
leserfinanziert.

Globalisierung
Die einen verteufeln sie, die anderen verharmlosen ihre Risiken:
Doch wer hinter die Maske blickt, könnte überrascht sein

greenpeace magazin.

4.18 Juli–August
konstruktiv.kritisch.
leserfinanziert.

Ich ess' Blumen

Für die Band Die Ärzte war es einst ein lustiger Songtitel. Heute machen immer mehr Menschen Ernst mit dem veganen Leben

National Geographic, 2015. Climate Change. Survival Guide. AD Lawson Parker.

The New York Times, 2011.
The Uncertain Future
of Nuclear Power.
Text Frank N. Von Hippel.
AD Gary Fogelson.

(1) *Pulmones*. CDN, 2019. **(2)** *The New York Times Magazine*, 2015. What We Don't See. "Pics or it didn't happen", falls short when it comes to describing the realities of American life. Text Colson Whitehead. AD Jason Sfetko.

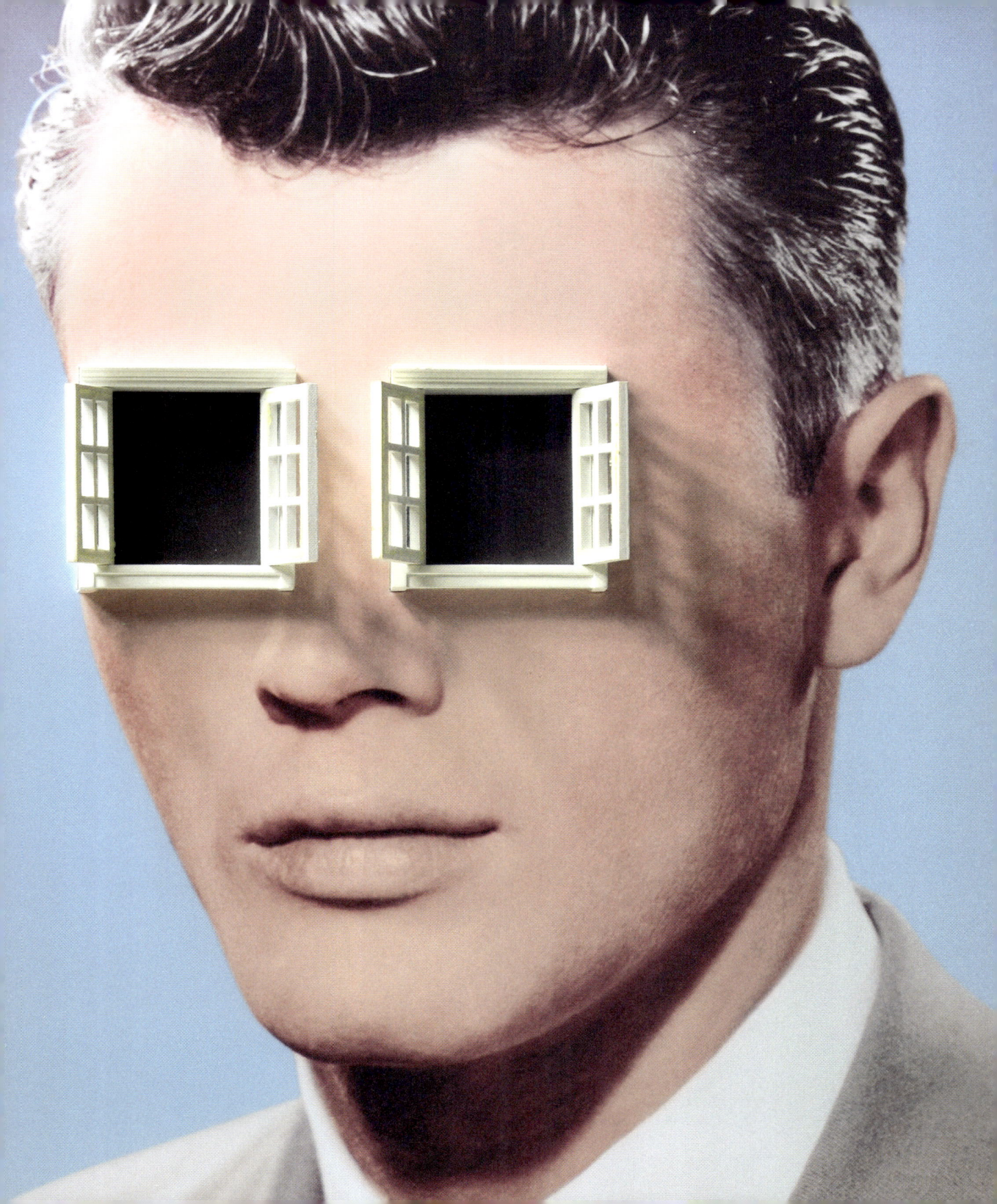

(1) *La Vanguardia,* 2011. In Praise of the Radio. Text Jordi Basté. (2) *M, Le Monde,* 2015. Interference with the CSA. Mathieu Gallet case, appointment to France Télévisions. AD Laurence Lagrange.

M Le magazine du Monde

Affaire Mathieu Gallet, nomination à France Télévisions…
Interférences au CSA

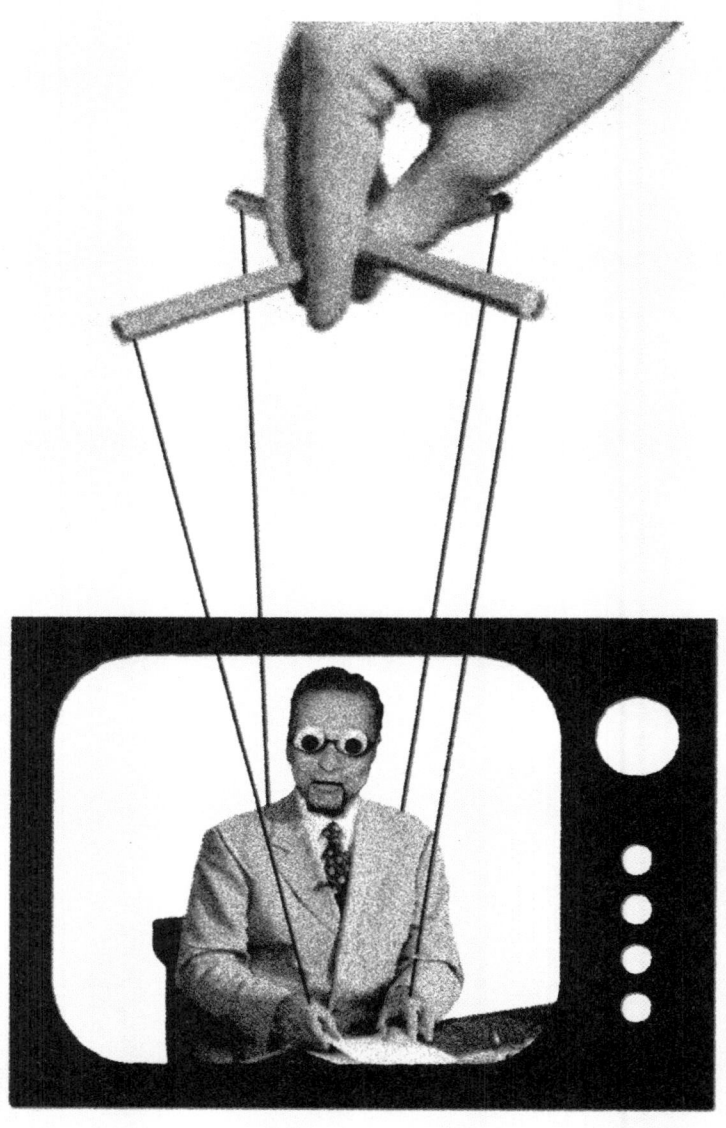

(1) *The New York Times*, 2011. Lies and Videotape. Text Christopher Walker and Robert W. Orttung. AD Alexandra Zsigmond. **(2)** *Titerescena*. CDN, 2018. *(Next spread)* *The New York Times Magazine*, 2016. The Problem With 'Self-Investigation' in a Post-Truth Era. The internet was supposed to democratize information, but instead it has democratized disinformation. Text Jonathan Mahler. AD Frank Augugliaro.

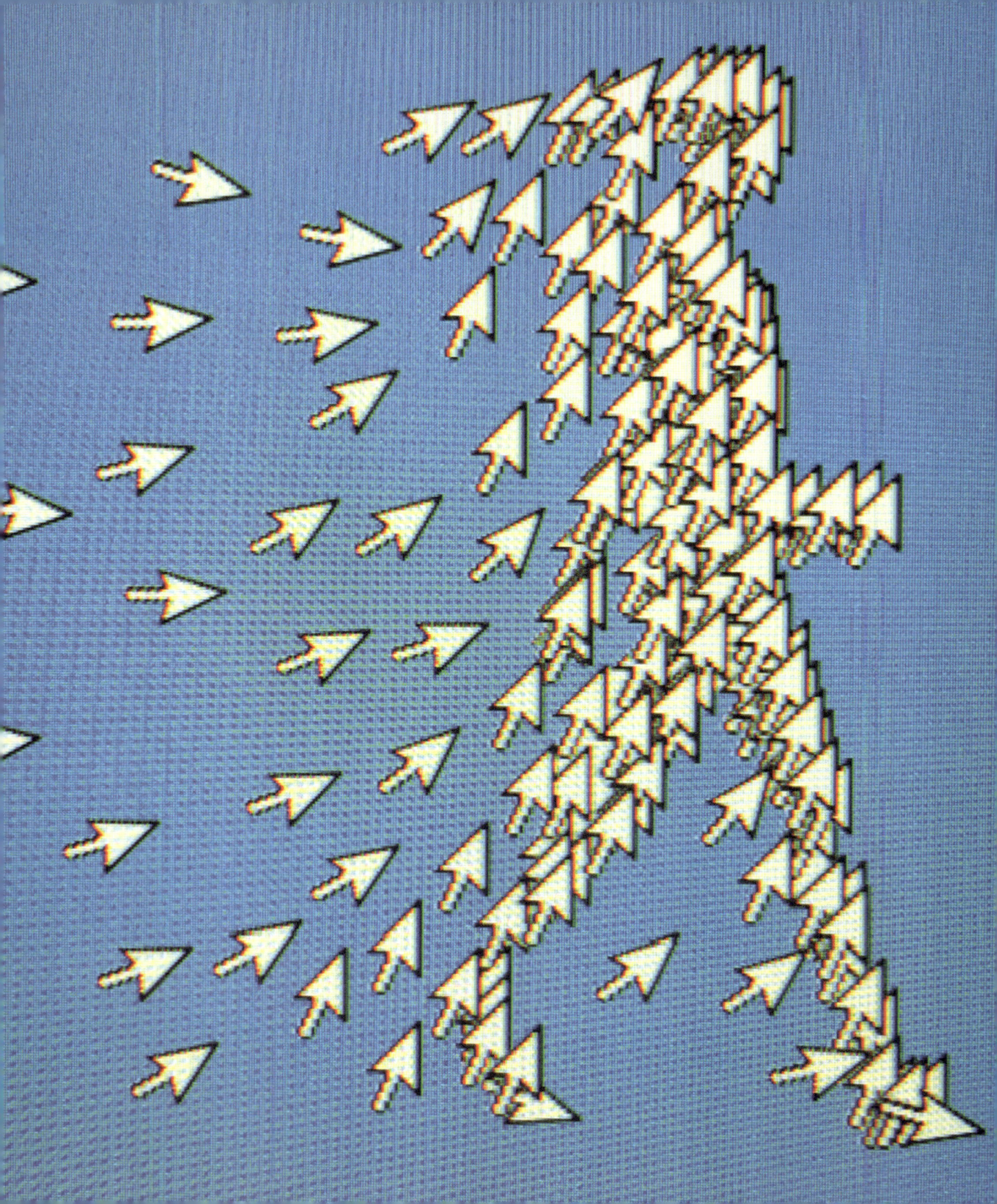

(1) *The New York Times Magazine*, 2015. The Rabbit-Hole of 'Relevant'. For years, the N.S.A.'s data grab has hinged on a reading of the word that encompasses every aspect of our lives. Text Mattathias Schwartz. AD Jason Sfetko. **(2)** *The New York Times Magazine*, 2015. The Murky Meaning of the Killer Selfie. What is it that we find so uniquely horrifying about people dying as they take pictures of themselves? Text Avi Steinberg. AD Jason Sfetko. *(Next spread)* **(1)** *The New York Times*, 2015. My Digital Cemetery. Text Rob Walker. AD Alexandra Zsigmond. **(2)** *The New Yorker*, 2018. Japan's Rent-a-Family Industry. People who are short on relatives can hire a husband, a mother, a grandson. The resulting relationships can be more real than you'd expect. Text Elif Batuman. AD Deanna Donegan.

2 OPINION	4 OPINION	5 OPINION		8 THE STONE
Trying to control the tourists. BY ELIZABETH BECKER	The moment of reckoning on race. BY ISABEL WILKERSON	We're not creating new treatments for mental illness. BY RICHARD A. FRIEDMAN		Beware the happiness obsession. BY CARL CEDERSTRÖM
4 OPINION	5 OPINION			10 EDITORIAL
New York should close Rikers. BY NEIL BARSKY	Are deadlines just a hoax? BY CARL HONORÉ			The morning after the Iran deal.

IDEAS | OPINION | NEWS ANALYSIS

SundayReview
The New York Times

SUNDAY, JULY 19, 2015

My Digital Cemetery

Our contact lists have accidentally acquired a memorial function.

SAVANNAH, GA.

MY digital address book lists 2,743 contacts. This is not because I'm popular or extroverted; I'm neither. It's because this collection of names stretches back two decades, the oldest contacts tracing to a 1996 Palm Pilot and preserved through transfers involving more devices than I care to remember. It covers life in four cities and work on countless reporting projects. The idea of organizing and pruning this slow-motion data dump is by now unthinkable.

One result is that when I start to tap in the name of someone I'm looking for, I often turn up several others as well. Maybe an expert source on a subject I'll never write about again. Or the best plumber in a place where I no longer live. Possibly a former colleague I have since learned actively dislikes me. Probably at least one name I just can't place. And, perhaps, someone who is dead.

I ought take that moment to delete one or more of those entries. But not the ones for the deceased. Those I keep.

I seldom talk about this habit, because I assume it sounds weird. But recently I was intrigued to read about an incident described in "Becoming Steve Jobs," the new book by Brent Schlender and Rick Tetzeli. A couple of years after Mr. Jobs died, the anecdote goes, John Lasseter, a founder of Pixar and a

OPINION
BY ROB WALKER

A writer on design and technology whose advice column, "The Workologist," appears every other weekend in the Sunday Business section of The Times.

Continued on Page 6

JAVIER JAÉN

How the West Overcounts Its Water

There's even less than people think there is.

NEWS ANALYSIS
BY ABRAHAM LUSTGARTEN

A senior reporter at ProPublica. This is an excerpt from a longer article published by ProPublica and Matter as part of their "Killing the Colorado" series.

PAUL MATUSKA is the closest thing the American West has to a water cop, and his beat includes Needles, Calif., a beleaguered desert town midway between Flagstaff, Ariz., and Los Angeles.

About 4,800 people live in Needles, on the western bank of the Colorado River where it cuts a swath in the mud between California and Arizona. The old railroad town is the gateway to the farmland of the Fort Mojave Indian Reservation across the river.

Mr. Matuska, a hydrologist, is one of about a dozen accountants for the federal Bureau of Reclamation, which controls water distribution along the lower half of the Colorado River. His job is to count the water used by cities like Needles and the farms around them — lands close to the essential Colorado — and make sure they don't take more than their share of the river.

As it happens, Needles gets most of its water from underground — pumping an average of about 700 million gallons a year from four wells it has drilled into the local aquifer. In recent years, such withdrawals have taken on more importance in the West, particularly in California and Arizona, as streams shrivel, rivers are fought over and reservoirs run dry. About 60 percent of California's water now comes from underground, according to estimates by NASA re-

Continued on Page 6

(1) *El País*, 2014. Who am I? Text Rita Abundancia. AD Andrew McConochie. **(2)** *La Republica*, 2018. These are social times, with 280-character rhythms of laughter, rivers of memes and gifs, but it is increasingly difficult to find your way around. *(Next spread)* **(1)** *WWD Magazine*, 2015. Overheated! All fashion, all the time. Chaos, crowds, hype, digital explosion: Is the system headed for a burnout? AD Robb Rice. **(2)** *Advertising Age*, 2015. Welcome to the Video Revolution. AD Erik Spooner.

AdvertisingAge

(1) *The New York Times Magazine*, 2015. Instagram's Graveyard Shift. Alone together with the warehouse workers, soldiers and paramedics of late-night social media. Text Jeff Sharlet. AD Jason Sfetko.
(2) *The Highlight by Vox*, 2021. The Pokémon Obsession. AD Lavanya Ramanathan & Apple News.

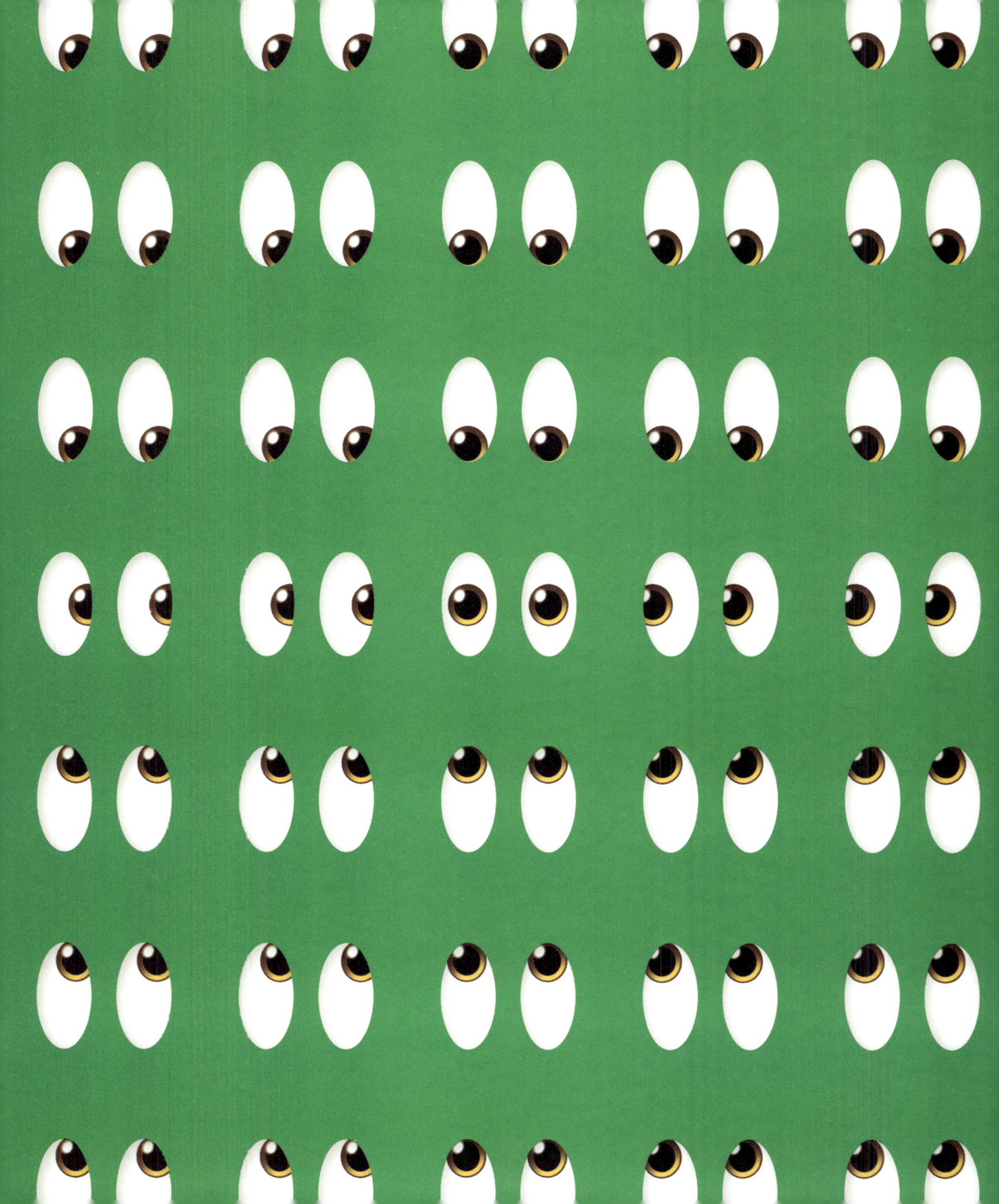

(1) *The Observers*, 2020. **(2)** *Vanity Fair*, 2015. Good Bye to "Hello". The phone call is dead. Can texting fill its void? Text A.A. Gill. AD Tonya Douraghy.

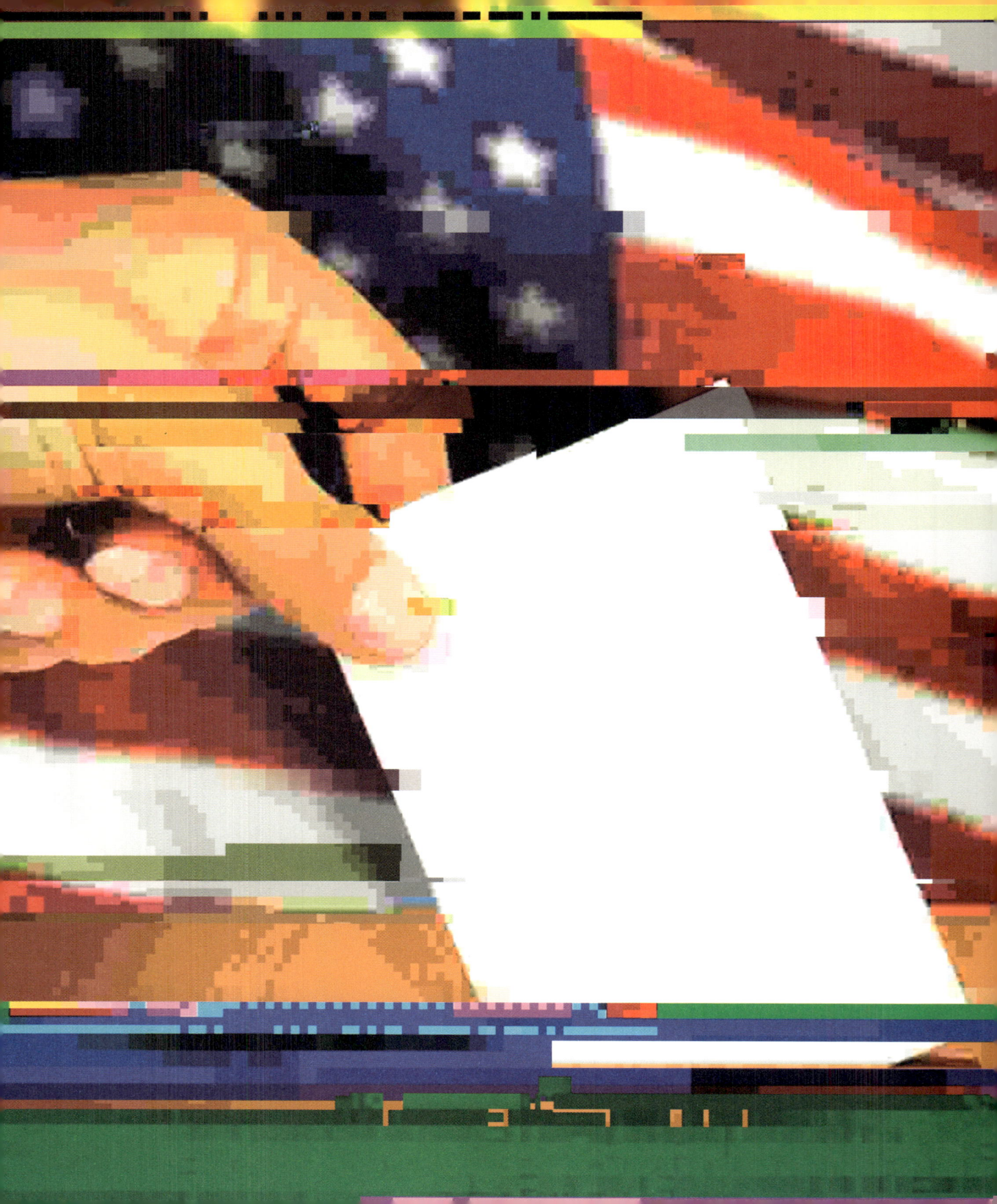

(1) *The New York Times Magazine,* 2018. The Crisis of Election Security. As the midterms approach, America's electronic voting systems are more vulnerable than ever. Why isn't anyone trying to fix them? Text Kim Zetter. AD Gail Blicher. **(2)** *Observatorio Obra Social "La Caixa",* 2017. Research and Innovation. What are we playing for?

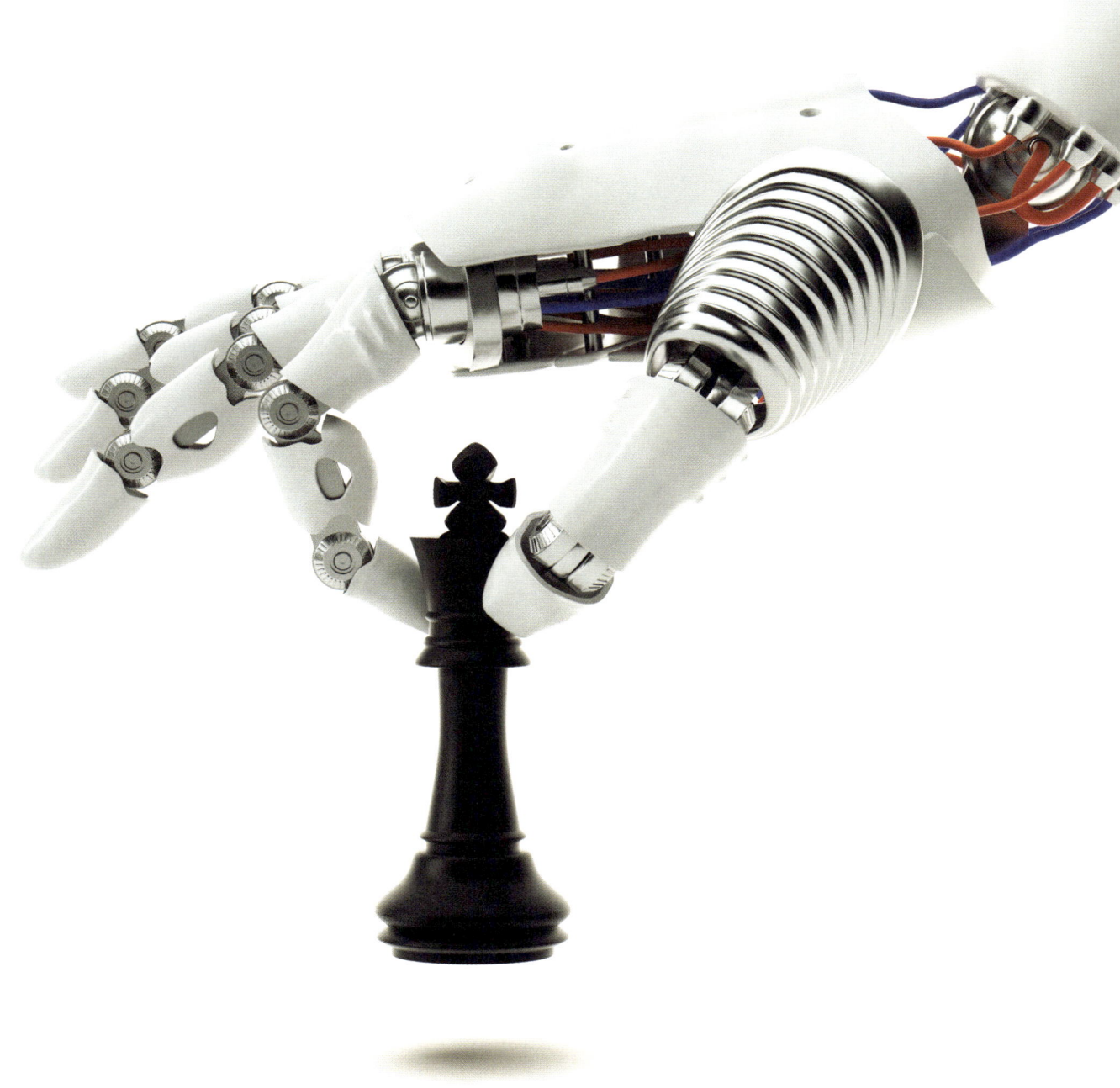

The New York Times, 2015.
How My Mom Got Hacked
Text Alina Simone.
AD Aviva Michaelov.

2 OPINION	10 COUCH	5 BEDSIDE	7 OPINION
Scientists are too timid on the climate. BY NAOMI ORESKES	 This is what it feels like to suffer from Dissociative Identity Disorder. BY VIVIAN CONAN	How to care for a criminal. BY THERESA BROWN	Can any good movie make it past China's censors? BY NURY VITTACHI
3 OPINION		6 OPINION	8 EDITORIAL
Don't nourish the body and neglect the mind. BY PICO IYER		You may be better off living in a red state. BY RICHARD FLORIDA	Afghanistan's overreach.

IDEAS | OPINION | NEWS ANALYSIS

SundayReview

SUNDAY, JANUARY 4, 2015

JAVIER JAÉN

How My Mom Got Hacked

Navigating the nefarious, shadowy world of ransomware criminals.

M Y mother received the ransom note on the Tuesday before Thanksgiving. It popped up on her computer screen soon after she'd discovered that all of her files had been locked. "Your files are encrypted," it announced. "To get the key to decrypt files you have to pay 500 USD." If my mother failed to pay within a week, the price would go up to $1,000. After that, her decryption key would be destroyed and any chance of accessing the 5,726 files on her PC — all of her data — would be lost forever.

Sincerely, CryptoWall.

CryptoWall 2.0 is the latest immunoresistant strain of a larger body of viruses known as ransomware. The virus is thought to infiltrate your computer when you click on a legiti-

mate-looking attachment or through existing malware lurking on your hard drive, and once unleashed it instantly encrypts all your files, barring access to a single photo or tax receipt.

Everyone has the same questions when they first hear about CryptoWall:

Is there any other way to get rid of it besides paying the ransom? No — it appears to be technologically impossible for anyone to decrypt your files once CryptoWall 2.0 has locked them. (My mother had several I.T. professionals try.)

But should you really be handing money over to a bunch of criminals? According to the Internet Crime Complaint Center, a partnership between the F.B.I. and the National White Col-

Continued on Page 4

OPINION

BY ALINA SIMONE

The author of the essay collection "You Must Go and Win" and the novel "Note to Self."

(1) *The New Yorker*, 2018. Can Mark Zuckerberg Fix Facebook Before it Breaks Democracy? The most famous entrepreneur of his generation is facing a public reckoning with the power of Big Tech. Text Evan Osnos. AD Nicholas Blechman. **(2)** *Hatching Twitter: A True Story of Money, Power, Friendship, and Betrayal*, 2014. Editorial Planeta (Not published).

The New York Times*,
2010. The Lost Art
of Reading. Text
Christopher R. Beha.
AD Nicholas Blechman.

**This was my first
illustration for them.
Thanks Nicholas.*

El Idiota. CDN, 2019.

Elephant Magazine, 2014. *Twitter* allows users to engage with the world in a unique dialect. The world's biggest museums and galleries aren't missing out on the phenomenon, shaping *Twitter* personalities for themselves that reflect the history and future of their institutions. AD Atlas.

Men's Health, 2020. Trivia Keeps Me Sane. It used to be for the geeky few, an activity hidden away in the recesses of dive bars everywhere. As it's gone online, the real question has become: Why are so many people flocking? Text Josh Ocampo. AD Justin O'Neill.

The New Yorker, 2013.
Anniversary Issue spots.
AD Chris Curry.

The New Yorker, 2019.
The Power Issue spots.
AD Aviva Michaelov.

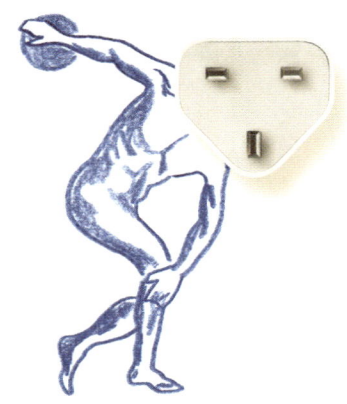

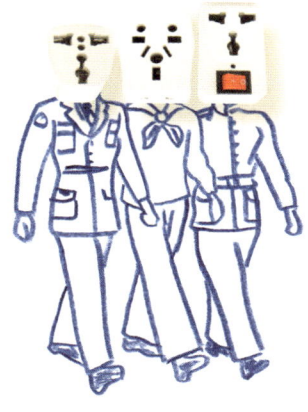

(1) *The New York Times Magazine*, 2016. From 'Hamilton' to Donald Trump: Are All 'Grievances' Created Equal? Airing and addressing them is a founding principle of American democracy. Text Jessic Lustig. AD Frank Augugliaro. **(2)** *Happy Valentine's*, 2015. *(Next spread)* **(1)** *The New Yorker*, 2013. Samsa in Love. Text Haruki Murakami. AD Chris Curry. **(2)** *Primer Amor*. CDN, 2018.

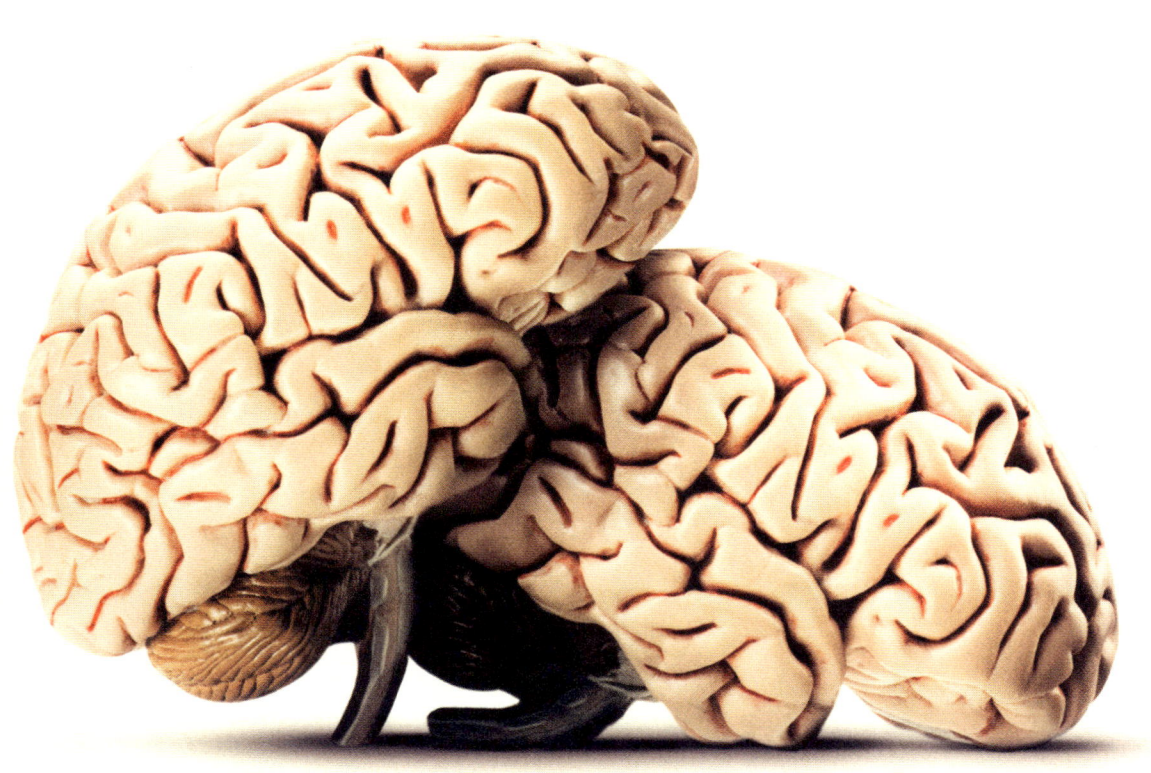

FICTION

Samsa in Love

Haruki Murakami

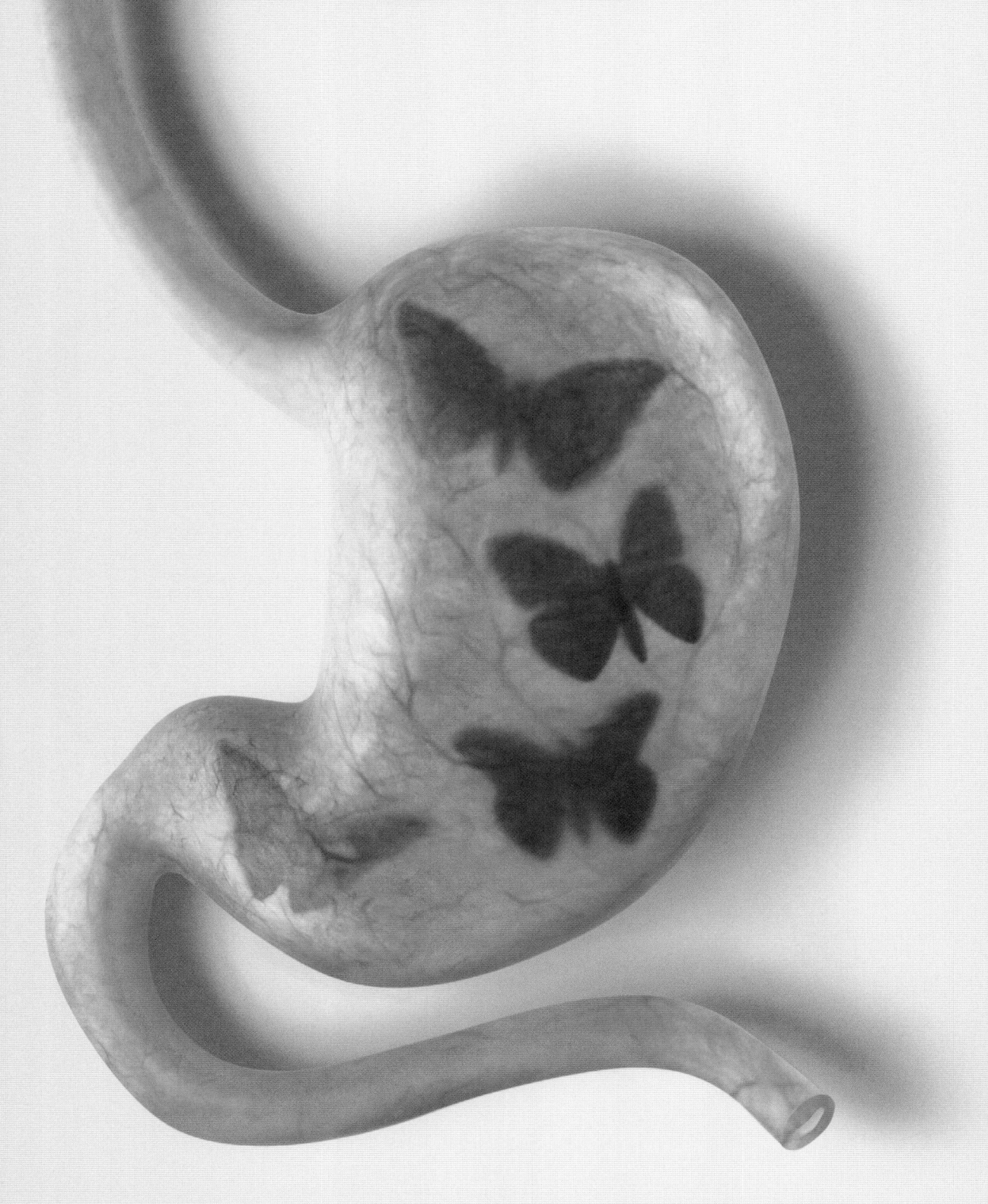

(1) *The Atlantic*, 2014. How Hard and Boring it is to be Faithful? Text Sandra Tsing Lohmar. AD Jackie Lay. **(2)** *Taxi Girl*. CDN, 2020. *(Next spread)* **(1)** *It's Not You, it's Me*, 2013. **(2)** *Caligula*. CDN, 2018.

**IT'S NOT YOU,
IT'S ME.
IT'S NOT YOU,
IT'S ME.
IT'S NOT YOU,
IT'S ME.
IT'S NOT YOU,
IT'S ME.
IT'S NOT ME,
IT'S YOU.**

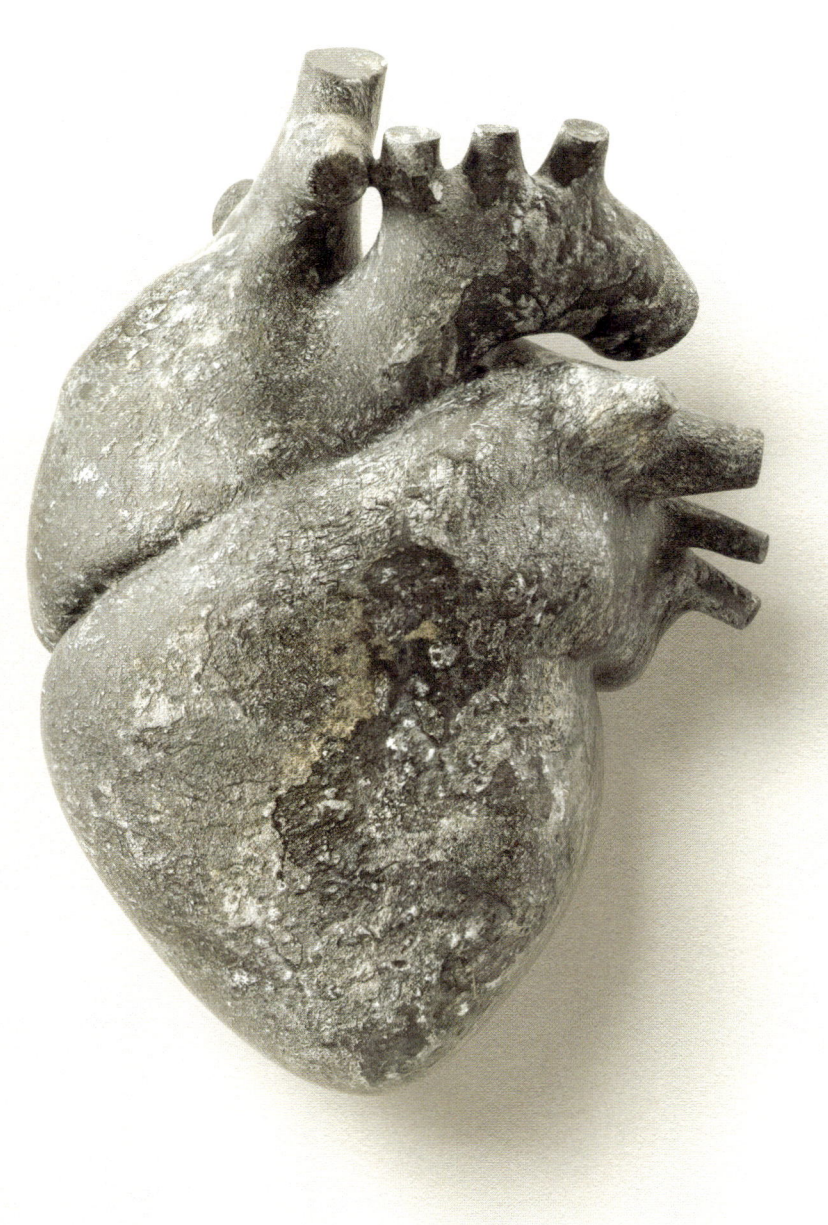

El Público. CDN, 2018.

Bestias de Escena. CDN, 2018.

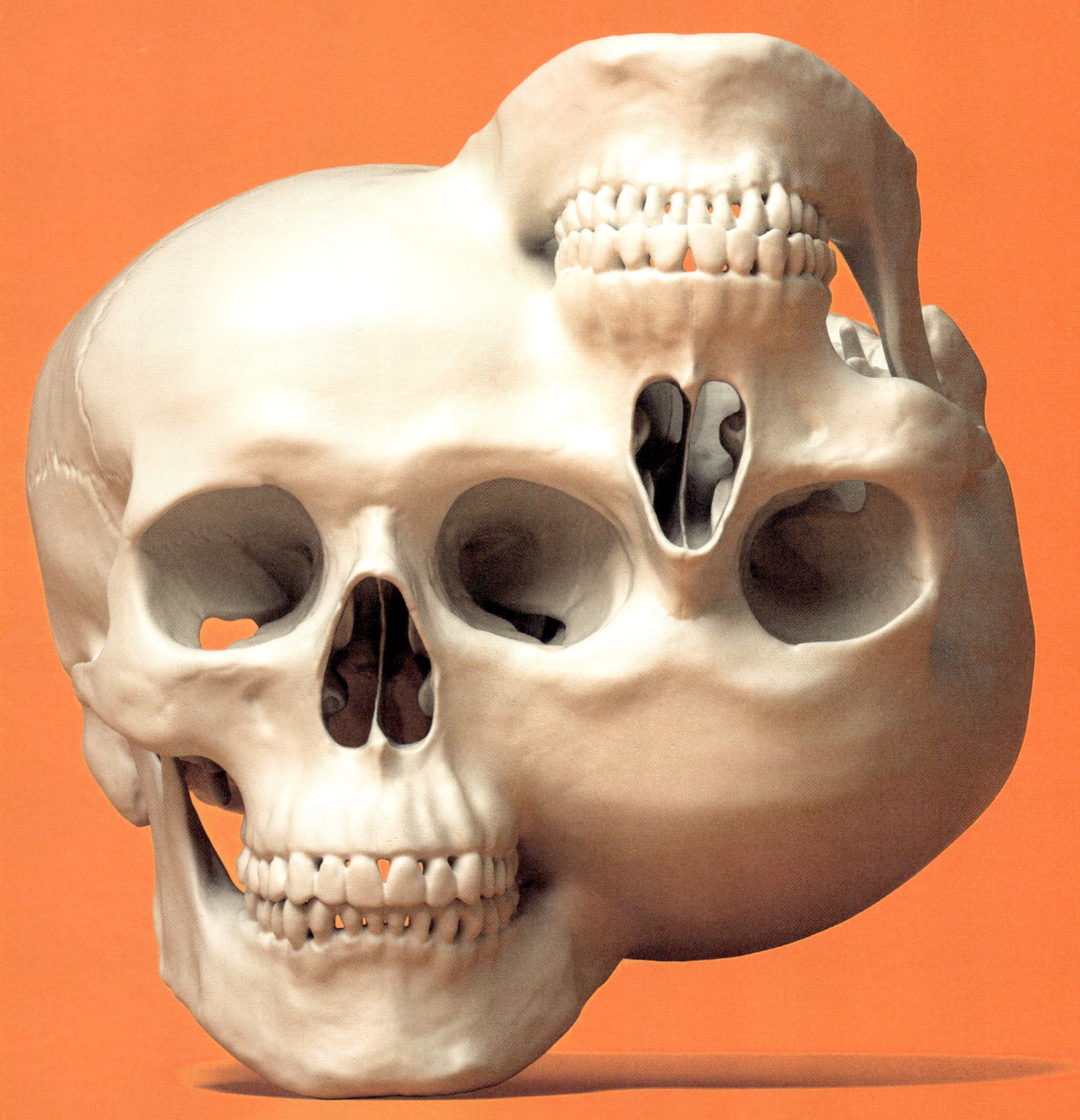

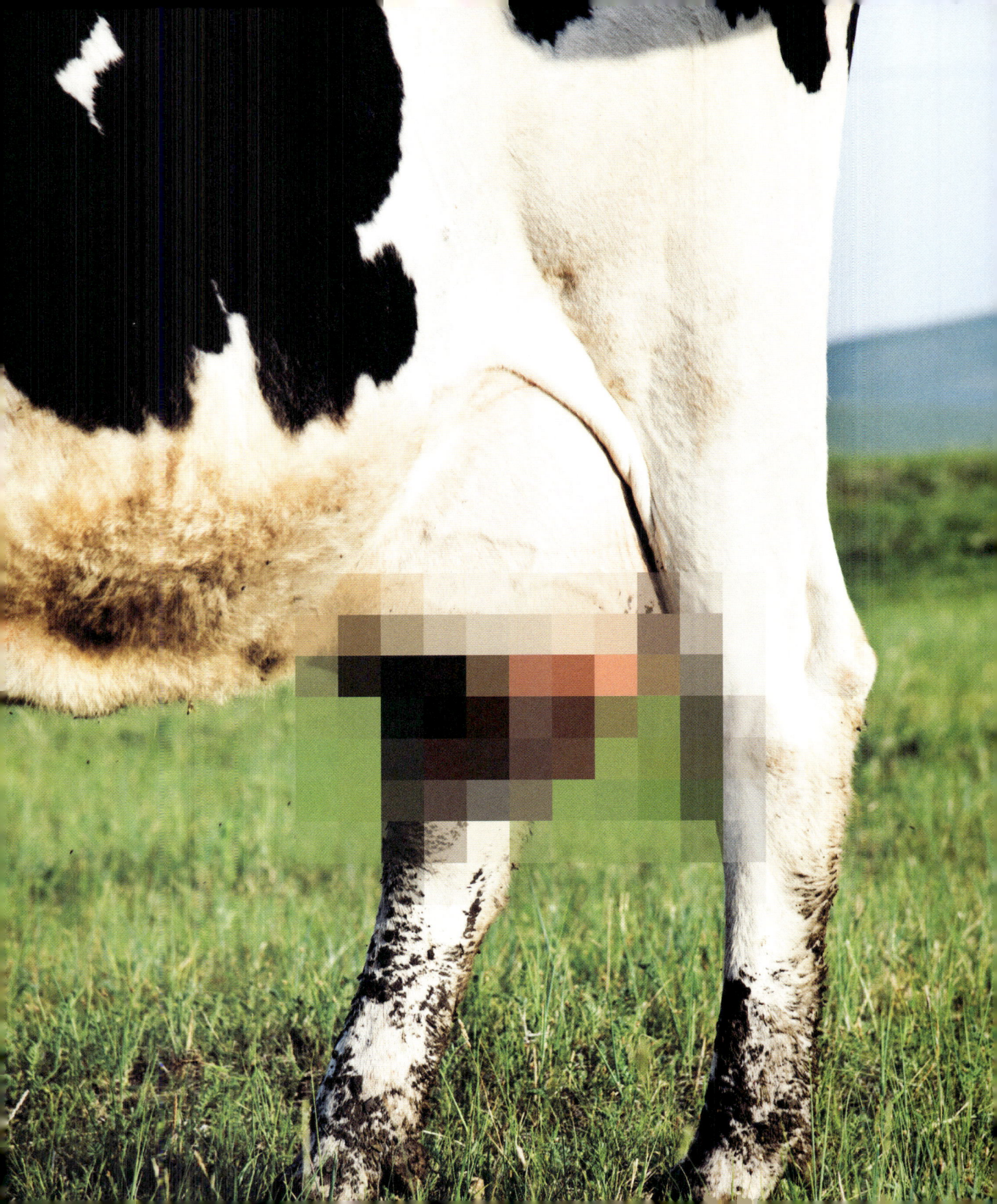

(Previous spread) **(1)** *Cosmopolitan*, 2016. How to Turn Yourself On. Do women really have a lower sex drive — or is that the wrong question? Text Esther Perel. AD Halsey Betsy. **(2)** *Elephant*, 2016. *(This spread)* **(1)** *Free the Nipple*, 2019. **(2)** *Ocultura*. Artafacta, 2009.

(1) *Bert and Ernie*, 2018. **(2)** *The New York Times Magazine*, 2015. Why 'Self-Identifying' is Different From Coming Out. In professional sports, where slurs are still tolerated, acting as if your homosexuality was never a secret is a bold counteroffensive move. Text Wesley Morris. AD Kimberly Sutherland. **(3)** *The New York Times Magazine*, 2015. Marriage of Convenience. Text Emily Bazelon. AD Jason Sfetko. **(4)** *The New York Times Magazine*, 2015. How 'Flawless' Became a Feminist Declaration. To be beautiful is to be pleasing to others, but to be 'flawless' is a statement of radical confidence: It means pleasing yourself. Text Parul Sehgal. AD Jason Sfetko. **(5)** *The New York Times Magazine*, 2016. When Everyone Can Be 'Queer', is Anyone? The word has gone from a slur to a radically inclusive term – but if anyone can join, does the identity lose its potency? Text Jenna Wortham. AD Frank Augugliaro.

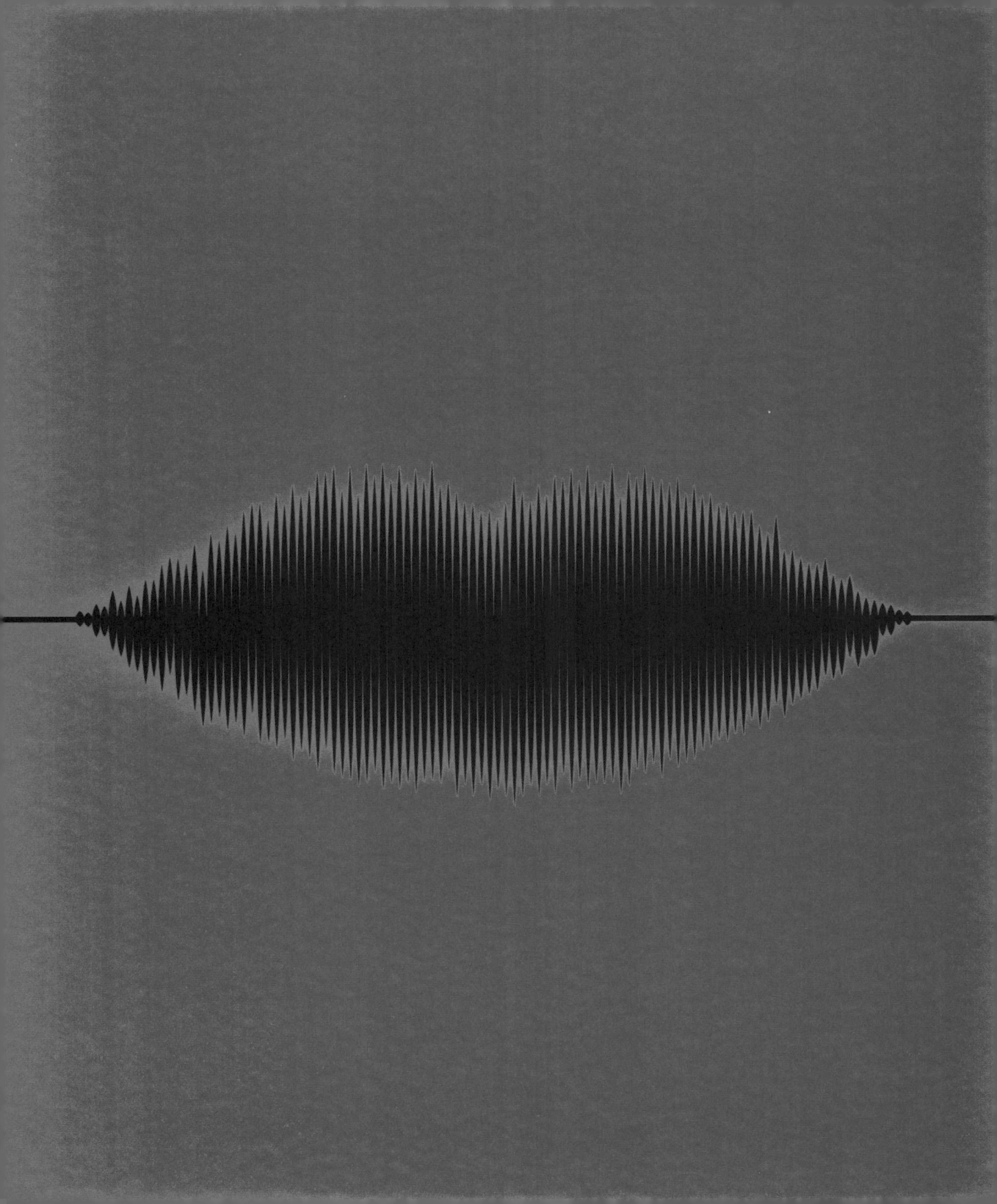

(Previous spread) **(1)** *Las Hermanas Macaluso.* CDN, 2020. **(2)** *Die Zeit*, 2019. Quiet, Please! AD Malin Schulz. *(This spread)* **(1)** *#Metoo*, 2019. **(2)** *The New York Times*, 2016. The Men Left Behind. Hillary Clinton's candidacy shows that women have changed. Men haven't. What happens next? Text Jill Filipovic. AD Alexandra Zsignond.

JAVIER JAÉN

The Men Left Behind

From Page 1

but abortion was mostly outlawed. Mrs. Clinton graduated as one of just 27 women in a class of 235, after being explicitly told that if accepted into law school, she would take the rightful place of a man.

Decades-long movements for women's rights have challenged that

lated. That many white men are struggling surely contributes to Mr. Trump's popularity, but the driving force of this election is not money — the median household income of Trump primary voters was about $72,000 a year, $16,000 more than the national median household income. It's power, and fury at watching it wane.

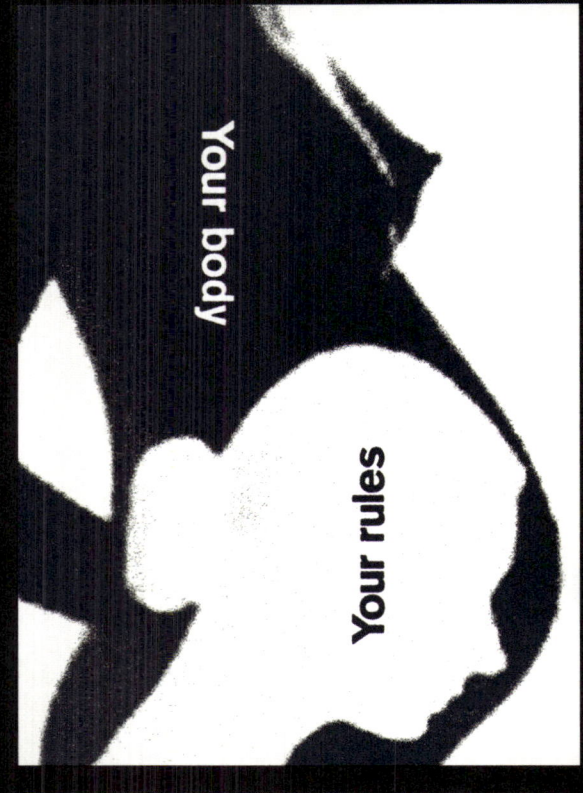

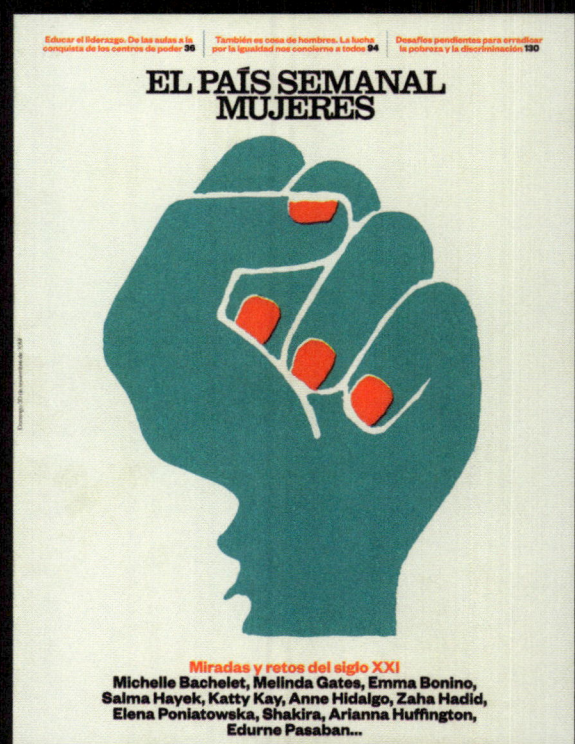

(1) *Your Body, Your Rules*, 2014. **(2)** *The New York Times Magazine*, 2016. How 'Empowerment' Became Something for Women to Buy. The corporate vision of female strength profits from the same old power dynamics. Text Jia Tolentino. AD Frank Augugliaro. **(3)** *The New York Times Magazine*, 2016. The Forced Heroism of the 'Survivor'. Can a single word ever encompass the experience of sexual violence? Text Parul Sehgal. AD Frank Augugliaro. **(4)** *El País Semanal*, 2014. Women, Perspectives and Challenges of the XXI Century. AD Solo Barcelona. **(5)** *Beatriz Galindo en Estocolmo*, CDN, 2017.

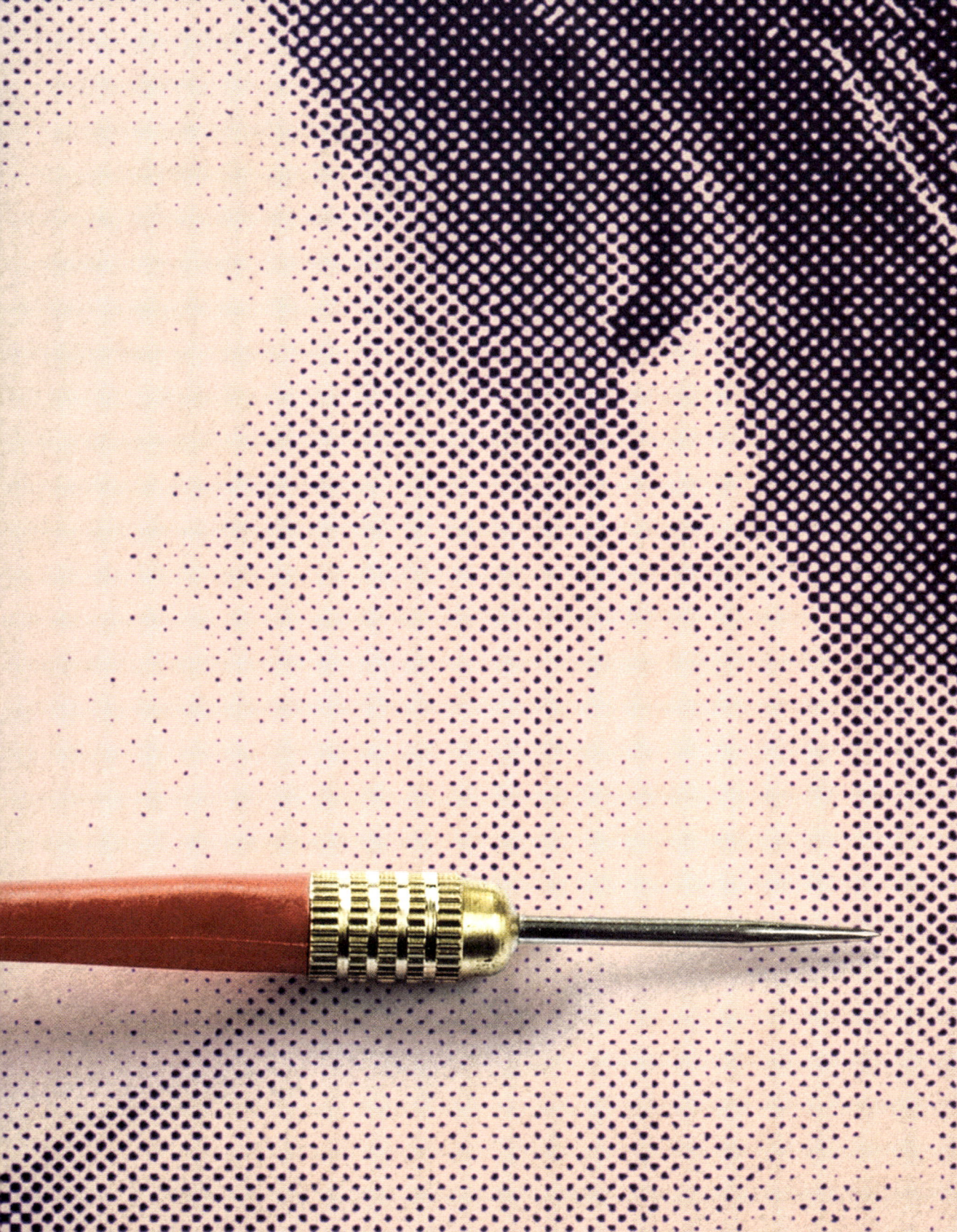

(Previous spread) The New York Times Magazine, 2015. The Underground Art of the Insult. Text Anna Holmes. AD Jason Sfetko. *(This spread)* (1) The New York Times Magazine, 2016. The Identity Politics of Whiteness. White Americans are starting, once again, to see themselves as a distinct identity group — and to wield power as one. Text Laila Lalami. AD Frank Augugliaro. (2) The New York Times, 2020. How Journalists Try to Stay Impartial. Times reporters and editors take careful measures in their personal lives to remain objective in their work. AD Andrew Sondern.

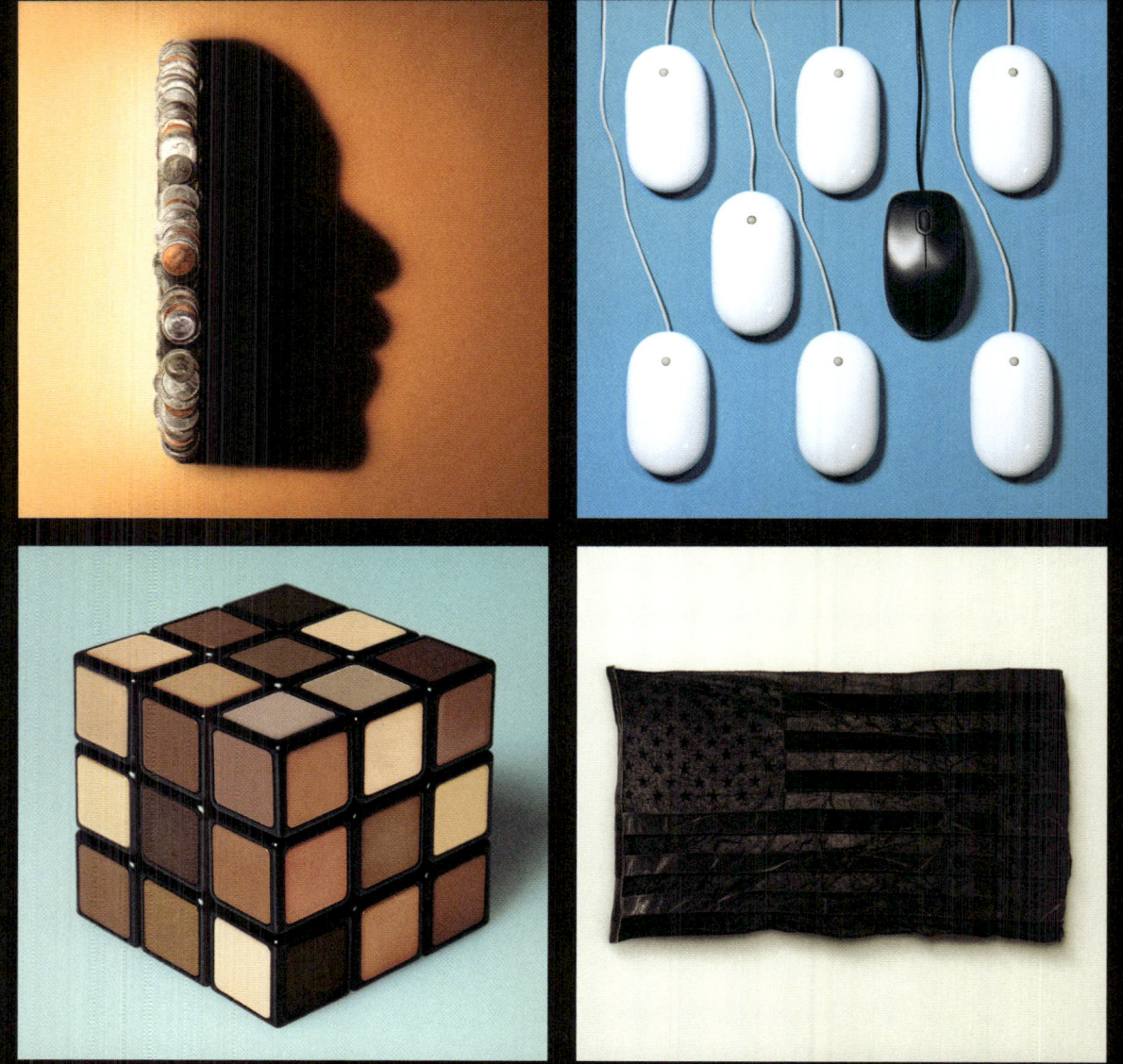

(1) *The New York Times*, 2014. The Worth of Black Men, from Slavery to Ferguson. Text Sharifa Rhodes-Pitts. **(2)** *The New York Times Magazine*, 2015. Has 'Diversity' Lost its Meaning? In the media, Hollywood and Silicon Valley, the word is invoked with increasing frequency, as if its simple utterance might be enough. Text Anna Holmes. AD Jason Sfetko. **(3)** *The New York Times Magazine*, 2015. America's 'Postracial' Fantasy. For millions of mixed-race people, identity fits more than one box, but we still see one another in black and white. Text Anna Holmes. AD Jason Sfetko. **(4)** *The New York Times Magazine*, 2016. Who Gets to Be Called a 'Patriot'? There are countless ways to show love for your country. So why does it feel as if you also need to be the right kind of person and show it in the right kind of way? Text Wesley Morris. AD Frank Augugliaro. **(5)** *The New York Times Magazine*, 2016. The Painful Consequences of 'Erasure'. Calling out the expunging of minorities' struggles and achievements from the record is an attempt to restore what has been lost. Text Parul Sehgal. AD Frank Augugliaro. *(Next spread)* *You are Welcome*, 2015.

The New York Times

CROSS CUTS | A. O. SCOTT

Looking the Other Way

JAVIER JAÉN

What are the responsibilities of culture to address a moment of

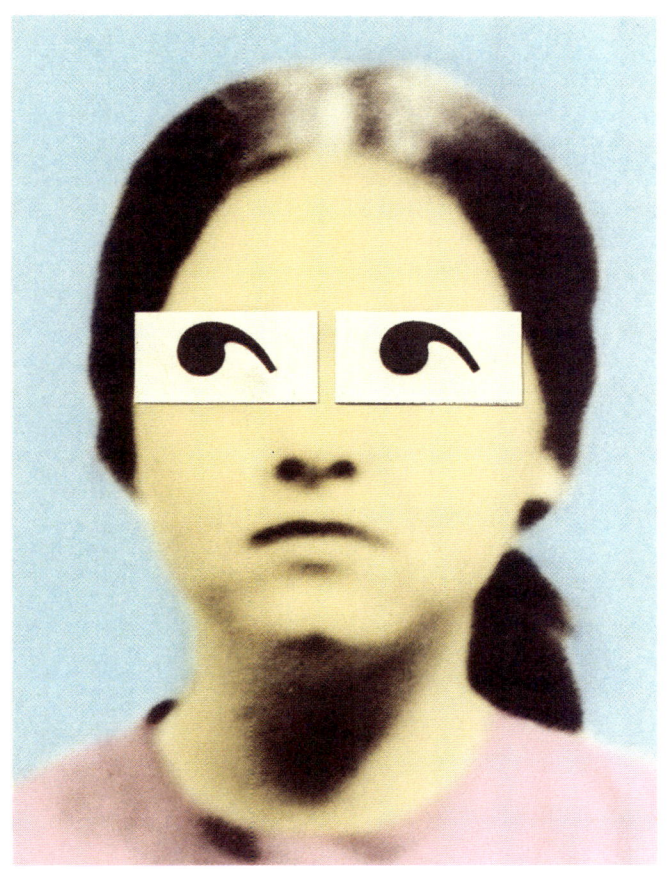

(1) *The New York Times*, 2014. Looking the other way. Is Our Art Equal to the Challenges of Our Times? We are in the midst of hard times now, and it feels as if art is failing us. Text A.O. Scott. AD Paul Jean. **(2)** *The New Yorker*, 2015. Confessions of a Comma Queen. Holy Writ. Learning to love the house style. Text Mary Norris. AD Chris Curry. *(Next spread)* **(1)** *Art Thief*, 2014. **(2)** *Garage*. CDN, 2018.

GOOD ARTIST ⌘C

GREAT ARTIST ⌘X

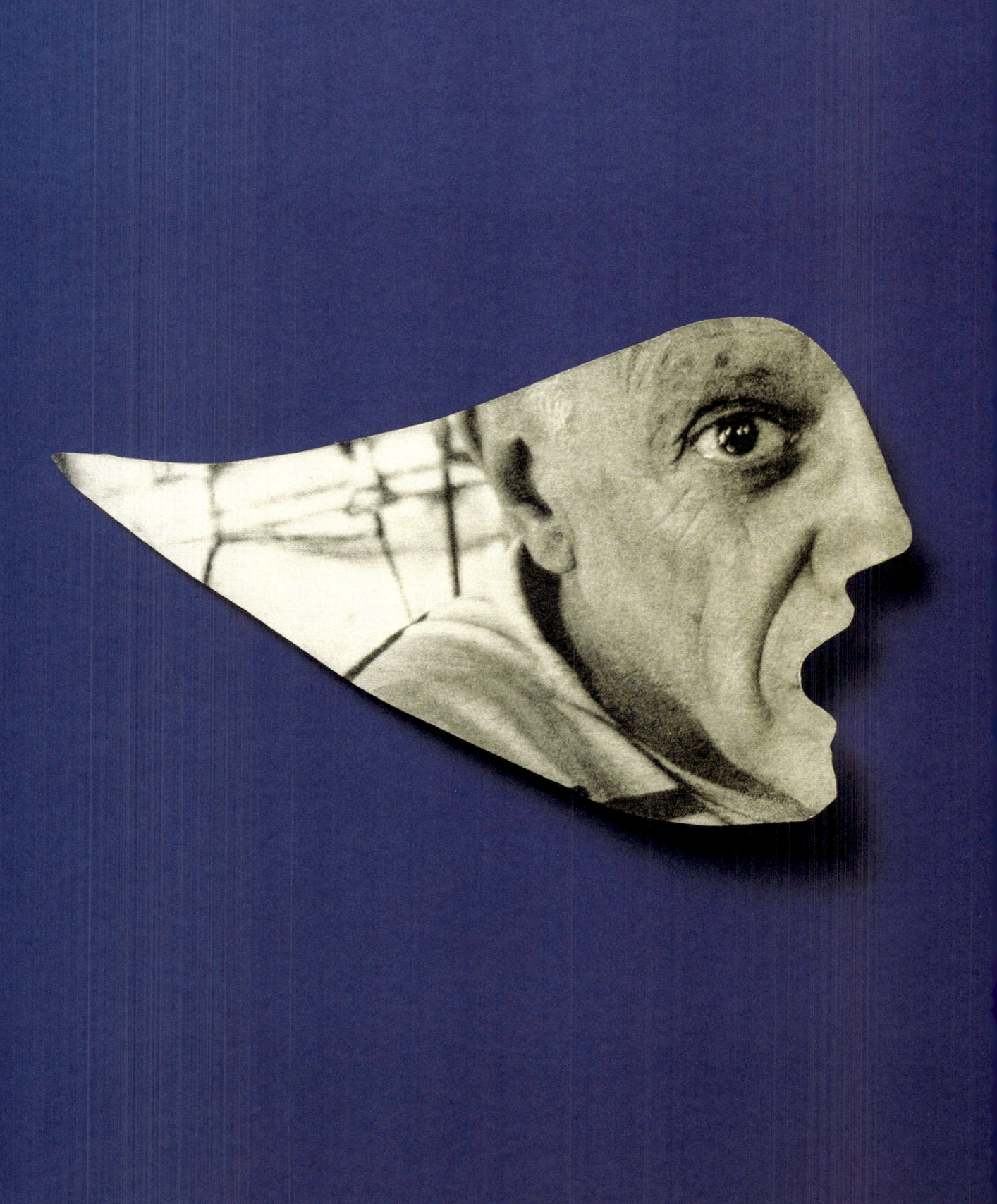

(1) *Peace Post*, Pablo Picasso, 2016. AD Selman Design. **(2)** *The Atlantic*, 2014. The Death of the Artist, and the Birth of the Creative Entrepreneur. Hard-working artisan, solitary genius, credentialed professional. What if the latest model to emerge means the end of art as we have known it? Text William Deresiewcz. AD Elisa Glass. *(Next spread)* **(1)** *The New Yorker*, 2016. Feel Me. What the new science of touch says about ourselves. Text Adam Gopnik. AD Chris Curry. **(2)** *Observatorio Obra Social "la Caixa"*, 2016. The Education Issue. AD Mucho.

Until one morning in mid-November of 1959, few Americans—in fact, few Kansans—had ever heard of Holcomb. Then a bru

ILLUSTRATIONS BY JAVIER JAÉN

ANNALS OF CRIME

IN COLD BLOOD
THE LAST TO SEE THEM ALIVE

An unspeakable crime in the heartland.

FROM THE SEPTEMBER 25, 1965, ISSUE

By Truman Capote

Editor's note: All quotations in this article are taken either from official records or from conversations, transcribed verbatim, between the author and the principals.

The village of Holcomb stands on the high wheat plains of western Kansas, a lonesome area that other Kansans call "out there." Some seventy miles east of the Colorado border, the countryside, with its hard blue skies and desert-clear air, has an atmosphere that is rather more Far West than Middle West. The local accent is barbed with a prairie twang, a ranch-hand nasalness, and the men, many of them, wear narrow frontier trousers, Stetsons, and high-heeled boots with pointed toes. The land is flat, and the views are awesomely extensive; horses, herds of cattle, a white cluster of grain elevators rising as gracefully as Greek temples are visible long before a traveller reaches them.

Holcomb, too, can be seen from great distances. Not that there is much to see—simply an aimless congregation of buildings divided in the center by the main-line tracks of the Santa Fe Railway, a haphazard hamlet bounded on the south by a brown stretch of the Arkansas (pronounced "Ar-kan-sas") River, on the north by a highway, Route 50, and on the east and west by prairie lands and wheat fields. After rain, or when snowfalls thaw, the streets, unnamed, unshaded, unpaved, turn from the thickest dust into the direst mud. At one end of the town stands a stark old stucco structure, the roof of which supports an electric sign—"DANCE"—but the dancing has ceased and the advertisement has been dark for several years. Nearby is another building with an irrelevant sign, this one in flaking gold on a dirty window—"HOLCOMB BANK." The bank failed in 1933, and its former counting rooms have been converted into apartments. It is one of the town's two "apartment houses," the second being a ramshackle mansion known, because a good part of the local school's faculty lives there, as the Teacherage. But the majority of Holcomb's homes are one-story frame affairs, with front porches.

Down by the depot, the postmistress, a gaunt woman who wears a rawhide jacket and denims and cowboy boots, presides over a falling-apart post office. The depot itself, with its peeling sulphur-colored paint, is equally melancholy; the Chief, the Super-Chief, the El Capitan go by every day, but these celebrated expresses never pause there. No passenger trains do—only an occasional freight. Up on the highway, there are two filling stations, one of which doubles as a meagerly supplied grocery store, while the other does extra duty as a café—Hartman's Café, where Mrs. Hartman, the proprietress, dispenses sandwiches, coffee, soft drinks, and 3.2 beer. (Holcomb, like all the rest of Kansas, is "dry.")

And that, really, is all. Unless you include, as one must, the Holcomb School, a good-looking establishment, which reveals a circumstance that the appearance of the community otherwise camouflages: that the parents who send their children

der stunned the country.

PHOTOGRAPH, COURTESY SPACINI

This was the first part of a four-part series. The pieces became the book "In Cold Blood," published by Random House. Part I is republished with permission of The Truman Capote Trust.

Whoops!

Has fiction lost its sense of humour?

Sam Leith

The Guardian

Review

Saturday 9 June 2018 · Issue №21

(Previous spread) **(1)** *The Guardian*, 2018. Has Fiction Lost its Sense of Humour? Text Sam Leith. AD Bruno Haward. **(2)** *Franz Kafka*, 2016. *(This spread)* **(1)** *Bird*, 2009. **(2)** *Sàpiens*, 2012. Cinema and Painting: How Art is Used in Film. Text Enric Calpena.

(1) *The New York Times*, 2013. The Selected Letters of Willa Cather. Reviewed by Tom Perrotta. AD Nicholas Blechman. **(2)** *Tablet Mag*, 2015. The Butcher of Desire; or Imagining Philip Roth. Tablet Original Fiction: Meet Phil the Kosher butcher, non-traditional writing student, counterfactual storyteller, Lothario. Text Sam Apple. *(Next spread)* Everything is Amazing and Nobody is Happy, (Louis C.K. Quote) 2012.

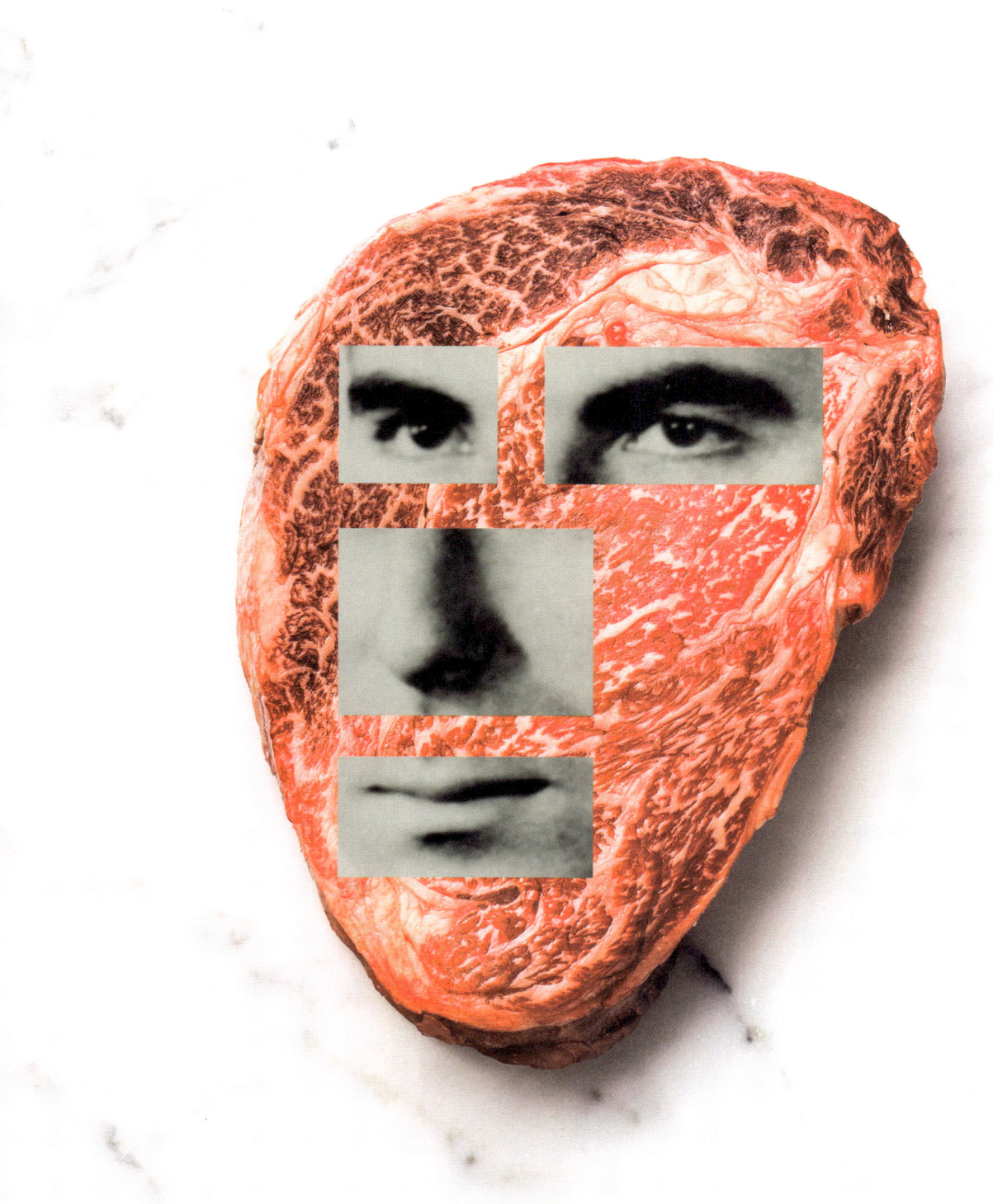

(1) *The New York Times Magazine*, 2015. Who's Really 'Radical'? Politicians and movements have long used the term to reference opposition or significant change. But these days, it's most often used to describe terrorists. Text Emily Bazelon. AD Kimberly Sutherland. **(2)** *The New York Times Magazine*, 2015. What Are the Limits of Religious Liberty? The law has always made room for the needs of believers, but lately doctrine is being invoked to justify intolerance. Text Emily Bazelon. AD Jason Sfetko. **(Next spread) (1)** *La Marea*, 2013. The Undeclared Income of the Church. AD Asier Barrio. **(2)** *The New York Times Magazine*, 2016. We Don't Talk About 'Radicalization' When an Attacker Isn't Muslim. We Should. Those on the path to mass destruction can be incited by ideology, conspiracy theories and the words of political leaders — including presidents. Text Jack Hitt. AD Frank Augugliaro.

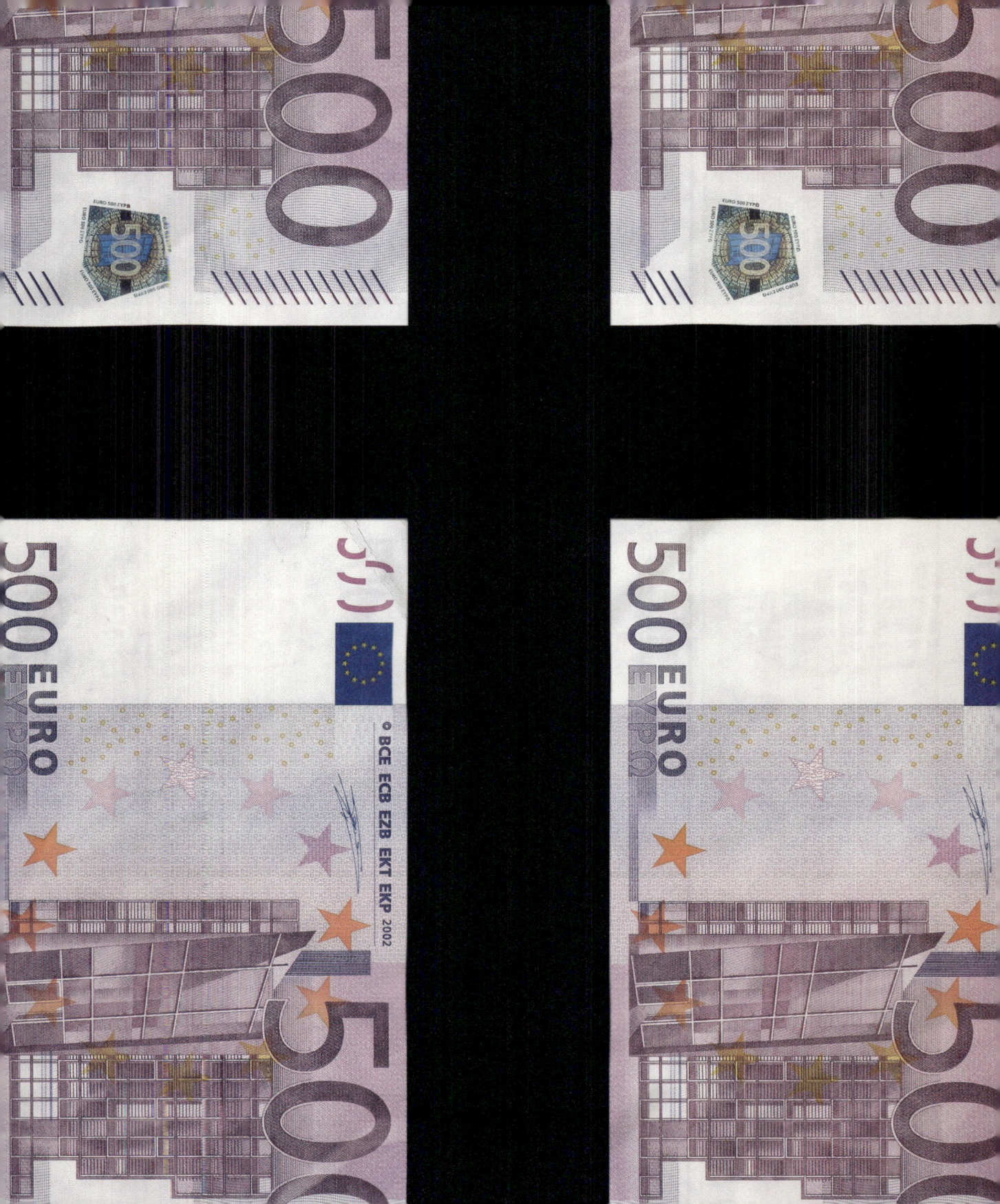

(Previous spread) **(1)** *Noche Oscura.* CDN, 2020. **(2)** *May the End of the World Catch You Dancing,* 2012. *(This spread)* **(1)** *Fukushima,* 2011. **(2)** *Público,* 2010. Behind the Burqa. AD Rapa Carballo. Text Carmen Domingo. *(Next spread)* *MIT Technology Review,* 2016. Hacking the Biological Clock. AD Jordan Awan.

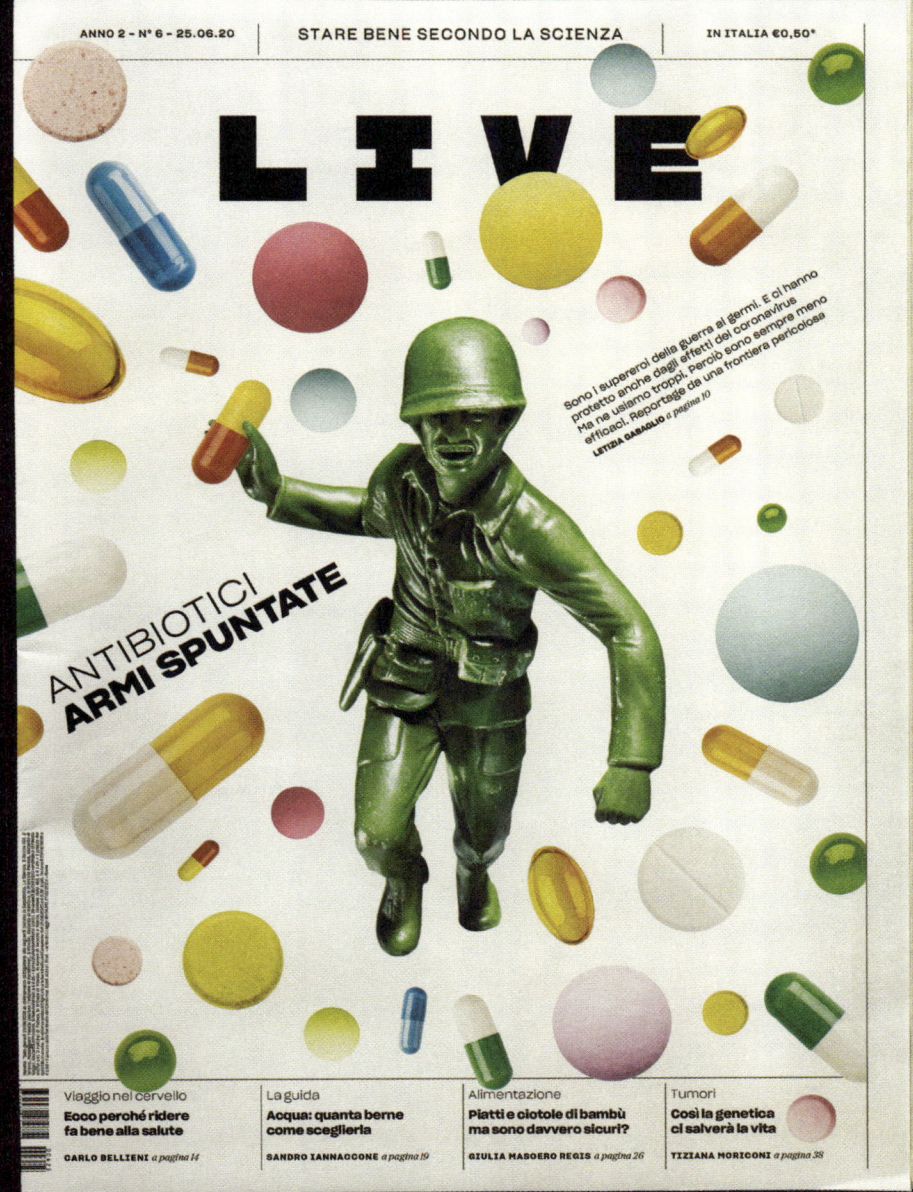

(1) *Wired*, 2017. Live Long and Prosper. Text Jason Pontin. AD Ben Bours. **(2)** *Live*, 2020. La Repubblica. Antibiotics: blunt weapons. The superheroes of the war on germs. But we use too many of them, and those we have are less and less effective. AD Paper Paper Studio.

(1) *The New York Times*. 2021. Our relationship to work is broken. So many Americans are burnt out and underpaid. Can we fix our broken relationship to work? . Text Jonathan Malesic. AD Jordan Awan.
(2) *Vanity Fair, 2022*. The year we decided to take care of our heads. Text Ana Arjona. AD Alberto Moreno.

VANITY FAIR

"El talento consiste en cómo vive uno la vida." – Ernest Hemingway

EL AÑO QUE DECIDIMOS CUIDAR DE NUESTRAS CABEZAS

POR ANA ARJONA Y JAVIER SÁNCHEZ   ILUSTRACIÓN JAVIER JAÉN

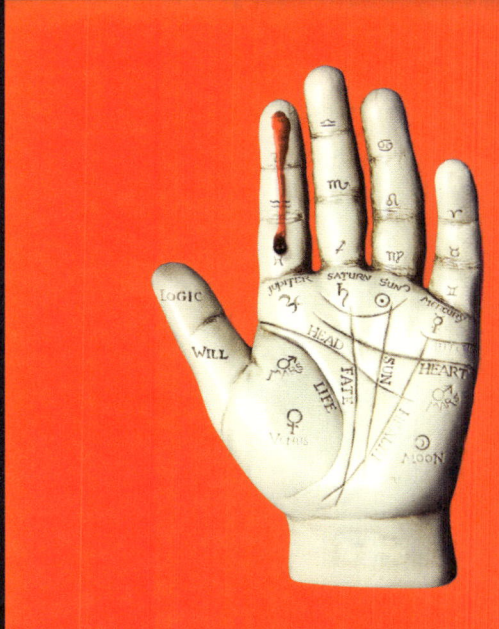

(1) *New York Times*, 2012. The Wrong Way to Stop Fake Drugs. Text Roger Bate. AD Matthew Dorfman.
(2) *MIT Technology Review*, 2015. Vol. 118. The Liquid Biopsy. Text Michael Standaert. AD Jordan Awan.
(3) *The New Yorker*, 2019. Is Marijuana as Safe as We Think? Permitting pot is one thing; promoting its use is another. Text Malcolm Gladwell. AD Christine Curry. **(4)** *Smoking Kills*, 2013.

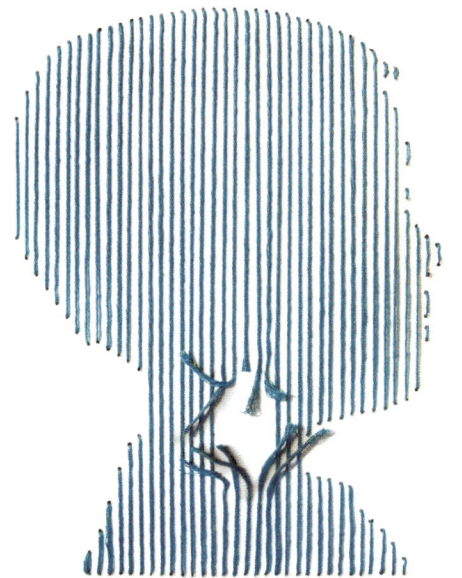

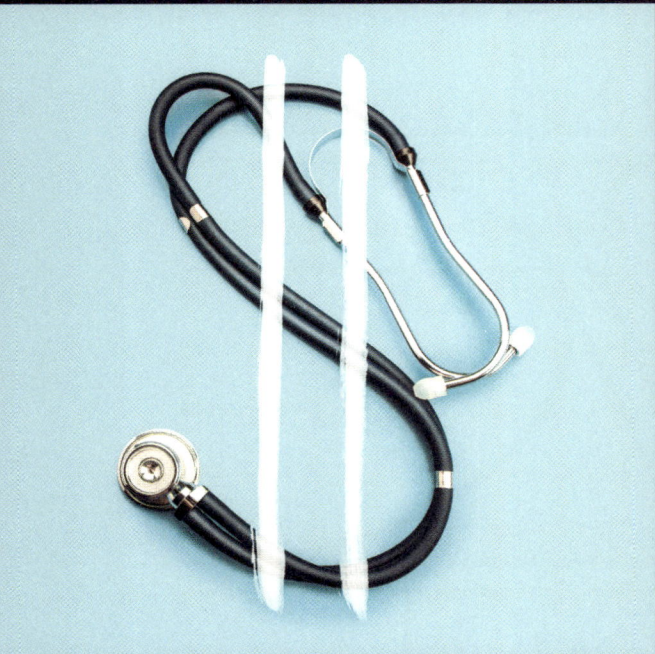

(1) *The Washington Post*, 2012. Asthma Didn't Explain Boy's Collapse. Text Janice Lynch Schuster. AD Brad Walters. **(2)** *The New Yorker*, 2015. Healthcare. **(3)** *The New Yorker*, 2019. The Hidden Cost of *GoFundMe* Health Care. When patients turn to crowdfunding for medical costs, whoever has the most heart-rending story wins. Text Nathan Heller. AD Chris Curry. **(4)** *Partida*, 2011.

BEAUTY TIPS

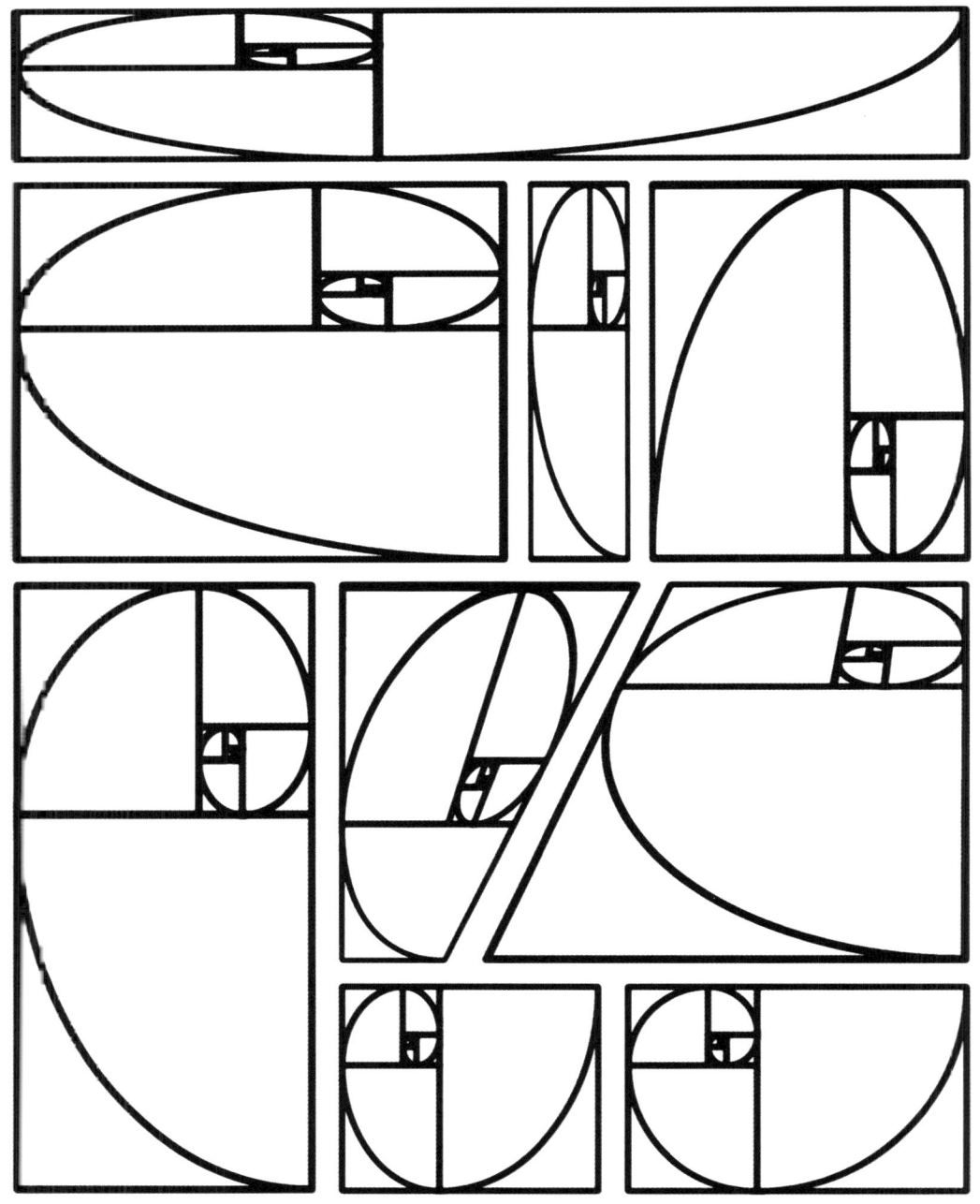

(1) *The Posttraumatic Fanzine*, 2021. Beauty Tips. (2) *The New York Times*, 2023. Many Personal Care Products Contain Harmful Chemicals. Here's What to Do About It. Take these small steps to lower your exposure. Text Knvul Sheikh. AD Deanna Donegan.

(1) *The New Yorker*, 2020. Seattle's Leaders Let Scientists Take the Lead. New York's Did Not. The initial coronavirus outbreaks on the East and West Coasts emerged at roughly the same time. But the danger was communicated very differently. Text Charles Duhigg. AD Aviva Michaelov. (2) *Die Zeit*, 2020. The Hour of Conspiracy Theories. *(Next spread)* (1) *Die Zeit*, 2020. Living with Corona. Which questions are moving people in Germany now. And why politics and science give different answers. (2) *The New York Times*, 2020. No One Knows What's Going to Happen. Stop asking pundits to predict the future after the coronavirus. It doesn't exist. Text Mark Lilla. AD Nathan Huang.

Das neue Heft. Jetzt im Handel.
Oder hier gratis testen: www.zeit.de/zw-aktuell

ZEIT WISSEN

PREIS DEUTSCHLAND 5,50 €

DIE ZEIT

WOCHENZEITUNG FÜR POLITIK WIRTSCHAFT WISSEN UND KULTUR

Leben mit Corona

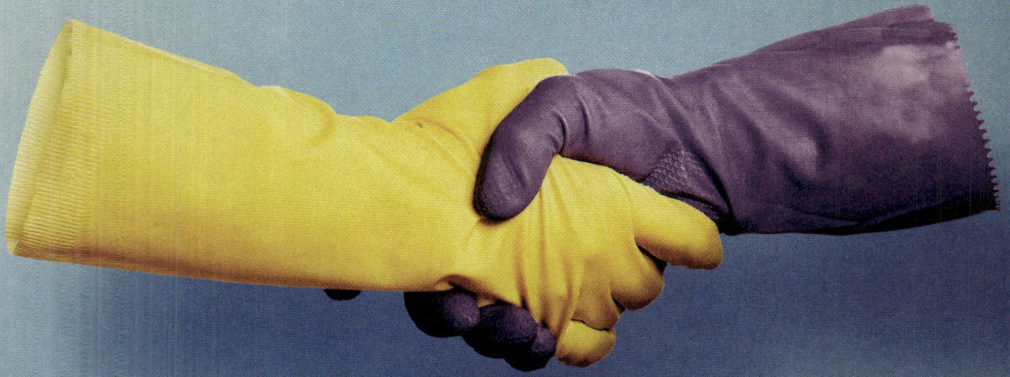

Welche Fragen die Menschen in Deutschland jetzt bewegen. Und warum Politik und Wissenschaft darauf unterschiedliche Antworten geben

DOSSIER, WIRTSCHAFT UND WISSEN

Titelbild: Javier Jaén

SCHMÄHUNGEN VON DEN TRIBÜNEN

Enttäuschte Liebe

Viele Fans wollen sich nicht damit abfinden, dass Fußball-Vereine zum großen Erfolg das große Geld brauchen VON CATHRIN GILBERT

Es ist kompliziert. Vor allem in der Liebe. Häufig fühlt sich derjenige ungerecht behandelt, der meint, mehr zu investieren. Bloß ist das Maß an Liebe selten die Grundlage einer intakten Beziehung. Wichtiger ist wohl die Fähigkeit, einander zuzuhören.
Im Fußball ist es gerade besonders kompliziert. Auch ein Fan liebt, er schenkt Zeit und Gefühle. Weil diejenigen, die besonders viel investieren, die Ultras, Dankbarkeit vermissen, könnte das Spiel, das für sie die Welt ist, nun stillstehen. Der Bundesliga drohen Spielabbrüche.
Wenn man etwas besonders gern hat, dann

Der DFB reagierte auf die Schmähungen mit einem »Drei-Punkte-Plan«, der als letzte Konsequenz den Spielabbruch vorsieht.
Es stehen sich nun also zwei Parteien gegenüber, die anscheinend nicht gewillt sind, aufeinander zuzugehen. Für die Ultras, die dem Wettkampf mit ihren Choreografien Folklore verleihen, ist Fußball ein Kulturgut, ihr Gut, das sie gegen den Ausverkauf an Finanziers wie Hopp verteidigen wollen. Für die Deutsche Fußball Liga, die das Spiel organisiert und vermarktet, ist die Kultur nur eine Facette. Aus ihrer Perspektive gehört der Fußball nicht den Fans – egal wie sehr sie ihn lieben –, sondern auch den Spielern und Vereinen.

FLÜCHTLINGSDRAMA

Unter unseren Augen

Wladimir Putin trägt Verantwortung für die Verbrechen in Syrien. Die Europäer machen sich zu Komplizen VON ALICE BOTA

Darf man schockiert sein, wenn man nicht überrascht sein kann – von den schrecklichen Bildern der Flüchtlinge aus Syrien? Diese Bilder erzählen eine Geschichte. Und Wladimir Putin hat sie ins Rollen gebracht.
Möge also niemand sagen, die Nachricht, Putins Militär verübe Kriegsverbrechen, sei ein Schock. Oder die Meldung, seine Luftwaffe habe gezielt zivile Einrichtungen bombardiert. Auf vier Krankenhäuser schoss sie im Mai vergangenen Jahres in der Provinz Idlib. Auf einem Marktplatz tötete sie nur zwei Monate später besonders per-

Nun zeigt sich, wie hilflos das Vorgehen der Europäer all die Jahre war; Assad ist bis heute kein Verhandlungspartner für sie. Aber sie ließen Putin gewähren, aus der militärischen Macht wurde eine politische. Die Ukrainer kennen das nur zu gut: Russland ist Kriegspartei, gibt sich aber als neutraler Makler. Auch dieses Mal ließ Putin internationale Konferenzen einberufen. Während dort der syrische Frieden verhandelt wurde, eroberte das russische Militär eine syrische Provinz nach der anderen zurück. Die Europäer hatten dem nichts entgegenzusetzen, also nahmen sie Putins Engagement hin. Aber der Glaube, Assad durch Putin mäßigen zu können, hat getrogen. Nun ist er voll-

6 OPINION
Yes, you really do have to stop eating animals.
BY JONATHAN SAFRAN FOER

2 OPINION
This single harlequin leaflet, no bigger than my fingernail, means that my strawberry seedling has been infected with a virus.
BY A. HOPE JAHREN

7 OPINION
They wanted a better world with CBD. They didn't expect what happened. BY AMANDA CHICAGO LEWIS

IDEAS | OPINION | NEWS ANALYSIS

SundayReview
The New York Times

SUNDAY, MAY 24, 2020

NO ONE KNOWS WHAT'S GOING TO HAPPEN

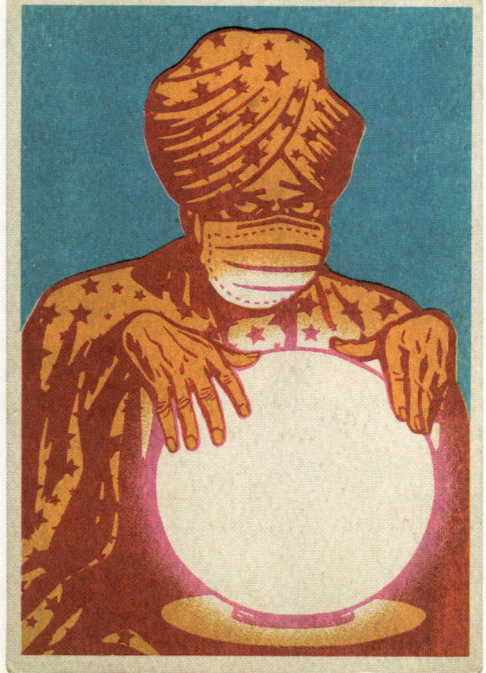

Why we should stop asking pundits to predict the future after the coronavirus.
BY MARK LILLA | PAGE 4

The Washington Post
OUTLOOK
SUNDAY, MARCH 29, 2020 · SECTION B

JAVIER JAEN FOR THE WASHINGTON POST

In October 1987, Jessica McClure, an 18-month-old girl in Midland, Tex., fell down a well. The nation followed with rapt attention for 58 hours as rescue workers, mining experts and local volunteers drilled a shaft parallel to the well, then tunneled horizontally through dense rock to reach Baby Jessica. Nobody fretted about the costly rush to free her. No one suggested that there were better charitable causes than the generous trust fund established for her by strangers and well-wishers.

Now imagine you receive an email inviting you to a community meeting to discuss whether to place fencing around local wells and other hazards. You are not likely to attend. Can you imagine anything more dull? Also, you wonder: Is it really smart to spend thousands of dollars blocking off small holes in the ground?

As humans, we don't know how to weigh the tragic trade-offs among money, health and life. Right now, policymakers are deciding whether to seriously damage our economy to stop the spread of the coronavirus, or to accept additional illnesses and deaths as the cost of warding off other suffering: Economists and public health researchers note the rising tide of suicides, fatal overdoses and other tragedies connected with deindustrialization, joblessness and poverty. Such "deaths of despair" are reminders that economic trauma, too,

Who lives, who dies, who decides

The virus makes us weigh the value of a life, says public health scholar **Harold Pollack**. We can't know if we've gotten it right.

destroys human lives.

President Trump himself struggled with the issue this past week when he argued that "we cannot let the cure be worse than the problem" and questioned the wisdom of a prolonged and costly strategy to slow the spread of the new coronavirus. His critics warned that hundreds of thousands could die if that strategy, including social distancing, business closures and stay-at-home orders, was abandoned too soon.

This seems like a monstrous choice. In fact, we make similar trade-offs all the time.

Sometimes we do spend too much to save or improve a small number of lives. Some of our fanciest medical centers, for instance, built huge, $100 million proton beam machines that provide only marginal benefit to prostate cancer patients. The cost of one such machine could have bought 100 million of the N95 masks now in short supply. Maybe shelter-in-place orders that damage the economy are another one of those measures.

An isolation-induced recession would reduce economic activity by roughly 21 percent, compared with 9 percent under a more lax approach, according to a ballpark estimate by economists Martin Eichenbaum, Sergio Rebelo and Mathias Trabandt. It's not unreasonable to assume that strict containment could cost $2 trillion.

SEE TRADE-OFFS ON B4

(1) The Washington Post, 2020. Who Lives, who dies, who decides. Text Harold Pollack. AD Elisabeth Hart. **(2)** *Mood*, 2020. ***(Next spread)*** **(1)** *Parenting*, 2020 **(2)** *Home*, 2020.

Home, sweet, salty, sour, bitter, home.

The New York Times, 2020.
Coronavirus postcards.
AD Jim Datz.

TIME Magazine, 2020. In a nightly community ritual during lockdown, our neighbours in Barcelona applaud healthcare workers. We projected an image of resilience and love on their buildings.

(Previous spread) Autumn Flavours, 2015 *(This spread)* **(1)** *The New York Times Magazine*, 2017. New Technology is Built on a 'Stack'. Is That the Best Way to Understand Everything Else, Too? People from nutrition geeks to philosophers are using a metaphor from software to describe the world. Text John Herrman. AD Chloe Scheffe. **(2)** *Why?* CDN, 2019.

Obeso, 2009.

Gluttony. Text Vaclav Smil.
AD Dennis Brack.

THE SUNDAY TIMES *magazine*

Who's making your lunch?
Matt Rudd goes inside the sandwich factory

(1) *Sunday Times*, 2015. Who's Making Your Lunch? AD Matt Curtis (Not published). **(2)** *The New York Times*, 2013. How America's Agricultural Programs Increase Inequality at Home and Abroad. Text Joseph E. Stiglitz. AD Aviva Michaelov. ***(Next spread)*** **(1)** *Saigon*. CDN, 2018. **(2)** *Summer in the City*, 2018.

(Previous spread) Otoño en abril. Verano en diciembre. CDN, 2020. *(This spread)* **(1)** *The New York Times Magazine.* 2015. The Muddied Meaning of 'Mindfulness'. Text Virginia Heffernan. AD Mike Ley. **(2)** *Tribus.* CDN, 2020. *(Next spread)* **(1)** *Somewhere,* 2016. **(2)** *Alba Paris,* 2013. Reflet de Lettres.

(1) *The New York Times*, 2012. Leaving the Atocha Station. Text Gary Sernovitz. AD Nicholas Blechman. **(2)** *I do*, 2015. ***(Next spread)*** **(1)** *The New York Times Magazine*, 2014. Why Are Americans So Fascinated With Extreme Fitness? Text by Heather Havrilesky. Art direction by Ben Grandgenett. **(2)** *The New Yorker*, 2021. A Botched Circumcision and Its Aftermath. The constant discomfort of a genital injury creates a covenant of pain. Men are not supposed to talk about pain or disfigurement; they must laugh it off or remain stoic about what happened. Text Gary Shteyngart. AD Nicholas Blechman.

```
I don't remember,
I don't remembe
I don't rememb
I don't rememm
I don't reme
I don't rem
I don't re
I don't r
I don't
I don
I do.
```

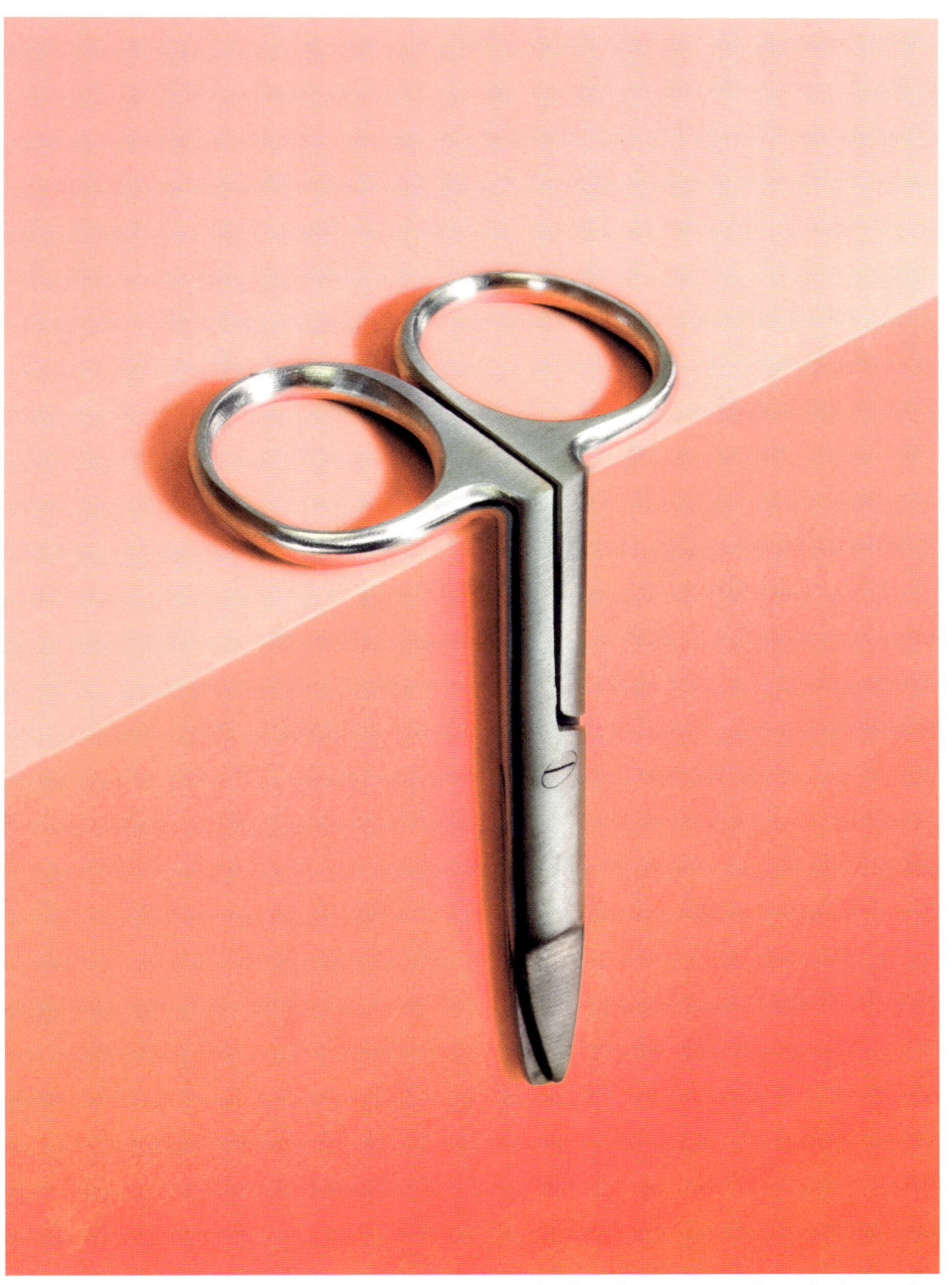

Men are not supposed to talk about pain or disfigurement; they must laugh it off or remain stoic about what happened.

Life, 2013.

(1) *Men's Health,* 2016. Men at Risk. What's Killing White Middle-Aged Men? Last summer a Princeton professor unearthed a shocking fact. While most American men are living longer, one group isn't. Text Laurence Roy Stains. AD Sally Berman. **(2)** *World Cup,* 2014. ***(Next spread)*** **(1)** *Free Verse,* 2018. Text Nicole Goodwin. AD Pablo Delcan **(2)** Wired, 2016. How Creativity Works Today.

+ COLIN KAEPERNICK'S AWAKENING
BY TIM KEOWN

ESPN

THE GENIUS OF BILL BELICHICK
AN EPIC ORAL HISTORY

BY DAVID FLEMING

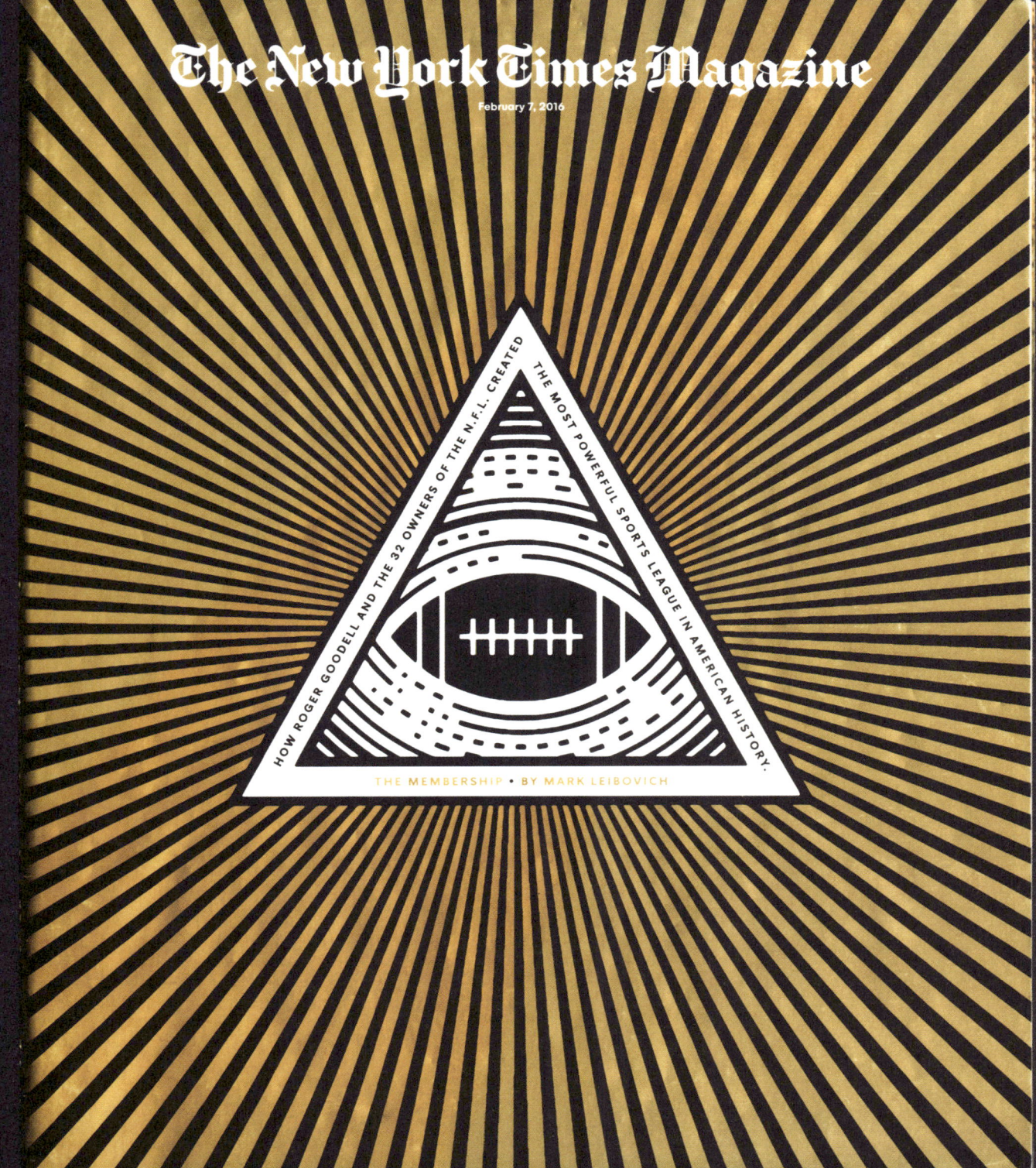

(Previous spread) **(1)** *ESPN*, 2016. The Genius of Bill Belichick. An Epic Oral History. Text David Fleming. AD Rami Moghadam. **(2)** *The New York Times Magazine*, 2016. How Roger Goodell and the 32 Owners of the N.F.L. Created the Most Powerful Sports League in American History. Text Mark Leibovich. Concept Javier Jaén. Illustration Dan Cassaro. AD Gail Bichler. *(This spread)* **(1)** *Barcelovers*, 2014. V is for Vote. AD Lamosca. **(2)** *Público*, 2010. The Neighbourhood Cohesion Threatened by Labour Reform. Text Joan Martínez. *(Next spread)* **(1)** *The New York Times Magazine*, 2017. A 'Resistance' Stands Against Trump. Text Beverly Gage. AD Frank Augugliaro. **(2)** *Borders*, 2017.

Público, 2011.
Pact for the Euro.

The New York Times, 2014. Can We Close the Pay Gap? Text Deborah Hargreaves. AD Aviva Michaelov.

(1) *The New York Times Magazine,* 2016. The Oppressive Gospel of 'Minimalism'. The movement turns possessions into objects of scorn and disgust – and self-denial into a virtue. Text Kyle Chayka. AD Frank Augugliaro. **(2)** *The New York Times,* 2013. Young and Isolated. Text Jennifer M. Silva. AD Aviva Michaelov. **(3)** *The New York Times,* 2013. The Great Stagnation of American Education. Text Robert J. Gordon. AD Aviva Michaelov. **(4)** *MIT Technology Review,* 2014. The disparity between the rich and everyone else is larger than ever in the United States and increasing in much of Europe. Text David Rotman. AD Colin Jaworski. **(5)** *International New York Times,* 2013. Premiere Edition. Inequality is a choice. Text Joseph E. Stigltz. AD Aviva Michaelov.

Opinion

TURNING THE PAGE

Inequality is a choice

The chasm in income and wealth results more from political decisions than economic forces.

Joseph E. Stiglitz

NEW YORK It's well known by now that income and wealth inequality in most rich countries, especially the United States, have soared in recent decades and, tragically, worsened even more since the Great Recession. But what about the rest of the world? Is the gap between countries narrowing, as rising economic powers like China and India have lifted hundreds of millions of people from poverty? And within poor and middle-income countries, is inequality getting worse or better? Are we moving toward a more fair world, or a more unjust one?

These are complex questions, and new research by a World Bank economist named Branko Milanovic, along with other scholars, points the way to some answers.

Starting in the 18th century, the industrial revolution produced giant wealth for Europe and North America. Of course, inequality within these countries was appalling — think of the textile mills of Liverpool and Manchester, England, in the 1830s, or the tenements of the Lower East Side of Manhattan and the South Side of Chicago in the 1890s — but the gap between the rich and the rest, as a global phenomenon, widened even more, right on through about World War II. To this day, inequality between countries is far greater than inequality within countries.

But starting around the fall of Communism in the late 1980s, economic globalization accelerated and the gap between nations began to shrink. The period from 1988 to 2008 "might have witnessed the first decline in global inequality between world citizens since the Industrial Revolution," Mr. Milanovic, who was born in the former Yugoslavia and is the author of "The Haves and the Have-Nots: A Brief and Idiosyncratic History of Global Inequality," wrote in a paper published last November. While the gap between some regions has markedly narrowed — namely, between Asia and the advanced economies of the West — huge gaps remain. Average global incomes, by country, have moved closer together over the last several decades, particularly on the strength of the growth of China and India. But overall equality across humanity, considered as individuals, has improved very little. (The Gini coefficient, a measurement of inequality, improved by just 1.4 points from 2002 to 2008.)

In while nations in Asia, the Middle East and Latin America, as a whole, might be catching up with the West, the poor everywhere are left behind, even in places like China where they've benefited somewhat from rising living standards.

From 1988 to 2008, Mr. Milanovic found, people in the world's top 1 percent saw their incomes increase by 60 percent, while those in the bottom 5 percent had no change in their income.

By embracing austerity, Europe seems to be following America's example: soaring inequality.

And while median incomes have greatly improved in recent decades, there are still enormous imbalances: 8 percent of humanity takes home 50 percent of global income; the top 1 percent alone takes home 15 percent. Income gains have been greatest among the global elite — financial and corporate executives in rich countries — and the great "emerging middle classes" of China, India, Indonesia and Brazil. Who lost out? Africans, some Latin Americans, and people in post-Communist Eastern Europe and the former Soviet Union, Mr. Milanovic found.

The United States provides a particularly grim example for the world. And because, in so many ways, America often "leads the world," if others follow America's example, it does not portend well for the future.

On the one hand, widening income and wealth inequality in America is part of a trend seen across the Western world. A 2011 study by the Organization for Economic Cooperation and Development found that income inequality first started to rise in the late '70s and early '80s in America and Britain (and also in Israel). The trend became more widespread starting in the late '80s. Within the last decade, income inequality grew even in traditionally egalitarian countries like Germany, Sweden and Denmark. With a few exceptions — France, Japan, Spain — the top 10 percent of earners in most advanced economies raced ahead, while the bottom 10 percent fell further behind.

But the trend was not universal, or inevitable. Over these same years, countries like Chile, Mexico, Greece, Turkey and Hungary managed to reduce (in some cases very high) income inequality significantly, suggesting that inequality is a product of political and not merely macroeconomic forces. It is not true that

inequality is an inevitable byproduct of globalization, the free movement of labor, capital, goods and services, and technological change that favors better-skilled and better-educated employees.

Of the advanced economies, America has some of the worst disparities in incomes and opportunities, with devastating macroeconomic consequences. The gross domestic product of the United States has more than quadrupled in the last 40 years and nearly doubled in the last 25, but as is now well known, the benefits have gone to the top — and increasingly to the very, very top.

Last year, the top 1 percent of Americans took home 22 percent of the nation's income; the top 0.1 percent, 11 percent. Ninety-five percent of all income gains since 2009 have gone to the top 1 percent. Recently released census figures show that median income in America hasn't budged in almost a quarter-century. The typical American man makes less than he did 45 years ago (after adjusting for inflation); men who graduated from high school but don't have a four-year college degree make almost 40 percent less than they did four decades ago.

American inequality began its upswing 30 years ago, along with tax decreases for the rich and the easing of regulations on the financial sector. That's no coincidence. It has worsened as we have under-invested in our infrastructure, education and health care systems, and social safety nets. Rising inequality reinforces itself by corroding our political system and our democratic governance.

And Europe seems all too eager to follow America's bad example. The embrace of austerity, from Britain to Germany, is leading to high unemployment, falling wages and increasing inequality. Officials like Angela Merkel, the newly

Some countries will have the wisdom and will to attack inequality, and others won't.

re-elected German chancellor, and Mario Draghi, president of the European Central Bank, argue that Europe's problems are a result of a bloated welfare spending. But that line of thinking has only taken Europe into recession (and even depression). That things may have bottomed out — that the recession may be "officially" over — is little comfort to the 27 million out of a job in the E.U. On both sides of the Atlantic, the austerity fanatics say, march on: those are the bitter pills that we need to take to achieve prosperity. But prosperity for whom?

Excessive financialization — which helps explain Britain's dubious status as the second-most-unequal country, after the United States, among the world's most advanced economies — also helps explain the soaring inequality. In many countries, weak corporate governance and eroding social cohesion have led to increasing gaps between the pay of chief executives and that of ordinary workers — not yet approaching the 500-to-1 level for America's biggest companies (as estimated by the International Labor Organization) but still greater than pre-recession levels. (Japan, which has curbed executive pay, is a notable exception.) American innovations in rent-seeking — enriching oneself not by making the size of the economic pie bigger but by manipulating the system to seize a larger slice — have gone global.

Asymmetric globalization has also exerted its toll around the globe. Mobile capital has demanded that workers make wage concessions and governments make tax concessions. The result is a race to the bottom. Wages and working conditions are being threatened. Pioneering firms like Apple, whose work relies on enormous advances in science and technology, many of them financed by government, have also shown great dexterity in avoiding taxes. They are willing to take, but not to give back.

Inequality and poverty among children are a special moral disgrace. They flout right-wing suggestions that poverty is a result of laziness and poor choices: children can't choose their parents. In America, nearly one in four children lives in poverty; in Spain and Greece, about one in six; in Australia, Britain and Canada, more than one in 10. None of this is inevitable. Some countries have made the choice to create more equitable economies: South Korea, where a half-century ago just one in 10 people attained a college degree, today has one of the world's highest university completion rates.

For these reasons, I see us entering a world divided not just between the haves and have-nots, but also between those countries that do nothing about it, and those that do. Some countries will be successful in creating shared prosperity — the only kind of prosperity that I believe is truly sustainable. Others will let inequality run amok. In these divided societies, the rich will hunker in gated communities, almost completely separated from the poor, whose lives will be almost unfathomable to them, and vice versa. I've visited societies that seem to have chosen this path. They are not places in which most of us would want to live, whether in their cloistered enclaves or their desperate shantytowns.

JOSEPH E. STIGLITZ, *a Nobel laureate in economics and a Columbia University professor, is a former chairman of the White House Council of Economic Advisers and a former chief economist for the World Bank.*

(1) *The New Yorker*, 2016. Is Gentrification Really a Problem? What the American ghetto reveals about the ethics and economics of changing neighborhoods. Text Kelefa Sanneh. AD Aviva Michaelov, Nicholas Blechman. **(2)** *The New Yorker*, 2019. The *Airbnb* Invasion of Barcelona. In the tourist-clogged city, some locals see the service as a pestilence. Text Rebecca Mead. AD Aviva Michaelov.

The New York Times, 2014.
Is Success In Our DNA?
AD Alexandra Zsigmond.

The New York Times, 2014.
Sympathy for the Toffs.
Text Chrystia Freeland.
AD Aviva Michaelov.

4 THE UPSHOT	5 OPINION	5 OPINION	9 GRAY MATTER
Peace makes us lazy. BY TYLER COWEN	Poetry: Who needs it? BY WILLIAM LOGAN	What I learned from staring my father's death in the face. BY JOSHUA MAX	Economic theories and the World Cup. BY IGNACIO PALACIOS-HUERTA
4 OPINION	7 DISPATCH		10 EDITORIAL
What Americans don't know about war. BY CHELSEA MANNING	A wedding and a funeral in Ukraine. BY SABRINA TAVERNISE		Hypocrisy on detainees.

IDEAS | OPINION | NEWS ANALYSIS

SundayReview
The New York Times

SUNDAY, JUNE 15, 2014

JAVIER JAEN

THE GREAT DIVIDE   MARIA KONNIKOVA

No Money, No Time
The poor are under a deadline that never lifts.

THE absurdity of having had to ask for an extension to write this article isn't lost on me: It is, after all, a piece on time and poverty, or, rather, time poverty — about what happens when we find ourselves working against the clock to finish something. In the case of someone who isn't otherwise poor, poverty of time is an unpleasant inconvenience. But for someone whose lack of time is just one of many pressing concerns, the

We make a mistake when we look at poverty as simply a question of financial constraint. Take what happened with my request for an extension. It was granted, and the immediate time pressure was relieved. But even though I met the new deadline (barely), I'm still struggling to dig myself out from the rest of the work that accumulated in the meantime. New deadlines that are about to whoosh by, a growing list of ignored errands, a rent check and insurance payment

of that promised light at the end of the tunnel.
My experience is the time equivalent of a high-interest loan cycle, except instead of money, I borrow time. But this kind of borrowing comes with an interest rate of its own: By focusing on one immediate deadline, I neglect not only future deadlines but the mundane tasks of daily life that would normally take up next to no time or mental energy. It's the same type of problem poor people encounter every day, mul-

LIBERT€€€
EGALIT€€€
FRATERNIT€€

(1) *The New York Times*, 2014. No Money, No Time. Text Maria Konnikova. AD Alexandra Zsigmond.
(2) *La Vanguardia*, 2014. New Values on French Politics. Text Mariano Guindal and Jose Manuel Garayoa.
(Next spread) *The New York Times*, 2013. Class Struggle in the Sky. Text James Atlas. AD Aviva Michaelov.

The New York Times, 2013. Who's Your Daddy? Text Miles Corak. AD Aviva Michaelov.

Penny Pig, 2019.

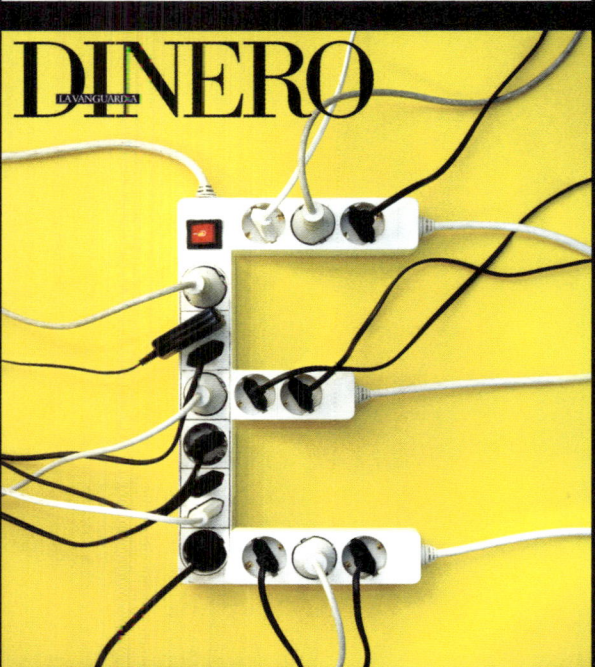

(1) *La Vanguardia*, 2012. Dinero Covers. What Does Germany Want?, Argentina's Economy, The Spanish Energy Reform, The Endless Financial Reform. AD Jaime Serra. (2) *La Vanguardia*, 2012. State Budget

Shop, 2017.

Present, 2018.

The New York Times, 2014.
No Accounting Skills?
No Moral Reckoning.
Text Jacob Soll
AD Matt Dorfman

La Vanguardia, 2012.
Banking Black Hole.

(1) *The New Yorker*, 2019. Private Mossad for Hire. Inside a plot to influence American elections, starting with one small-town race. Text Adam Entous and Ronan Farrow. AD Aviva Michaelov. **(2)** *The New York Times Magazine*, 2016. How 'Bias' Went From a Psychological Observation to a Political Accusation. One of this presidential election's most profound disagreements is over what our unconscious judgments say, or don't say, about who we are. Text Emily Bazelon. AD Frank Augugliaro. *(Next spread)* **(1)** *The New York Times*, 2012. The Deafness Before the Storm. Text Kurt Eichenwald. AD Matt Dorfman. **(2)** *The New York Times Magazine*, 2015. What Do We Really Know About Osama bin Laden's Death? The history of Obama's most important foreign-policy victory is still being written. Text Jonathan Mahler. AD Ben Grandgenett.

JOE NOCERA

In Chicago, It's a Mess, All Right

"This is going to be a hot, buttery mess."

So said Karen Lewis, the fiery president of the Chicago Teachers Union, when Mayor Rahm Emanuel named a new chief executive of the city's sprawling school system, the third largest in the nation.

It was April 2011. The new man was Jean-Claude Brizard, who had cut his teeth working with one of the country's best-known school reformers, Joel Klein in New York City, before becoming superintendent of schools in Rochester. There he promoted charter schools and merit pay, pushed for performance standards — and so infuriated the teachers' union that it overwhelmingly gave him a vote of no confidence two months before he left for Chicago.

In naming Brizard, Emanuel was sending a clear signal: He was going to push the same kind of aggressive reform agenda as Mayor Michael Bloomberg had in New York. And Emanuel has — lengthening Chicago's notoriously short school day, backing charter schools and promoting tougher evaluations of teachers. He has not done this with any particular finesse. The move to extend the school day had even many parents complaining about how it was handled. Then again, neither did Bloomberg.

Yet, even in Bloomberg's New York, where the pushback from the teachers' union was fierce, the teachers never went on strike. Across the country, teachers complained of being unfairly vilified, and unfairly scrutinized, but, in general, they grudgingly accepted that there was too much momentum to stop things like charter schools and performance standards. Democrats and Republicans alike supported them.

In Chicago, on Monday, Lewis and her 26,000-member union appear to have drawn a line in the sand and said: We're done with reform. Though the Chicago school district is expected to have a $3 billion shortfall over the next three years, according to Reuters, the issues that separate the teachers and the Emanuel administration have very little to do with money. They almost completely revolve around reform: whether the teachers will agree to the performance standards the city wants; whether teachers who lose their jobs when a school closes can have first dibs on new openings; whether pay should be based on merit or seniority. I don't know how hot or buttery it is, but it sure is a mess.

After the teachers' strike ends, will anything really change?

As regular readers know, I have been somewhat skeptical of the reform movement. For those disadvantaged students who get into a good charter school or land in a program that can help them succeed, that's wonderful. In the grand scheme of things, though, the number of students who get that kind of attention is small. There really isn't much evidence that introducing choice and competition — an important rationale for charter schools — has forced the big-city public schools to improve. Until somebody figures out how to create reforms that work for all, and not just the lucky few, American public education will continue to suffer. The reform movement hasn't come close to that goal.

On the other hand, the status quo

The Deafness Before the Storm

By Kurt Eichenwald

It was perhaps the most famous presidential briefing in history.

On Aug. 6, 2001, President George W. Bush received a classified review of the threats posed by Osama bin Laden and his terrorist network, Al Qaeda. That morning's "presidential daily brief" — the top-secret document prepared by America's intelligence agencies — featured the now-infamous heading: "Bin Laden Determined to Strike in U.S." A few weeks later, on 9/11, Al Qaeda accomplished that goal.

On April 10, 2004, the Bush White House declassified that daily brief — and only that daily brief — in response to pressure from the 9/11 Commission, which was investigating the events leading to the attack. Administration officials dismissed the document's significance, saying that, despite the jaw-dropping headline, it was only an assessment of Al Qaeda's history, not a warning of the impending attack. While some critics considered that claim absurd, a close reading of the brief showed that the argument had some validity.

That is, unless it was read in conjunction with the daily briefs preceding Aug. 6, the ones the Bush administration would not release. While those documents are still not public, I have read excerpts from many of them, along with other recently declassified records, and come to an inescapable conclusion: the administration's reaction to what Mr. Bush was told in the weeks before that infamous briefing reflected significantly more negligence than has been disclosed. In other words, the Aug. 6 document, for all of the controversy it provoked, is not nearly as shocking as the briefs that came before it.

The direct warnings to Mr. Bush about the possibility of a Qaeda attack began in the spring of 2001. By May 1, the Central Intelligence Agency told the White House of a report that "a group presently in the United States" was planning a terrorist operation. Weeks later, on June 22, the daily brief reported that Qaeda strikes could be "imminent," although intelligence suggested the time frame was flexible.

But some in the administration considered the warning to be just bluster. An intelligence official and a member of the Bush administration both told me in interviews that the neoconservative leaders who had recently assumed power at the Pentagon were warning the White House that the C.I.A. had been fooled; according to this theory, Bin Laden was merely pretending to be planning an attack to distract the administration from Saddam Hussein, whom the neoconservatives saw as a greater threat. Intelligence officials, these sources said, protested that the idea of Bin Laden, an Islamic fundamentalist, conspiring with Mr. Hussein, an Iraqi secularist, was ridiculous, but the neoconservatives' suspicions were nevertheless carrying the day.

In response, the C.I.A. prepared an analysis that all but pleaded with the White House to accept that the danger from Bin Laden was real.

Kurt Eichenwald, a contributing editor at Vanity Fair and a former reporter for The New York Times, is the author of "500 Days: Secrets and Lies in the Terror Wars."

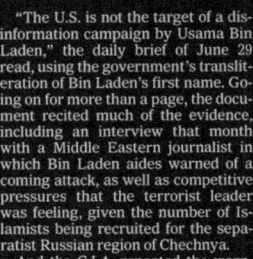

JAVIER JAÉN BENAVIDES

"The U.S. is not the target of a disinformation campaign by Usama Bin Laden," the daily brief of June 29 read, using the government's transliteration of Bin Laden's first name. Going on for more than a page, the document recited much of the evidence, including an interview that month with a Middle Eastern journalist in which Bin Laden aides warned of a coming attack, as well as competitive pressures that the terrorist leader was feeling, given the number of Islamists being recruited for the separatist Russian region of Chechnya.

And the C.I.A. repeated the warnings in the briefs that followed. Operatives connected to Bin Laden, one reported on June 29, expected the planned near-term attacks to have "dramatic consequences," including major casualties. On July 1, the brief stated that the operation had been delayed, but "will occur soon." Some of the briefs again reminded Mr. Bush that the attack timing was flexible, and that, despite any perceived delay, the planned assault was on track.

Yet, the White House failed to take significant action. Officials at the Counterterrorism Center of the C.I.A. grew apoplectic. On July 9, at a meeting of the counterterrorism group, one official suggested that the staff put in for a transfer so that somebody else would be responsible when the attack took place, two people who were there told me in interviews. The suggestion was batted down, they said, because there would be no time to train anyone else.

That same day in Chechnya, according to intelligence I reviewed, Ibn Al-Khattab, an extremist who was known for his brutality and his links to Al Qaeda, told his followers that there would soon be very big news. Within 48 hours, an intelligence official told me, that information was conveyed to the White House, providing more data supporting the C.I.A.'s warnings. Still, the alarm bells didn't sound.

On July 24, Mr. Bush was notified that the attack was still being readied, but that it had been postponed, perhaps by a few months. But the president did not feel the briefings on potential attacks were sufficient, one intelligence official told me, and instead asked for a broader analysis on Al Qaeda, its aspirations and its history. In response, the C.I.A. set to work on the Aug. 6 brief.

In the aftermath of 9/11, Bush officials attempted to deflect criticism that they had ignored C.I.A. warnings by saying they had not been told when and where the attack would occur. That is true, as far as it goes, but it misses the point. Throughout that summer, there were events that might have exposed the plans, had the government been on high alert. Indeed, even as the Aug. 6 brief was being prepared, Mohamed al-Kahtani, a Saudi believed to have been assigned a role in the 9/11 attacks, was stopped at an airport in Orlando, Fla., by a suspicious customs agent and sent back overseas on Aug. 4. Two weeks later, another co-conspirator, Zacarias Moussaoui, was arrested on immigration charges in Minnesota after arousing suspicions at a flight school. But the dots were not connected, and Washington did not react.

Could the 9/11 attack have been stopped, had the Bush team reacted with urgency to the warnings contained in all of those daily briefs? We can't ever know. And that may be the most agonizing reality of all.

DAVID BROOKS

Why Men Fail

You're probably aware of the basic trends. The financial rewards to education have increased over the past few decades, but men failed to get the memo.

In elementary and high school, male academic performance is lagging. Boys earn three-quarters of the D's and F's. By college, men are clearly behind. Only 40 percent of bachelor's degrees go to men, along with 40 percent of master's degrees.

Thanks to their lower skills, men are dropping out of the labor force. In 1954, 96 percent of the American men between the ages of 25 and 54 worked. Today, that number is down to 80 percent. In Friday's jobs report, male labor force participation reached an all-time low.

Millions of men are collecting disability. Even many of those who do have a job are doing poorly. According to Michael Greenstone of the Hamilton Project, annual earnings for median prime-age males have dropped by 28 percent over the past 40 years.

Men still dominate the tippy-top of the corporate ladder because many women take time off to raise children, but women lead or are gaining nearly everywhere else. Women in their 20s outearn men in their 20s. Twelve out of the 15 fastest-growing professions are dominated by women.

Over the years, many of us have embraced a certain theory to explain men's economic decline. It is that the information-age economy rewards traits that, for neurological and cultural reasons, women are more likely to possess.

To succeed today, you have to be able to sit still and focus attention in school at an early age. You have to be emotionally sensitive and aware of context. You have to communicate smoothly. For genetic and cultural reasons, many men stink at these tasks.

But, in her fascinating new book, "The End of Men," Hanna Rosin posits a different theory. It has to do with adaptability. Women, Rosin argues, are like immigrants who have moved to a new country. They see a new social context, and they flexibly adapt to new circumstances. Men are like immigrants who have physically moved to a new country but who have kept their minds in the old one. They speak the old language. They follow the old mores. Men are more likely to be rigid; women are more fluid.

This theory has less to do with innate traits and more to do with social position. When there's big social change, the people who were on the top of the old order are bound to cling to the old ways.

Too much Achilles, not enough Odysseus.

The people who were on the bottom are bound to experience a burst of energy. They're going to explore their new surroundings more enthusiastically.

Rosin reports from working-class Alabama. The women she meets are flooding into new jobs and new opportunities — going back to college, pursuing new careers. The men are waiting around for the jobs that left and are never coming back. They are strangely immune to new options. In the Auburn-Opelika region, the median female income is 140 percent of the median male income.

FRANK BRUNI

The Washington Post

Guns kill more people. Why does terrorism get more attention?

JAVIER JAÉN BENAVIDES
FOR THE WASHINGTON POST

people were killed in terrorist attacks against the United States or its interests abroad. By comparison, about 30,000 people were killed by guns in the United States every year between 1986 and 2010. This means that about five times as many Americans are killed every year by guns than have been killed in terrorist attacks since Richard Nixon took office.

The Transportation Security Administration has an annual budget of about $8 billion and has spent about $60 billion on aviation security since 2001. The TSA employs about 62,000 people, of whom 47,000 are airport screeners.

The Bureau of Alcohol, Tobacco, Firearms and Explosives — the principal federal agency charged with regulating the gun industry — has a budget of about $1.2 billion. It employs roughly 5,000 workers, about half of whom are special agents charged with carrying out criminal inves-

of risk on its head. In the nine years after 2001, 340 people were killed and 267 injured in attacks on civil aviation worldwide.

Our perception of the relative dangers of terrorism and gun violence is distorted. We don't know it, and our leaders don't bother to tell us. Indeed, they conspire with the gun industry to hide it.

Beyond immediate danger, humans are poor judges of risk — witness texting drivers and iPod-entranced jaywalkers. Yet, with education, risk perception can change. We've altered risk perceptions about smoking, unprotected sex, seat-belt use and the need for police to wear body armor. These changes were driven by fact-based research and clear advice on how to lower risk.

Americans needed no further evidence of the risk of terrorism than the collapsing towers of the World Trade Center on Sept.

sparked a national consensus about what to do. That consensus has been sustained by a vast, federally funded security industry that extends even into academia. The Department of Homeland Security's Center for Homeland Defense and Security lists 375 colleges and universities that offer homeland security programs. Platoons of security experts from the industry and its academic branch continually warn us in seminars and congressional hearings of the need to keep the money flowing.

The greater risk of gun violence is masked. The media report lavishly on mass shootings but often fail to cover the much higher number of Americans killed and injured in gun violence daily. In Chicago last month, Obama said that 443 people were killed by guns in that city in 2012, and 65 of them were children — "a Newtown every four months." Every day,

(1) *The Washington Post*, 2013. Guns Kill More People. So Why Does Terrorism Get All the Attention? Text Tom Diaz. AD Marianne Seregi. **(2)** *The New York Times Magazine*, 2016. The 'Active Shooter' is Never Far Away. How the rampaging gunman became a defining feature of 21st-century American life. Text Charles Homans. AD Frank Augugliaro.

(1) *The New York Times Magazine*, 2014. Off Target on Toy-Gun Regulation. AD Elisa Glass. **(2)** *The New Yorker*, 2017. What Happens When War is Outlawed. Did a largely forgotten peace pact transform the world we live in? Text Louis Menand. AD Christine Curry. *(Next spread)* Horror. CDN, 2018.

Afrikaans: Vrede
Albanian: Paqe
Amharic: Selami
Arabic: سلام
Armenian: խաղաղություն
Azerbaijani: Sülh
Basque: Bakea
Belarusian: паду
Bengali: শান্তি
Bosnian: Mir
Burmese: ငြိမ်းချမ်းရေး
Catalan: Pau
Chinese: 和平
Corsican: Di paci
Croatian: Mir
Czech: Mír
Dutch: Vrede
English: Peace
Estonian: Rahu

Filipino: Kapayapaan
Finnish: Rauha
French: Paix
Galician: Paz
Georgian: მშვიდობა
German: Friede
Greek: Ειρήνη
Gujarati: શાંતિ
Haitian Creole: Lapè
Hawaiian: Ka maluhia
Hebrew: שלום
Hindi: शांति
Hungarian: Béke
Icelandic: Friðurlgbo
Indonesian: Perdamaian
Irish: Síocháin
Italian: Pace
Japanese: 平和
Kannada: ಶಾಂತಿ

Kazakh: бейбітшілік
Korean: 평화
Kurdish: aşîtî
Kyrgyz: тынчтык
Lao: ສັນຕິພາບ
Latvian: Miers
Lithuanian: Taika
Malay: Keamanan
Malayalam: സമാധാനം
Maltese: Paċi
Maori: Te rongo
Marathi: शांतता
Nepali: शान्ति
Norwegian: Fred
Persian: صلح
Polish: Pokój
Portuguese: Paz
Punjabi: ਸ਼ਾਂਤੀ
Russian: мир

Scottish Gaelic: Sith
Serbian: мир
Shona: Runyararo
Slovak: Mier
Somali: Nabadda
Spanish: Paz
Swahili: Amani
Swedish: Fred
Tamil: அமைதி
Telugu: శాంతి
Thai: ความสงบสุข
Turkish: Barış
Ukrainian: світ
Urdu: امن
Vietnamese: Hòa bình
Welsh: Heddwch
Xhosa: Uxolo
Yiddish: פרידן
Zulu: Ukuthula

(1) *Colombia Peace Project*, 2017. **(2)** *Greenpeace Magazin*, 2017. Stickers. *(Next spread)* **(1)** *Berliner Zeitung*. Struggling for Peace. One year of war in Ukraine and no end in sight. What can help: more weapons, less weapons – or none at all? AD Uros Pajovic. **(2)** *Internazionale*, 2022. The Victory of the Right as seen by the Foreign Press. AD Maysa Moroni.

B

Berliner Zeitung

UM DEN FRIEDEN RINGEN

WOCHENENDE 25./26. FEBRUAR 2023

Wenn Sie den QR-Code scannen, gelangen Sie auf berliner-zeitung.de

Postvertriebsstück A6517 I Entgelt bezahlt. Preis 2,60 € (Mo-Fr), 4,00 € (Sa)

Ein Jahr Krieg in der Ukraine und kein Ende in Sicht. Was hilft: mehr Waffen, weniger Waffen – oder gar keine? Seiten 23–29

Anzeigen: +49 (0)30 2327-50
anzeigen@berlinerverlag.com
(Mo-Fr von 8-16 Uhr)

Leserservice: +49 (0)30 2327-77
leserservice@berlinerverlag.com
(Mo-Fr 8-17 Uhr, Sa 8-14 Uhr)

Berliner Verlag GmbH, 11509 Berlin
Redaktion: +49 (0)30 633 311 457
(Mo-Fr 13-14 Uhr)

„Die ganz großen Schauspieler schreien nicht": Intendant Thomas Ostermeier im Interview
Seiten 12/13

Ein Italiener in Berlin: Unser Autor suchte nach dem besten Espresso der Stadt – und wurde fündig!
Seiten 38/39

(Previous spread) **(1)** *The New Yorker*, 2018. How Trump, Israel, and the Gulf States Plan to Fight Iran and Leave the Palestinians and the Obama Years Behind. Text Adam Entous. AD Aviva Michaelov. **(2)** *The New Yorker*, 2017. Are China and The United States Headed for a War? Professors, pundits, and journalists weigh in on a heated topic. Text Ian Buruma. AD Christine Curry. *(This spread)* **(1)** *El cóndor y el puma*. CDN, 2019. **(2)** *The Washington Post*, 2014. Not Worth the Fight. Text Ramzy Mardini. AD Chris Barber.

The Washington Post
OUTLOOK

SUNDAY, SEPTEMBER 14, 2014

WORST WEEK
Pity the poor Tyrannosaurus rex
It has new competition for the "king of the dinosaurs" title. **B2**

BOOK WORLD, B6-8
Big data is watching you The social-science experiments of OkCupid. **B6**
Sins of the father The son of a terrorist reckons with his father's fanaticism. **B7**
Agony and ecstasy Could psychedelic drugs relieve PTSD? **B7**

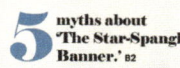 myths about 'The Star-Spangled Banner.' **B2**

NOT WORTH THE FIGHT

Mideast scholar **Ramzy Mardini** says the Islamic State threat is overhyped

The United States has a tradition of misinterpreting the Middle East. President George W. Bush invaded Iraq in 2003 with misplaced certainty, misconstrued assumptions and poor foresight. After the Arab revolts began in 2011, Washington misdiagnosed the problems and opportunities, and overestimated its influence to steer outcomes in its favor. Now, as the United States prepares to escalate military action against the Islamic State, misinterpretation is leading to another tragic foreign policy mistake.

In his prime-time address Wednesday, President Obama said that U.S. airstrikes targeting militants in Iraq over the past month "have protected American personnel and facilities, killed [Islamic State] fighters, destroyed weapons, and given space for Iraqi and Kurdish forces to reclaim key territory. These strikes have also helped save the lives of thousands of innocent men, women and children."

A more accurate assessment would be that U.S. military intervention has tremendous propaganda value for the Islamic State, helping it to rally other jihadists to its cause, possibly even Salafists who have so far rejected its legitimacy. Moreover, to the extent that the group poses any threat to the United States, that threat is magnified by a visible U.S. military role. Obama's restraint in the use of military power in recent years has helped keep the Islamic State's focus regional — on its efforts to establish an Islamic caliphate in the Middle East rather than on launching attacks against the United States. It's only with the U.S. military's return to Iraq and the prospect of U.S. intervention in Syria that the

ISLAMIC STATE CONTINUED ON **B4**

We shouldn't stay on the sidelines

Sen. **Marco Rubio** (R-Fla.) says President Obama's isolationist policies have led the world into chaos

President Obama's call on Wednesday for the United States to lead an international military campaign in the Middle East has the potential to begin a departure from the isolationism that he and former secretary of state Hillary Rodham Clinton have advocated during their years in office. There is a risk, however, that the president's focus on a counterterrorism campaign akin to those waged in Yemen and Somalia, and his reliance on regional partners to deal with the challenge posed by the Islamic State, could lead to the continuation of what has been the most disengaged presidential foreign policy in modern American history.

From his focus on prematurely ending wars in the interest of "nation-building here at home" to his abandonment of America's traditional allies in an effort to placate America's enemies, President Obama has made it clear that he is different from his post-World War II predecessors. The question now is whether, facing this new threat, the president will rise to the occasion and truly reassert American leadership.

Five and a half years of the Obama/Clinton worldview has given Americans a graphic and often horrific view of the chaos that is unleashed in the world when America walks away from its traditional role as the guarantor of global security. From Syria and Iraq to eastern Ukraine and the South China Sea, we are seeing what the world will look like if our leaders continue choosing detachment; more violence, rivals and partners alike taking advantage of

RUBIO CONTINUED ON **B4**

JAVIER JAÉN FOR THE WASHINGTON POST

He held a gun to my head. I loved him.

Leslie Morgan Steiner says Janay Rice's loyalty to Ray Rice seems all too familiar

Just before I fell in love with a man who abused me, I spouted off to my New York City roommate that I'd never be stupid enough to stay with a man who hit me. Like most people who are naive about the complexities of relationship violence — victims and bystanders alike — my dismissal of the dangers of abusive love cost me dearly.

When I see footage of Ray Rice knocking his then-fiancee, Janay Palmer, unconscious in an Atlantic City elevator — and her subsequent defense of Rice after he was cut from the Baltimore Ravens and suspended indefinitely from the National Football League this past week — I recognize how hard it can be to leave a violent relationship.

Here are the times I wish I'd left my abusive husband, an Ivy League graduate and Wall Street trader I met in New York when I was 22 and a recent Harvard graduate:

Three months into our relationship, the night he choked me during sex and I wrote it off as weird but somehow erotic (for him; not for me).

The day we moved in together and he wouldn't talk to me because a male friend from college called to congratulate me on the milestone.

The Saturday he said I looked better without any makeup and told me not to wear it anymore.

VIOLENCE CONTINUED ON **B3**

A celebrity writer's cautious tell-all

Book review by **Liza Mundy**

DARING
My Passages
By Gail Sheehy
Morrow. 484 pp. $29.99

BY LIZA MUNDY

For a professional writer, there are few truly good reasons to write a memoir. Most writers lead boring lives, spending swaths of time sitting at their desks or in coffee shops, rifling through notes, gazing about, looking with despair at the sentence or two they have eked out, wondering if it's lunchtime yet, and finding other ways to procrastinate.

Given the uneventfulness of the average writer's workday, the only valid reasons to publish a soup-to-nuts autobiography are (1) to chronicle historic events they have witnessed; (2) to explain things they did that might need justification; (3) to settle scores; and, related to that, (4) to share noteworthy gossip about other writers they have known and perhaps warred with.

All of these motivations seem to lie behind Gail Sheehy's decision to chronicle her life — that, and the fact that an editor suggested she do it — but the upshot is a rather cautious passage. The memoir is titled "Daring," yet there is little material in it that is truly, rashly daring. During her prolific career —

DARING CONTINUED ON **B5**

Families, 2018.
AGI México.

ijes

DE **ADVOCAAT** DIE NOG WEL SPRAK MET JIHADIST ABDESLAM **P9**

ALS JE EENMAAL **SCHULDEN** HEBT, KOM JE ER HEEL MOEILIJK AF **P12**

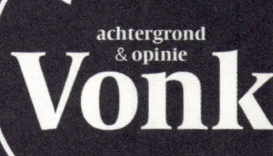

achtergrond & opinie
Vonk

Hij bijt niet hoor

▸ TRUMPS PLANNEN BEDREIGEN JUIST DE DIEPSTE WENS VAN ZIJN KIEZERS **P2**

▸ HOOGOPGELEIDE AANHANGERS HOUDEN ZICH STIL **P4**

▸ EN ALS HET NOU NIET MEEVALT? **P6**

de Volkskrant ZATERDAG 12 NOVEMBER 2016

Illustratie Javier Jaén

(Previous spread) The New York Times Magazine, 2015. What it Really Means to Call Hillary Clinton 'Polarizing'. Text Mark Leibovich. AD Jason Sfetko. *(This spread)* **(1)** De Volkskrant, 2016. He Won't Bite. AD Koos Jeremiasse. **(2)** Dove of War, 2014. *(Next spread)* Público, 2011. Europe. Text Joan Subirats.

(1) *The New York Times*, 2020. Justice is Incomplete at Best When it Benefits Only the Few. AD Matt Dorfman.
(2) *The Washington Post*, 2013. How the Court Made You Less Free. Text David Cole. AD Marianne Seregi.

The Washington Post

OUTLOOK

SUNDAY, JUNE 30, 2013

INSIDE
Four stars, one investigation
Why retired Marine Gen. James Cartwright had a bad week. **B3**

BOOK WORLD, B6-8
Kind of a loner, keeps to himself
Does Obama's inability to schmooze help or hurt his presidency? **B6**

From kite running to endless war
A memoir of growing up under Afghan warlords, then the Taliban. **B7**

Mommie dearest
A very forgiving biography of Rose Kennedy. **B8**

5 myths about the burning of Washington. B3

JAVIER JAÉN BENAVIDES FOR THE WASHINGTON POST

How the court made you less free

Don't let DOMA fool you, says law professor **David Cole**. The justices are limiting your rights.

Mandela's political genius, one letter at a time

The Post's **Steven Mufson** says the anti-apartheid leader's correspondence from prison helped reconcile a nation

In the mid-1980s, I spent two years covering South Africa and the black township uprising that would mark the beginning of the end of apartheid. Twice the government declared a state of emergency, jailing tens of thousands of people and sending troops to the townships in a futile effort to quell the rebellion against the country's system of racial segregation.

Throughout that time, I never met or even saw Nelson Mandela; he was still

The Supreme Court's 5 to 4 decision to strike down a key part of the Defense of Marriage Act was undeniably historic, a victory not just for gay rights advocates but for anyone committed to advancing equal rights in America. ¶ It was also an anomaly. ¶ For all the celebration Wednesday — and who will forget the Gay Men's Chorus of Washington singing the national anthem outside the court? — the underlying theme of the Supreme Court's term was not the recognition of rights, but their dilution. Time

Meet the first women who approached the bench

Book review by **Emily Bazelon**

REBELS AT THE BAR
The Fascinating, Forgotten Stories of America's First Women Lawyers
By Jill Norgren
New York Univ. 268 pp. $29.95

When Clara Foltz began studying to become a lawyer in the late 1860s, she was trying to feed her five children. Foltz's husband had run off, and she'd turned in succession to teaching, sewing and taking in boarders, but none of it brought in much income. Hoping for better, she studied law with the help of her father, who was

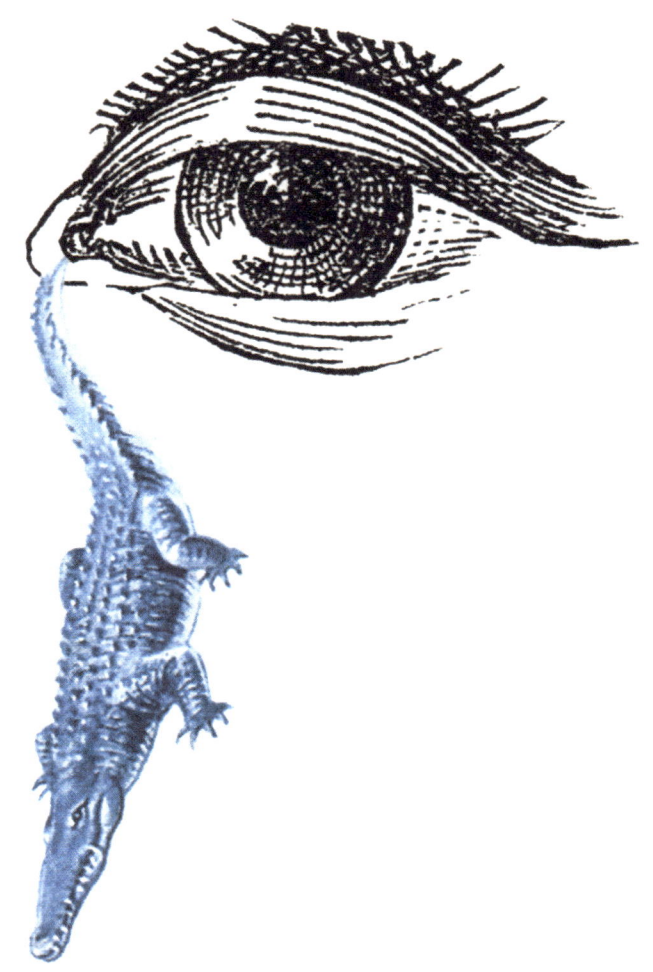

(Previous spread) Community, 2019. San Francisco Design Week. *(This spread)* **(1)** *The New York Times Magazine,* 2015. Crying 'Gotcha'. A once-legitimate media critique is now shorthand for any question a politician doesn't want to answer. Text Mark Leibovich. AD Jason Sfetko. **(2)** *Público,* 2009. How the Right Wing Uses the Crisis. AD Rapa Carballo. Text José Andrés Torres Mora.

(1) *New York Times Magazine*, 2016. What Makes a Politician 'Authentic'? We spend a lot of time trying to discern the inner lives of our presidential candidates, even though what we find is in the eye of the beholder. Text Jennifer Szalai. AD Frank Augugliaro. (2) *Vraiment*, 2018. E-justice. How Computers Will Help Justice. AD Léo Pico. (3) *New York Times Magazine*, 2016. The 'Normalization' of Trump, and What Comes After. The candidate has brought views that used to be unthinkable to the main stage of American politics. Is the damage permanent? Text Charles Homans. AD Frank Augugliaro. (4) *Público*, 2010. Politics Becomes a Battlefield. Text Eduard Vinyamata.

(1) *The New York Times*, 2012. How We Finance Political Campaigns. AD Alexandra Zsigmond. **(2)** *The New York Times Magazine*, 2015. Should We Fear the Political 'Crazies'? When John McCain referred to people who attended an anti-immigration rally as "crazies", he was trying to marginalize supporters of Donald Trump. But is the political status quo any saner? Text Mark Leibovic. AD Jason Sfetko. **(3)** *The New York Times Magazine*, 2017. The Media's Risky Love Affair With Leaks. In a hyperpartisan news environment, spilled secrets can destabilize those in power – and those in the Editorial. Text John Herrman. AD Frank Augugliaro. **(4)** *Travel+Leisure*, 2014. New Year's Resolutions. AD Julia Moburg.

The Economist

- The Fourth of July—with tanks
- Foreign savers mob China
- The epic haggle over who runs the EU
- Our annual supplement: The World If

JULY 6TH–12TH 2019

The global crisis in CONSERVATISM

---

(1) *The Economist*, 2019. The Global Crisis in Conservatism. +Matt Withers. AD Stephen Petch
(2) *The New York Times*, 2011. Bring the Iron Lady Back. Text Richard Vinen. AD Matt Dorfman.

THE NEW YORK TIMES OP-ED THURSDAY, DECEMBER 8, 2011

Bring the Iron Lady Back

By ...ard Vinen

JAVIER JAÉN

LONDON

...RET THATCHER has ...een reviled by the British ... much so that the singer ...Costello once fantasized ...stomping on her grave in ...p the Dirt Down." But ...ved more than any other ...ime minister of the 20th ...that, when she dies, she ...neral — an honor rarely ...except monarchs. There ...blic celebration.

...spiration for a new movie ...month, starring Meryl ...Lady." It chronicles Mrs. ...olicies as prime minister ...rough the economic dol- ...It was a time when the

---

problems
another
Thatcher.

...cial ruin and politicians ...ke hard choices.
...vas a tough, adversarial ...er liked, even by those ...olicies, and she was hat- ...sed her.
...style may be just what ...ow. The country is in the ...crisis that will force the ...difficult, unpopular deci- ...at Mrs. Thatcher did so ...m economic decline and ...of the Soviet Union, she ...s, sold off nationalized ...imbue British capital- ...e that they had not felt since the ...ia.
...est when the odds seemed against ...clear enemies. In 1982, she sent an ...rgentines in the Falkland Islands. ...eld out against a strike by the Na- ...workers, which had been powerful ...a government 10 years before. ...Thatcher has become a respected

comment leaked, the Labour opposition seized upon it, keen to circulate the quote in the hopes that it would stir up old anti-Thatcher feelings. And despite being in power today, Conservative leaders still worry that they are associated with the bitterness of the Thatcher years. They speak of changing their image as "the nasty party" and the need to "detoxify the brand."

One reason British politicians feel uncomfortable

Mrs. Thatcher came to power became leader of the Conser 2005, when the current ed seemed almost unimaginable. Cameron became prime minis financial crisis still felt, to mo electorate, like something vaguely unreal.

But British politics has with its post-Thatcher embra and optimism. Thatcherism w force. It mobilized right-wing such as selling off huge state tions, that many of them would sidered impossible. It also mo develop radical alternatives: the Labour Party veered tow unilateral nuclear disarma creased state intervention in t

Unlike today, voters in choices. A vote for Thatcher vote for large-scale privatiza Labour was a vote for sociali tive vote meant keeping Brit pean Economic Community; meant withdrawal. A Tory vot ing American cruise missiles bour vote meant that they wou

There are no longer choices. Explicit talk of class equality have been replaced b less divisive language of "equal opportunity."

The major political parti ably similar today. All are led somethings who blend social port for same-sex marriage a the death penalty) with accep market. Indeed, the Conserv themselves governing with lows, in a coalition with th Democrat Party, whose presid scribed Thatcherism as "org ness." Mrs. Thatcher hated most likely would have prefe election than to govern with parliamentary majority.

Unlike Mr. Cameron, came to power at a time wher perate. This desperation, and the sense be the last chance to restore Britain counted for much of her success.

Thatcherism was not an alien invas a consensus by many members of the lishment that things could not go on as is why so many supported Mrs. Tha even when they disliked her personally.

Mr. Cameron is certainly a more li

(1) *The New York Times Magazine*, 2014. Mitt Isn't Ready to Call it Quits. Text Mark Leibovich. AD Jason Sfetko. **(2)** *The New Yorker*, 2019. How Brexit Will End. Until recently, it was possible to believe that there was a middle way, or to be in denial that a decisive moment would come. That's no longer the case. Text Sam Knight. AD Aviva Michaelov.

(1) *Público*, 2010. Storm Clouds Over Iran. Text Noam Chomsky. **(2)** *Fortune*, 2016. Lin-Manuel Miranda Thought 'Hamilton' Would Only Appeal to History Teachers. Text Kia Kokalitcheva. AD Peter Herbert.

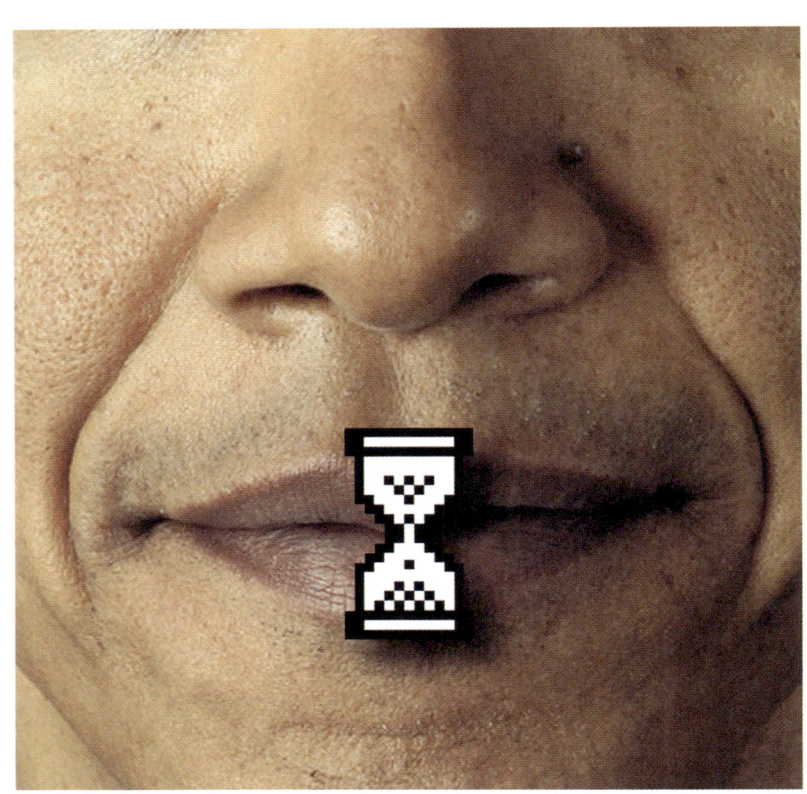

(1) *The New York Times Magazine*, 2015. You and I Change Our Minds. Politicians 'Evolve'. There is an immediate rush to portray politicians as "flip-floppers" when they shift position on anything, but some are starting to employ a nifty new rhetorical disguise. Text Mark Leibovich. AD Jason Sfetko.
(2) *Vladimir*, 2017.

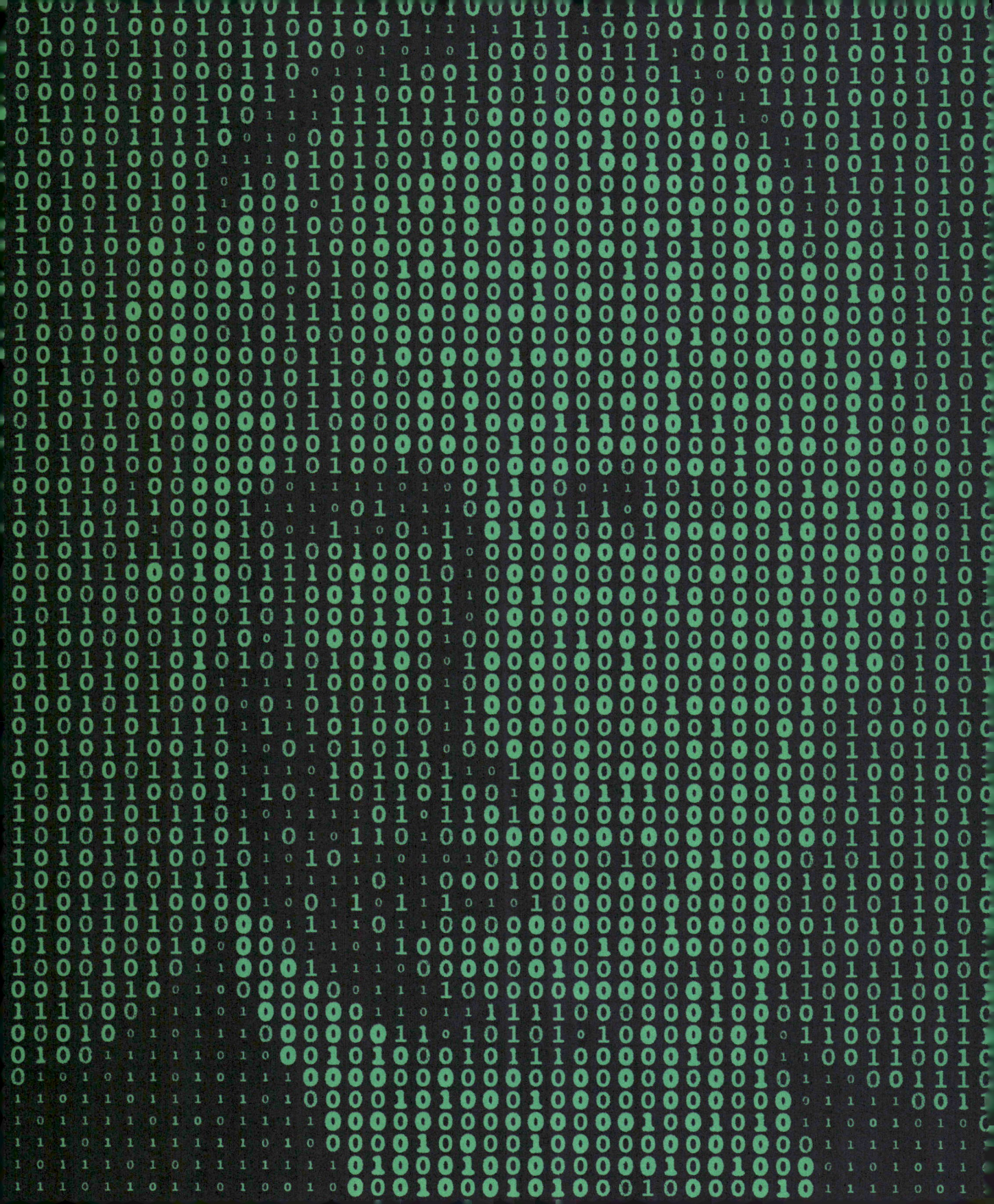

(1) *The New York Times Magazine*, 2014. What an Uncensored Letter to Martin Luther King Reveals. Would the F.B.I.'s smear campaign against Martin Luther King Jr. work today? Text Beverly Cage. AD Jason Sfetko. **(2)** *The Washington Post*, 2013. What if Oswald Had Missed?. AD Marianne Seregi. **(Next spread) (1)** *The New York Times Magazine*, 2021. The Orban Effect: Inside the Right-Wing Romance With Hungary. Some U.S. conservatives are taking a cue from Prime Minister Viktor Orban — how to use the power of the state to win the culture wars. Text Elisabeth Zerofsky. AD Ben Grandgenett. **(2)** *The Telegraph Magazine*, 2022. Platinum Jubilee. 70 Years, 70 Stories. AD Sinéad Ham, CD Kuchar Swara.

THE BOOKS OF JFK

THE WHAT-IFS   REVIEW BY H.W. BRANDS

What if Oswald had missed?

IF KENNEDY LIVED
The First and Second Terms of President John F. Kennedy: An Alternate History
By Jeff Greenfield
Putnam. 249 pp. $26.95

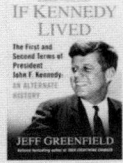

Would Rocky Marciano have beaten Muhammad Ali if their primes had overlapped? Could Ted Williams have hit Bob Gibson's fastball? Would John Kennedy have defeated Barry Goldwater in a race for president?

Jeff Greenfield is silent on boxing and baseball, but his current contribution to fantasy politics includes a Kennedy victory over Goldwater in 1964, following Kennedy's survival of the assassination attempt by Lee Harvey Oswald 50 years ago this November. Fantasists will find "If Kennedy Lived" intriguing — students of the real world less so.

There are two reasons to engage in counterfactual history. Greenfield prefers the more lenient label "alternate history." One is to identify critical events, hinge points of history, and analyze why they turned out the way they did. To ask whether there would have been a Cold War if Franklin Roosevelt had lived to complete his fourth term is to conduct a thought experiment on the causes of the breakdown of the Grand Alliance of World War II. Were personal considerations crucial — was Harry Truman overly suspicious, perhaps? Or were larger factors decisive?

The key to the usefulness of such experiments is controlling for everything but one variable. This is impossible, of course, but approximations can nevertheless be revealing. The trouble is that the approximations attenuate as the experiment progresses, for fiddling with reality creates its own context. In Greenfield's case, he can imagine, with some confidence, what Nov. 23, 1963, would have looked like whether Kennedy had lived or died the day before. But as to November 1964, or July 1965, or any other date after that, he is just guessing.

Yet guessing can be fun, which is the second reason to engage in counterfactualism. Historical fiction has a long lineage. Homer, Shakespeare and Dickens indulged, as did countless authors less distinguished. Greenfield amuses himself concocting a second inaugural gala at which the Beach Boys sing "Fun, Fun, Fun (in a Second Term With JFK)" and Roy Orbison croons "Oh, Pretty Woman" ("This one's for you, Jackie," he says). Kennedy brings the Beatles to the executive mansion and declares, "Not since the British burned the White House in 1812 has a foreign invader conquered our land as swiftly and thoroughly as have John, Paul, George, and Ringo."

More seriously (to the extent fantasy can be serious), Greenfield's Kennedy successfully resists broad pressure to escalate the war in Vietnam. This has been the touchstone of the Camelot claque since the 1960s: that Kennedy would have had the wisdom and strength to keep America out of the morass that Vietnam became. The argument is not implausible. The real Kennedy did hint at a basic review of U.S. policy in Southeast Asia. And if he had won a second term, his lame-duck status would have granted him a certain political freedom denied to presidents who have another race to run.

But it's worth remembering that the American effort in Vietnam looked promising to most observers until very late in what would have been that second term. Of course, Greenfield's Kennedy is blessed with the author's hindsight. Real presidents aren't so fortunate.

In Greenfield's telling, Kennedy pays for withdrawal from Vietnam with a decision not to press Southern conservatives on civil rights. He does win passage of a voting rights act with the assistance of Lyndon Johnson, who was forced off the second-term ticket after revelations of corruption in Johnson's rise to power. Here Greenfield quietly acknowledges LBJ's crucial role in the most important development of the Kennedy-Johnson decade: the revolution in civil rights. Absent Johnson — a Southerner who could speak to Southerners in their own language, and a legislator in chief par excellence — the Jim Crow system would have lasted longer, perhaps much longer.

Greenfield doesn't ignore Kennedy's indefensible personal behavior and failing health. His extramarital affairs imperiled his presidency and conceivably national security; Greenfield's Kennedy survives his second term with his reputation intact, but barely. His health is another matter. By the end, the degeneration of his spine makes it almost impossible for him to walk. Like Franklin Roosevelt a generation earlier, he resorts to subterfuge to hide his disability from the American people. As for Kennedy's marriage — on this subject the reviewer must be silent, lest the drama be spoiled.

Greenfield's approach includes quoting historical figures, using their actual words but lifting them from context and setting them down to suit his fabricated tale. Knowledgeable readers will appreciate the artfulness of the method; others won't notice the difference, sometimes to their detriment.

In this solemn season of Kennedy remembrances, and after decades of dark conjectures of conspiracies surrounding the assassination, Greenfield's alternate history takes readers on a lighthearted romp through a fraught decade. But as they enjoy the ride, they should bear in mind the words of Thomas Brackett Reed, the legendary Gilded Age speaker of the House of Representatives, who said of a political opponent that he could not open his mouth without subtracting from the sum of human knowledge.

Greenfield courts a comparable feat here. His work engages and entertains, but by the very plausibility of its fictions, it risks leaving readers knowing less than they did before they picked it up.

bookworld@washpost.com

H.W. Brands, a professor of history at the University of Texas and author of 25 books, has written about several presidents, including John F. Kennedy.

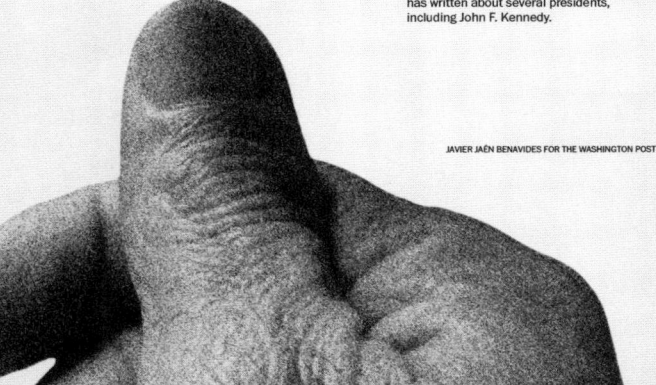

Jeff Greenfield amuses himself concocting a second inaugural gala at which the Beach Boys sing "Fun, Fun, Fun (in a Second Term With JFK)" and Roy Orbison croons "Oh, Pretty Woman" ("This one's for you, Jackie," he says).

JAVIER JAÉN BENAVIDES FOR THE WASHINGTON POST

The Telegraph Magazine

70 YEARS · 70 STORIES · 04.06.22

PLATINUM JUBILEE

SPECIAL ISSUE

(1) *The New York Times Magazine*, 2016. Trump Versus the 'Haters'. The Republican nominee borrowed the language of the rappers who once idolized him and turned it into another weapon in his rhetorical arsenal. Text Wesley Morris. AD Frank Augugliaro. **(2)** *The New Yorker*, 2016. Trump's Ghostwriter Tells All. "The Art of the Deal" made America see Trump as a charmer with an unfailing knack for business. Tony Schwartz helped create that myth—and regrets it. Text Jane Mayer. AD Christine Curry.

de Volkskrant

Donald Trump is, among many other things, the character I have had to portray the most times for work. This image was originally published in 2016 by the Dutch newspaper *de Volkskrant* where they wondered what would happen "after the blow" once he had won the elections in the United States.

Unfortunately, some of the worst suspicions came true during his tenure. His divisive rhetoric, his contempt for democratic institutions, and his lack of respect for the truth led to an unprecedented polarisation in American society.

The image was published in various traditional media, newspapers, magazines and ended up becoming a popular meme on social networks. As the image spread online, people began creating their own versions and adding humorous or satirical text. Some memes focused on Trump's arrogant and belligerent persona, while others mocked his politics and controversial public statements.

Donald Trump es, entre otras muchas cosas, el personaje que más veces he tenido que retratar por trabajo. Esta imagen la publicó originalmente en 2016 el diario holandés *de Volkskrant* donde se preguntaban qué pasaría "después del golpe" al ganar las elecciones en Estados Unidos.

Desafortunadamente, algunas de las peores sospechas se hicieron realidad durante su mandato. Su retórica divisiva, su desprecio por las instituciones democráticas y su falta de respeto por la verdad llevaron a una polarización sin precedentes en la sociedad estadounidense.

La imagen se publicó en varios medios tradicionales, periódicos, revistas y acabó convertido en un popular meme en redes sociales. A medida que la imagen se difundía en línea, la gente comenzó a crear sus propias versiones y a agregar texto humorístico o satírico. Algunos memes se centraron en la personalidad arrogante y beligerante de Trump, mientras que otros se burlaron de su política y de sus controvertidas declaraciones públicas.

Ebony Magazine

In the 1980s Bill Cosby produced and starred in the comedy *The Cosby Show*. He was known as "America's Dad". For several years the number one show in the United States focussed on an influential African-American family, breaking down all racial barriers in the world of television.

In 2015, more than 60 women accused Cosby of rape, sexual assault with narcotics, child sexual abuse and sexual assault committed over decades. He was found guilty.

Ebony Magazine commissioned me to cover the issue where they contrasted the figures of Bill Cosby and his character in the series, Cliff Huxtable, an exemplary doctor. The issue proposed a necessary revision of Cosby's legacy. Many readers felt that the magazine should show only positive images of African Americans and that this cover helped perpetuate negative stereotypes.

Some people were offended by the image, accusing the magazine of defamation and even calling for a boycott. Several international media outlets spoke of the controversial cover. Many of them applauded *Ebony*'s courageous decision in opening a pending debate.

En los años 80 Bill Cosby produjo y protagonizó la comedia *The Cosby Show*. Se le conocía como el "padre de América". Durante varios años el programa número uno en Estados Unidos giró en torno a una influyente familia afroamericana, rompiendo con todas las barreras raciales en el mundo de la televisión.

En 2015, más de 60 mujeres acusaron a Cosby de violación, asalto sexual con estupefacientes, abuso sexual infantil y agresiones sexuales cometidos durante décadas. Fue declarado culpable.

La revista *Ebony* me encargó la portada del número donde ponían en contraste las figuras de Bill Cosby y su personaje en la serie, Cliff Huxtable, un médico ejemplar. La publicación proponía una necesaria revisión del legado de Cosby. Muchos lectores consideraron que la revista debería enseñar únicamente imágenes positivas de afroamericanos y que esta portada ayudaba a perpetuar estereotipos negativos.

Algunas personas se sintieron ofendidas por la imagen, acusando a la revista de difamación e incluso llamando al boicot. Varios medios internacionales hablaron de la polémica portada. Muchos de ellos aplaudieron la valiente decisión de *Ebony* al abrir un debate pendiente.

EBONY

THE FAMILY ISSUE(S)

COSBY VS. CLIFF

KANDI & TODD'S BLENDED BLISS

HOW TO BUILD A LEGACY

THE OBAMAS: END OF AN ERA

COMING OUT AT HOME

DEBATING THANKSGIVING

NOVEMBER 2015
USA $3.99 CANADA $4.99
A JOHNSON PUBLICATION
EBONY.COM

FROM *JULIA* TO *EMPIRE*: THE BLACK FAMILY ON TV

The New York Times Book Review

In 2012, I was commissioned to illustrate the cover of the issue dedicated to Mother's Day. In his first email, the art director said that he thought the image should have a light and humorous tone. He asked me to make proposals freely, but attached for reference an old photograph where Joan Crawford was holding a couple of girls in her arms.

I think I just read the "do what you want" part and came up with some sketches that included spoons with airplane propellers, maternal love sailor tattoos, and a sow nursing her piglets. For obvious reasons, all those horrible ideas were scrapped. I reread the original commission and got down to work. I made an appeal on social networks (digital and analog) for my contacts to send me photos of when they were little. In a few hours I received a hundred memories. With that base material, I built a collage where my friends became a tree where Mother Nature sustains us all. The one in the photo is, of course, my mother. It was my first cover for the *Book Review* and one of the projects that I have the most affection for.

En 2012, me encargaron ilustrar la portada del número dedicado al día de la madre. En su primer correo, el director de arte decía que había pensado que la imagen tuviese un tono ligero y humorístico. Me pidió que hiciera propuestas libremente, pero adjuntaba como referencia una antigua fotografía donde Joan Crawford sostenía un par de niñas en sus brazos.

Creo que solo leí la parte de "haz lo que quieras" y propuse algunos esbozos que incluían cucharas con hélices de avión, tatuajes marineros de amor materno, y una cerda amamantando a sus lechones. Por motivos obvios, todas esas horribles ideas fueron descartadas. Volví a leer el encargo original y me puse manos a la obra. Hice un llamamiento en redes sociales (las digitales y las analógicas) para que mis contactos me mandasen fotos de cuando eran pequeños. En pocas horas recibí un centenar de recuerdos. Con ese material base, construí un collage donde mis amistades se convierten en un árbol donde es la madre naturaleza la que nos sostiene a todos. La de la foto es, por supuesto, mi madre. Fue mi primera portada para el *Book Review* y uno de los proyectos a los que más cariño le tengo.

The New York Times Book Review

MAY 13, 2012

CHRISTOPHER BUCKLEY | Page 10
Alida Becker reviews his new book.

JOHN IRVING'S 'IN ONE PERSON' | Page 11
Jeanette Winterson on his novel.

ROGER ROSENBLATT | Page 43
On being the writer in the family.

CHILDREN'S BOOKS PAGE 17

Family Way

By Judith Newman

MAKING BABIES Stumbling Into Motherhood. *By Anne Enright. 207 pp. W. W. Norton & Company. $24.95.*

No subject offers a greater opportunity for terrible writing than motherhood. Men, of course, have their painful sportswriters, fellows who don't just document the mildew and peeling paint on a boxing gym's walls but go on to liken it to the weeping of fetid tears over the tragedies they've seen. But women? Just as the sports guys mythologize the athlete, mommy writers mythologize the child, the bond, the late nights and the little toothless grin breaking out like sunshine from

Continued on Page 13

By Judith Warner

THE CONFLICT How Modern Motherhood Undermines the Status of Women. *By Elisabeth Badinter. Translated by Adriana Hunter. 208 pp. Metropolitan Books/Henry Holt & Company. $25.*

THE NEW FEMINIST AGENDA Defining the Next Revolution for Women, Work, and Family. *By Madeleine M. Kunin. 288 pp. Chelsea Green Publishing. $26.95.*

Just as everyone was getting ready to throw out the Baby Bjorns and start practicing detachment parenting *à la française* comes a new book, from the esteemed philosopher Elisabeth Badinter, warning that French motherhood isn't all it's cracked up to be.

Continued on Page 14

JAVIER JAÉN BENAVIDES

(Previous spread) *The New York Times*, 2012. Family Way. Text Judith Newman. AD Nicholas Blechman. (This spread) (1) *The New York Times*, 2013. The Selected Letters of Willa Cather. Text Tom Perrotta. AD Nicholas Blechman. (2) *The New York Times*, 2015. The 10 Best Books of 2015. AD Matt Dorfman. (3) *The New York Times*, 2018. Politics & Poetry. Text Tracy K. Smith. AD Matt Dorfman.

The New York Times Book Review

JUNE 23, 2019

WAS HERMAN WOUK UNDERRATED?
Adelle Waldman makes the case.

TINA BROWN checks in to New York's grand Plaza Hotel.

EMILY ST. JOHN MANDEL reads Karen Russell's new story collection.

JAVIER JAÉN

One Small Step

By Jill Lepore

THE FOOTPRINTS ARE STILL THERE, the striped tread of Neil Armstrong's boots, caked into dust. There's no atmosphere on the moon, no wind and no water. Footprints don't blow away and they don't wash away and there's no one up there to trample them. Superfast micrometeorites, miniature particles traveling at 33,000 miles per hour, are bombarding the surface of the moon all the time, but they're so infinitesimal that they erode things only at the more or less unobservable rate of 0.04 inches every million years. So unless those footprints are hit by a meteor and blasted into a crater, they'll last for tens of millions of years.

This summer marks half a century since Armstrong first walked on the moon, though cosmologically, that was a mere snap of the fingers ago. "Man on the moon!" cried Walter Cronkite on CBS television news, gasping, while the world watched, rapt. Kids away at summer camp were marched from their tents deep in the woods to mess halls to plop down in front of a little screen, while camp counselors tinkered with rabbit-ear antennas. "That's one small step for man," Armstrong said, immortally, as he stepped off the ladder of the Lunar Module on July 20, 1969, "one giant leap for mankind." And then Armstrong pressed his gray-and-white boot into the dust, and left that first trace.

But what really lasts from that moment? What was the mission for? And what did it leave behind, here on Earth? Fifty years later, floods made more frequent by the changing of the climate have begun to wash away the Kennedy Space Center in Florida, from which Apollo 11 was

CONTINUED ON PAGE 14

---

(4) *The New York Times*, 2016. Running Through Time. James Gleick's "Time Travel: A History" is a fascinating mash-up of philosophy, literary criticism, physics and cultural observation. Text Anthony Doerr. AD Matt Dorfman. **(5)** *The New York Times*, 2019. One Small Step. Text Jill Lepore. AD Matt Dorfman.

El País Semanal

Some magazines are part of the lives of their readers, they grow up with them and establish an emotional relationship that is difficult to explain. Sunday magazines are a whole genre in that area. *El País Semanal* belongs to that select group. Since 1976 it has been an icon of quality journalism in Spain. On their 40th anniversary they commissioned me for the cover. In a first conversation with Diego Areso, the art director, he considered building a number 40 with some material that would refer to the celebration. On other anniversaries, the cover spotlight had been on celebrities featured in the magazine. In this case the intention was to give prominence to the reader. With the total certainty that it would never be accepted, I proposed a double cover die-cut like a *gruyère* cheese. Doing such a project requires the courage and complicity of a team willing to spend much more on production and deal with publishers and advertisers for days. I remain grateful to them. There is no good project without a good client. A few days before launch, we assured on social networks that each and every one of the readers would be the protagonist of the cover in the next issue. Many thought it would be through a super-technological digital system. It was just a hole in the paper, but we had a great time doing it. It was not only well received by the readers, it also became a collective celebration in the editorial office of the newspaper.

Algunas revistas son parte de la vida de sus lectores, crecen con ellas y establecen una relación emocional difícil de explicar. Los dominicales son todo un género en ese ámbito. *El País Semanal* pertenece a ese selecto grupo. Desde 1976 ha sido un icono del periodismo de calidad en español. En su 40 aniversario me encargaron la portada. En una primera conversación con Diego Areso, el director de arte, se planteó construir un número 40 con algún material que remitiera a la celebración. En otros aniversarios se había puesto el foco de portada en celebridades aparecidas en la revista. En este caso la intención era dar protagonismo al lector. Con la total seguridad de que nunca sería aceptada, propuse una doble portada troquelada como un queso *gruyère*. Hacer un proyecto de este tipo requiere de la valentía y complicidad de un equipo dispuesto a gastar mucho más en producción y lidiar con editores y anunciantes durante días. Les sigo estando agradecido. No hay buen proyecto sin un buen cliente. Unos días antes, aseguramos en redes sociales que todos y cada uno de los lectores serían protagonistas de la portada en el siguiente número. Muchos pensaron que sería a través un super tecnológico sistema digital. Era solo un agujero en un papel, pero lo pasamos muy bien haciéndolo. No solo fue bien recibida por los lectores, también se convirtió en una celebración colectiva en la redacción del propio diario.

National Geographic

New Assignment. I have to think about the cover image of the magazine on the right. It is a great opportunity, no pressure. The cover story is "How we can stop the theft and looting of ancient treasures around the world, but especially in the Middle East by groups like ISIS". Journalists are still working on the text. At the moment, there is no headline or more information. I have 48 hours to present ideas in any technique and a little less than a million dollars of budget. By the way, the image has to work in more than 40 countries. I accept instantly. I take a deep breath.

Me proponen un encargo. Tengo que pensar la imagen de portada de la revista de la derecha. Es una gran oportunidad, sin presión. El tema de portada es "Cómo podemos detener el robo y el saqueo de los tesoros antiguos en todo el mundo, pero especialmente en el Medio Oriente por grupos como ISIS." Los periodistas están trabajando todavía en el texto. De momento, no hay titular ni más información. Tengo 48h para presentar ideas, técnica libre y algo menos de un millón de dólares de presupuesto. Por cierto, la imagen tiene que funcionar en más de 40 países. Acepto al instante. Respiro hondo.

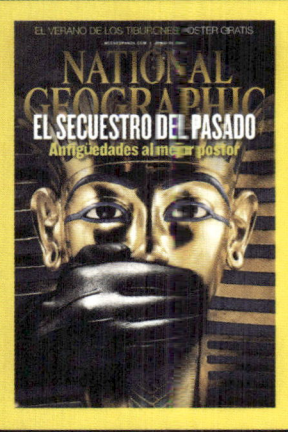
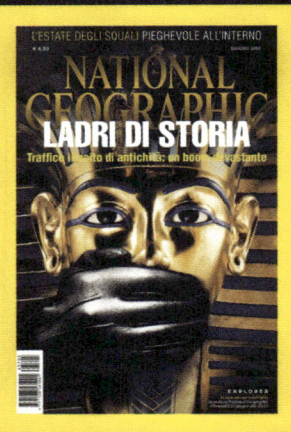
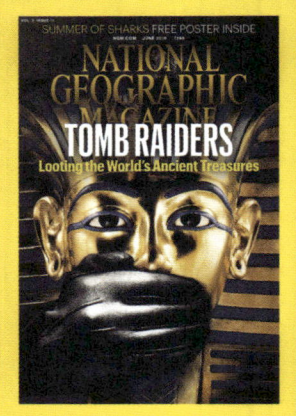

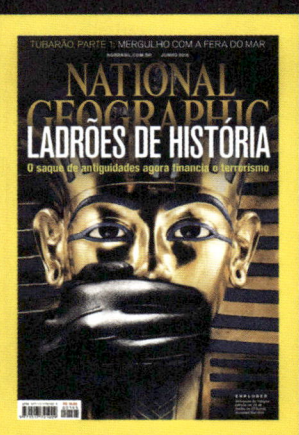
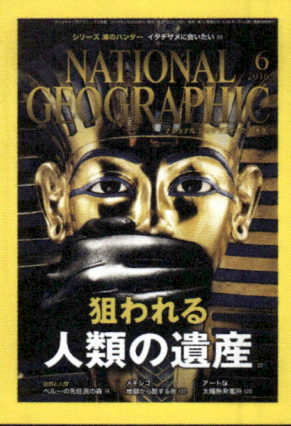
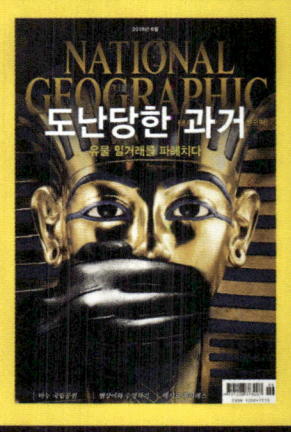
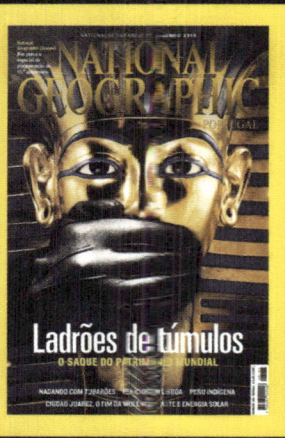
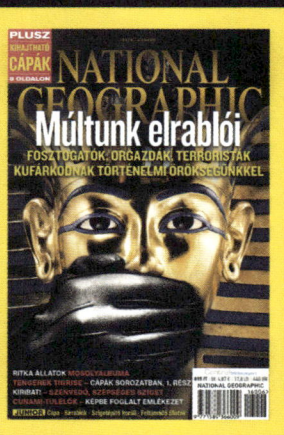
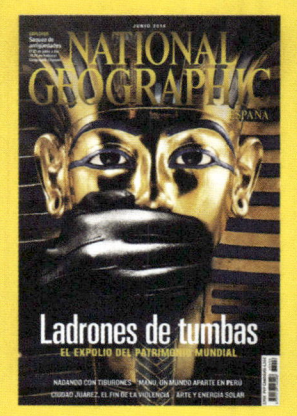
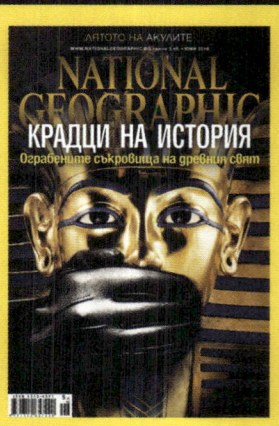

National Geographic, 2016. Tomb Raiders. Looting the World's Ancient Treasures. The illegal antiquities trade is booming, wreaking havoc on the world's archaeological heritage. Text Tom Mueller. AD Emmet Smith.

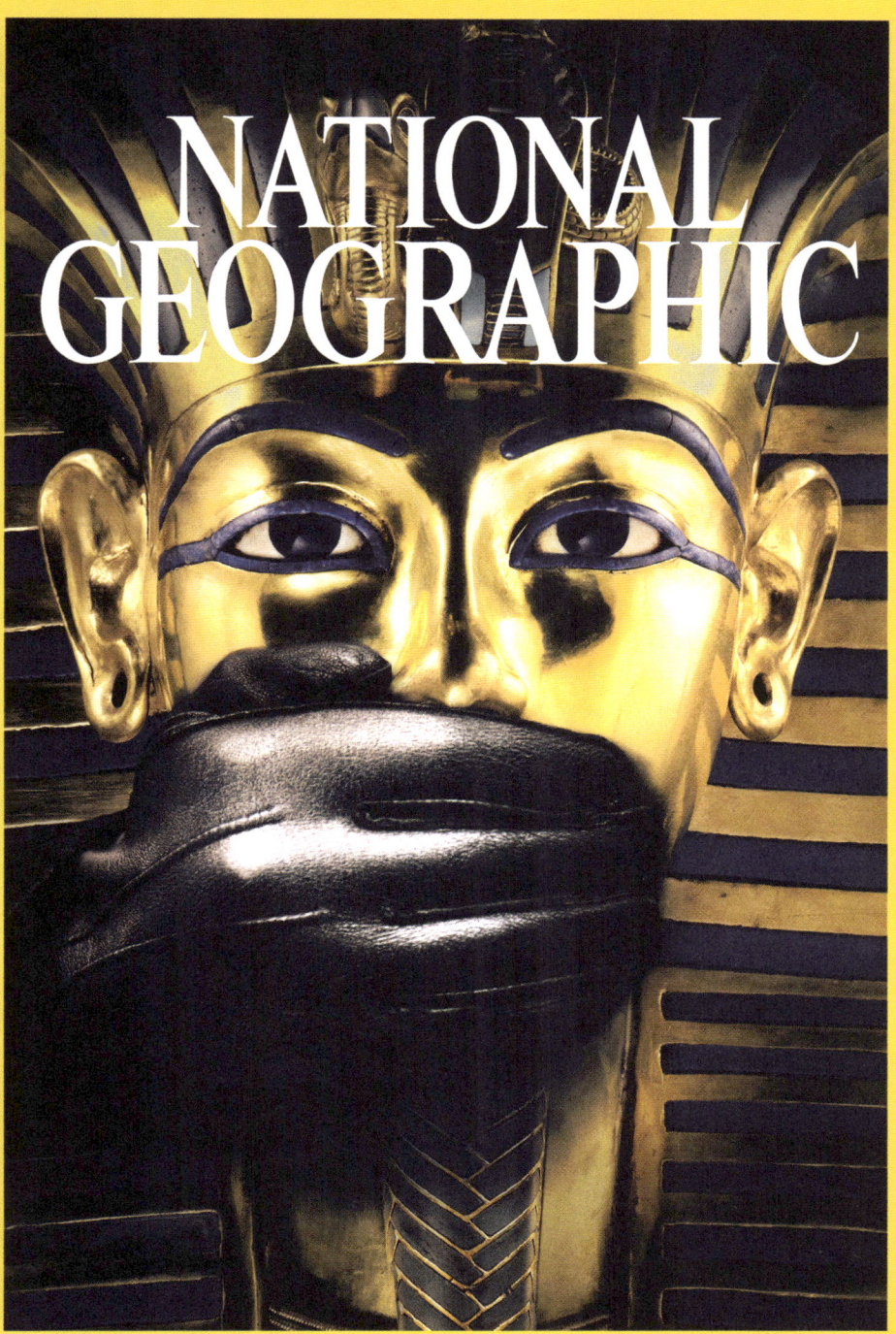

Patrias de Nailon

One morning in 2016 I received a call from a hidden number. The first thing they said when I picked up the phone was that they were proposing a project that I couldn't refuse. For the same reason I thought of rejecting it immediately, but curiosity got the better of me. I don't think it's curiosity that kills cats, but if that's true, isn't it worth spending three or four lives being curious? They asked me to make a 'falla' in the city of Valencia.

Fallas are popular festivals in which immense sculptures made of paper, cardboard, wood, or the less noble polyurethane or expanded polystyrene, are exhibited in the street for a week. They usually have a critical, political or satirical comment on current issues and consist of one or more figures in compositions several meters high. Fallas is classified as a festival of International Tourist Interest, and considered Intangible Cultural Heritage of Humanity by Unesco.

Una mañana de 2016 recibí la llamada de un número oculto. Lo primero que dijeron al descolgar es que me proponían un proyecto que no podría rechazar. Por ese mismo motivo pensé en rechazarlo inmediatamente, pero la curiosidad me pudo. No creo que sea la curiosidad la que mata a los gatos, y de ser cierto, ¿no vale la pena gastar tres o cuatro vidas siendo curioso? Me proponían hacer una falla en la ciudad de Valencia.

Las fallas son unas fiestas populares en las que durante una semana se exponen en la calle inmensas esculturas construidas con papel, cartón, madera, o los menos nobles poliuretano o poliestireno expandido. Habitualmente tienen sentido crítico, político o satírico sobre temas de actualidad. Suelen constar de una o varias figuras en composiciones de varios metros de altura. Las Fallas están catalogadas como fiesta de Interés Turístico Internacional, y consideradas Patrimonio Cultural Inmaterial de la Humanidad por la Unesco.

Fallas artists dedicate themselves throughout the year to make the monuments that the different committees of the city commission. In recent years, some committees have chosen to divide the project between two artists: one develops the concept and form, and the other executes it technically. After a week of street exposure, floral offerings and long nights of mobile-discos and fireworks, they burn them in the middle of the street.

Although I felt admiration and respect for this tradition, the preconceived idea of what "a falla" is was something that was far from my interests. Maybe it wasn't for me. I often try turning the projects around until I find an interesting approach. What do you want to burn? This was a much more challenging question.

Los artistas falleros se dedican durante todo el año a realizar los monumentos que las diferentes comisiones de la ciudad contratan. En los últimos años, algunas comisiones han optado por dividir el proyecto entre dos artistas: uno desarrolla el concepto y la forma, y otro la ejecuta técnicamente. Después de una semana de exposición en la calle, ofrendas florales y largas noches de *disco-móvil* y pirotecnia, las queman en plena calle.

Aunque sentía admiración y respeto por esta tradición, la idea preconcebida de todo lo que significa "una falla" era algo que quedaba lejos de mis intereses. Quizá no era para mí. A menudo trato de darle la vuelta a los proyectos hasta encontrar un enfoque sugerente. ¿Qué quieres quemar? Ésta era una pregunta mucho más estimulante.

Unlike the vast majority of projects in which I have participated, here I was not working as a "translator", but as an author. I have always been interested in the difference between the image on the left and the right. That obsession so human and so stupid to delimit and label what you know. From *this* line to *that* line we are all the same, and from *there* on you are all different. The idea that all people born in a thousand kilometer area have a common character seems to me as absurd as those all born on the same day. Americans, Mexicans, Europeans, Africans, Koreans, divided by imaginary lines. The more you think about it, the more ridiculous it sounds.

A diferencia de la gran mayoría de proyectos en los que he participado, aquí no estaba trabajando como "traductor", sino como autor. Siempre me ha interesado la diferencia entre la imagen de la izquierda y la de la derecha. Esa obsesión tan humana y tan estúpida de delimitar y etiquetar cuanto conoce. Desde *esta* línea hasta *esa* otra somos todos iguales, y a partir de *ahí* sois todos diferentes. La idea de que todas las personas nacidas en mil kilómetros a la redonda tengan un carácter común me parece tan absurda como que lo tengan los nacidos en el mismo día. Americanos, mexicanos, europeos, africanos, coreanos, divididos por líneas imaginarias. Cuanto más te alejas del hormiguero, más ridícula es la discusión.

After a year of work, the project finally materialised in a falla of double meaning. During the day it represented a large white flag, an international symbol used during periods of war or conflict. It has several meanings: surrender, request to parley with the enemy, ceasefire or abandonment of hostilities of all kinds. Under international law, their inappropriate or misleading use is even considered a war crime.

During the night, a video mapping system projected the flags of all the countries of the world on it, while their anthems sounded. All ended up burning to the sound of the last movement of *Symphony No. 9 in D minor, op. 125* by Ludwig Van Beethoven.

Después de un año de trabajo, el proyecto se materializó finalmente en una falla de doble significado. Durante el día representaba una gran bandera blanca, símbolo internacional usado durante periodos bélicos o de conflicto. Posee varios significados: rendición, solicitud de parlamentar con el enemigo, alto el fuego o cese de las hostilidades de todo tipo. Según el derecho internacional, su uso inapropiado o engañoso es incluso considerado un crimen de guerra.

Durante la noche, un sistema de *video mapping* proyectaba sobre ella las banderas de todos los países del mundo mientras sonaban sus himnos. Todas acabaron ardiendo al son del último movimiento de la *Sinfonía n.º 9 en re menor, op. 125*, de Ludwig Van Beethoven.

Patrias de Nailon, 2016.
Falla Mossén Sorell-Corona.
+ José Lafarga.

Plans for tomorrow:
Exercise, learn something new, save some money, spend more time with my family, travel more, eat healthier, I don't smoke but if I did I should quit immediately, sleep better, call my parents more, be more organised, be less obsessive, complain less, listen more, be more grateful, stay away from the phone, do not forget to water the plants or take out the garbage, read more, draw more, laugh more, kiss more, dance more, write a child, plant a book and give birth to a tree.

Planes para mañana:
Hacer ejercicio, aprender algo nuevo, ahorrar algo de dinero, pasar más tiempo con mi familia, viajar más, comer más sano, no fumo pero si lo hiciera debería dejarlo inmediatamente, dormir mejor, llamar más a mis padres, ser más ordenado, ser menos obsesivo, quejarme menos, escuchar más, ser más agradecido, estar menos pendiente del teléfono, no olvidarme de regar las plantas ni de bajar la basura, leer más, dibujar más, reir más, besar más, bailar más, escribir un niño, plantar un libro y dar a luz un árbol.

Incomplete list of acknowledgments

Alberto Jaén, Alexandra Zsigmond, *Alliance Graphique Internationale*, Álvaro Carmona, Álvaro Domínguez, Andreu Meixide, Anna Parini, Aviva Michaelov, Ben Grandgenett, Chris Curry, Cristina Sardà, Céline Leterme, Dani Rubio, Diego Areso, *Domestika*, Edmon de Haro, Enric Jardí, Ester Ferruz, Fernando Rapa, Frank Augugliaro, Gail Bichler, *Gràffica*, Guille Mendia, Iván Bravo, Ibán Ramón, Jaime Serra, Jason Sfetko, Javier Mariscal, Javi Royo, Jon Dowling, Juan Pajares, Júlia Jarne Sardà, Lluis Ricart, Lucas Doerre, Malika Favre, Mamá y Papá, Mario Eskenazi, Marçal Vaquer, Marianne Seregi, Matt Dorfman, Matt Willey, Miguel Ángel Pérez, Nacho Clemente, Nicholas Blechman, Peter Mendelsund, Pedro Almodóvar, Raquel Pelta, Ricardo Rey, Scott Stowell, Stefan Sagmeister, Victoria Salsas and you.

Borja Alegre (CGI)
74, 79, 109, 148, 165, 190, 244, 344, 350

Elena Claverol (Photographer)
94, 98, 99, 104

Lucas Doerre (CGI)
13, 17, 38, 55,
68 *(1,3,4,5,6,8,9,11,12)*,
69 *(1,2,3,5,6,7,10,11,12)*,
70 *(2,5,6,7,8,12)*, 71 *(2,4,5,6,9, 10,11)*, 75, 107, 112, 77, 103, 140, 141, 169, 185, 189, 193, 205, 209, 217, 236, 270, 275, 309, 316, 328, 332, 342, 351, 353

Marta Felipe (Motion Graphics)
124, 127

Guille Mendia (Photographer)
126, 127

Laia Pallarès (Modeler)
70(3), 265, 373

Marçal Vaquer (Photographer)
2, 6, 18, 20, 67, 68 *(2,7,10)*, 69 *(8)*, 70*(3,4,10)*, 71*(3)*, 118-119, 153, 192, 200, 272, 273, 313, 324

Ricardo Rey (CGI)
30, 73, 249

Six N. Five (CGI)
70 *(5)*, 372 *(4)*

Yippiehey (CGI)
70 *(1)*, 194, 221, 271, 287, 301, 331

Ivan Castro (Lettering)
Cover

Proofreader
Cristina Sardà
Jon Dowling

**Prod Manager
and Studio Archive**
Ester Ferruz

Studio Manager
Victoria Salsas

Counter-Print
© 2020 Counter-Print
counter-print.co.uk

British Library cataloguing-in-publication data: A catalogue of this book can be found in the British Library.

ISBN
9781916126169

First published in the United Kingdom in 2020 by Counter-Print. Reprinted in 2023.

Edited and produced by Counter-Print.

Design
Jon Dowling
Céline Leterme
Javier Jaén

Typefaces
Washington Heights
& Vulf Mono

Printing and Binding
10|10 International

Paper
Dunder Mifflin

Lucky number
Three

Copyright on projects and their related imagery is held by Javier Jaén.

Javier Jaén
javierjaen.com
shopjavierjaen.com

All rights reserved. No part of this book may be reproduced, stored in a retrieval system, or transmitted in any form or by any means without prior written permission from the publisher.